Is Higher Education Fair?

Is Higher Education Fair?

Papers presented
to the 17th annual conference of the
Society for Research into Higher Education
1981

Edited by David Warren Piper

SOCIETY FOR RESEARCH INTO HIGHER EDUCATION

Research into Higher Education Proceedings

The Society for Research into Higher Education
At the University, Guildford, Surrey GU2 5XH

First published 1981

ISBN 0 900868 82 1

Printed in England by
Direct Design (Bournemouth) Ltd. Printers
Sturminster Newton,
Dorset   DT10 1AZ

TYRRELL BURGESS

Reader in the Philosophy of Social Institutions at the North East London Polytechnic, he was the first head of the School for Independent Study. He has written extensively on education topics and recent books include *Education After School* (Gollancz and Penguin 1977).

GORDON BROTHERSTON

A professor in the Department of Literature at the University of Essex, he was dean of the School of Comparative Studies from 1976 to 1980. He has written several books and articles in the fields of Comparative Literature, Latin American and Native American Studies. His work has led to an inquiry into the role of literacy and language ability in higher education.

JOHN GAY

Director of Culham College Institute whose purpose is to examine the role of the Church in statutory education in this country, he was previously on the staff of Culham College of Education and of the Department of Educational Studies of the University of Oxford. Publications include *The Geography of Religion in England* (Duckworth 1971) and *The Christian Campus? The Role of the English Churches in Higher Education* (1979, obtainable from Culham College Institute).

ALAN LITTLE

Lewisham Professor of Social Administration, University of London, and head of the School of Social Sciences at Goldsmiths' College, he was director of the Community Relations Commission and previously director of Research and Statistics at the Inner London Education Authority. Publications include *Strategies of*

Compensation: A review of Educational Projects for the Disadvantaged in the United States (Centre for Educational Research and Innovation, with George Smith 1973); *Urban Deprivation, Racial Inequality and Social Policy* (A Report, HMSO 1977).

JOHN RICHARDSON

Lecturer in Psychology at Brunel University, his extensive works on human learning and memory include *The Grammar of Justification: An Interpretation of Wittgenstein's Philosophy of Language* (Sussex University Press 1976) and *Mental Imagery and Human Memory* (Macmillan 1980). He is currently engaged in a comparative study of systems of higher education in countries of the European Economic Community.

DIANA ROBBINS

Research officer at the Disablement Income Group, she was previously a member of the Community Relations Commission's Reference Unit. She has undertaken freelance research, principally on discrimination and disadvantage, recently with Professor Little on transmitted deprivation and affirmative action.

DALE SPENDER

Editor of *Women's Studies International* and the Athene Monograph series, she is a member of the Women's Research and Resources Centre, and author of books and articles on feminism in relation to language, education, and philosophy.

RONALD STURT

Assistant provost of the City of London Polytechnic, he was first director of the National Bureau for Handicapped Students and Chairman, now president of the Talking Newspaper Association of the United Kingdom.

BILL WILLIAMSON

Lecturer in Sociology at the University of Durham, his main research and teaching interest is in the sociology of education. Publications include *The Poverty of Education: A Study in the Politics of Opportunity* (with

D. S. Byrne and B. Fletcher. Martin Robertson 1975) and *Education, Social Structure and Development* (Macmillan 1979).

ALAN WOODLEY

Research fellow in the Survey Research Department of the Open University, he is currently working on a national study of mature students which is funded by the Department of Education and Science. His publications include an evaluation of the Open University Younger Student Pilot Scheme, *The Door Stood Open* (Falmer Press 1980).

DAVID WARREN PIPER
(Editor)

Head of the University Teaching Methods Unit, University of London Institute of Education, he is a member of the Governing Council of the Society for Research into Higher Education who commissioned this book. Previous publications include *Efficiency and Effectiveness in Higher Education* (ed UTMU 1978); *The Changing University* (with Ron Glatter, NFER 1977).

ACKNOWLEDGEMENTS

In producing this volume the authors no doubt have their unsung heroes or, more likely, heroines. As editor I have had immense support from Kate Tierney, the secretary of UTMU, and Sally Kington, the Society's publications officer.

The book was produced in association with a conference, 'Biases in Higher Education', organized by the Society in December 1981. A number of bodies assisted, either financially or in practical ways, with the conference. They include the Equal Opportunities Commission, the Commission for Racial Equality, the Commission of European Communities and the International Year of Disabled People. The conference was hosted by the Staff Development Unit, Manchester Polytechnic.

CONTENTS

The authors contributing to this book were asked to review evidence of various forms of bias in the British higher education system. The word 'bias' was chosen to suggest a characteristic of the system rather than the prejudices which individuals might exercise. Authors were also asked to consider Britain within a European context and to draw evidence where it seemed appropriate from other parts of the world. Partly this is because the characteristics of a system become clear in comparison with alternatives, partly because evidence from other countries suggests lessons for us, partly because for some topics most of the research has been done abroad. Thus Bill Williamson compares the class structure of the British system with that of other European countries, Alan Little describes at some length the working of the discrimination laws in the United States, and John Richardson draws on work from countries where geographical distances are so great that the effect on people's chances of becoming students is more obvious than in a small island.

Finally, authors were invited to interpret the evidence they reviewed and to take a position on its implications. Although asked to do so in a manner befitting a learned society, avoiding polemic, the subjects of 'bias' and 'fairness' are, by definition, ones in which a neutral position cannot exist. 'Bias' exists only in relation to some notion of normality, rightness or straightness. 'Fairness' is an expression of values which make up part of social awareness, and reflect the ethics of a particular society at a particular time. The authors are necessarily taking ethical positions, some very strongly so.

The relativity implicit in these notions and their social origins ensures a certain reflexiveness when it comes to applying them to education; the education system itself is deeply implicated in setting the ideals and standards by which bias and fairness may be judged. I will return to the point later.

Many different forms of bias could be explored, and choices had to be made in planning this book. There are, for instance, biases in the functions an education system plays in society. Is its primary purpose to offer educational opportunities to individuals, or rather to produce a mixture of qualified people which matches the demands of employers? Of course, a system can do both, but not equally well; the reality of the choice is demonstrated by changes in government policy in the United Kingdom in the past twenty years. The Robbins principle of places in higher education for all who were qualified and wanted them in whatever subjects they chose, led in the sixties and seventies to a mismatch between the jobs on offer and the aspirations of graduates. The policies first of 'level funding' and then of cuts in the university budgets marked a change of view about the function of the higher education system from that of providing individuals with opportunity to one of producing a system with 'relevance' to the national economy.

Even with this change, other biases persist, such as the Protestant work ethic which may be seen as compounding the psychological stress on the unemployed, or the views of women's social role stoking the guilt felt by women employed outside the home. Perhaps an education truly relevant to the modern world would address such issues and, as Dale Spender argues, we would come to see as biases some matters which at present we hardly see at all, so completely do we accept their normality.

Other biases of a more academic sort exist. The secular nature of British higher education, developing through the Reformation, the Enlightenment and industrialization, is outlined by John Gay. The Catholic Church may be seen to be still deeply divided on its response to finding itself no longer at the centre of Western education. Within its own education system, one might point to the antipathy between the departments of Theology and Spirituality in the Pontifical Gregorian University; the first focusing on an abstract system of ethics, the second on human experience, each implying fundamentally different views of the role of the Church in education. On a wider scale, one might explore the extent to which the notions of the Enlightenment inform teaching in modern Latin America where the route from Paris was via Madrid and where Jesuit universities form an influential part of higher education. Such studies would, by contrast, give further insight into the biases of our own system.

Another 'academic' bias of historical significance is towards English rather than classics, a definitive characteristic of the modern university; others, the relative emphases on arts and science, on pure and applied study. None of these issues was taken directly as the subject for a chapter of this book. Instead, education is considered as a service to the community. The question is then asked: which sections of that community are disadvantaged? Different ways of classifying the community are considered: by social class, where people live, race, age, sex, able bodiedness, religion, and language. How does each of these factors affect the chances of individuals applying for, being accepted by, succeeding in and benefiting from the education system? Each chapter reviews and interprets the evidence.

To structure the book in this way is not to abandon consideration of those other biases discussed above. First, the social biases for or against certain groups of people are intimately bound up with the philosophical basis of what is taught. As a demonstration of this direct connection, Tyrrell Burgess in his chapter links the Popperian paradigm of scientific method to the practical possibility of a non-exclusive education system.

Second, the interpretation of evidence itself rests on a theoretical stance and, as Gordon Brotherston points out at the end of the book, different theories can lead to quite contrary interpretations of the evidence.

The eight areas of bias chosen are not the only ones. It is perhaps a notable exception that there is no chapter on political bias. Three reasons why it does not arise naturally in the context of the British education system are: the absence of any policy such as *berufsverbot* in Germany; the explicit separation of the universities from political institutions; and the claim of the disinterestedness of scholarly inquiry. The same, however, could be said of religious bias, and that does find a place here.

Although conceptually different, some of the category systems do empirically correlate. Thus, political affiliation would relate closely to religion in Northern Ireland and rather less closely to social class in the rest of the United Kingdom. Within higher education there is a correlation between age and sex: there is an above-average proportion of women among 'mature students', which leads to some tendency for the problems statistically associated with the older students to be those experienced by virtue of womanhood. Other category systems employed are conceptually related. The most obvious is that language and religion are both aspects of culture which are subsumed under problems of race. Indeed, strictly speaking the term 'race', in a biological sense, is not very helpful when trying to identify causes and effects of disadvantage. A biological view of race would lump together West African and West Indians, Maoris and Polynesians, Pakistanis and Indians, whose problems with Western education are different. In effect, 'race' is used as a convenient shorthand for minority cultures, in fact defined by self-identity, language, religion and a whole range of social ritual and value systems. But such self-identity, social ritual and value systems define any sub-culture, including those differentiated under 'class'. Thus it is that many of the things which may be said about class may also be said about ethnic minorities.

Some of the things which ethnic minorities and the working class have in common are also shared by women. First is a lack of involvement in centres of power, not entirely compensated for through trade unions, political representation or pressure groups. Consequently, all three are in a dependent position in our society. Secondly, all three are offered an education which springs naturally from none of their cultures. This is plainly so in the case of ethnic minorities. It is true also of the working class; the education we offer is not designed by the working class to perpetuate working-class values; it is designed by the middle class. Those who teach in it, whatever their origins, become middle class by virtue of their position; and its purpose is to give people an opportunity for social mobility or, put in another way, to universalize middle-class culture. In the case of women, the position is rather more complicated. It cannot be said that women are not part of the culture which produced our education system, and they clearly have been among the key contributors to its development; but the feminist argument is that, even so, education reflects a male orientated culture. In so far as that is true, so is it true that education does not spring from the culture feminists are fighting to create. Thirdly, all three are offered an education which is the conventional path from their present culture to that of the dominant group. It is the way which promises West Indians they can become so English that they are fully integrated into the general community, promises the working class social mobility, and women success in terms conceived of by men.

As the chapters in this book detail, all three groups are educationally disadvantaged to varying degrees in the same ways. A smaller proportion aspire to higher education. A smaller proportion become eligible for entry. The criteria by which students are selected may tell against them. The educational experience offered is fashioned primarily to suit the dominant group. The assessment system may incidentally underrate them. The extent to which their life chances are improved by education may be less than for others.

If the problems which beset these groups have much in common, the solutions which are offered have rather less. We might consider the differences and the reasons for them. In general terms, the feminists' solution to the disadvantaging of women is to change the education system: not only the selection system and the content of the courses but, more fundamentally, the educational aims and the very structure of knowledge. At the same time, primary and secondary education would tackle the attitudes which lead to the reluctance of girls to enter higher education. Strictly speaking, this is not a move to make education more relevant to women or some notion of a woman's culture; it is an intention to develop an education system relevant to a new society in which men and women are equally influential.

The key point is that education is always an induction into a given culture. Feminists seek to change the culture and the education system with it. Thus, with the working class the solution offered is crucially different. The higher education system may be altered to make it easier for working-class people to enter, and its content made more attractive and accessible, but its *purpose* cannot be compromised; not in the way that it must be when trying to create a society where the sexes are equal. The reason is that the inequality is incidental to the definition of the sexes, but it is essential to the definition of class. The concept of making middle- and working-class equal, in the way that men and women may some day be equal, has no sense. Class is a way of describing inequality. Further, in so far as there is an egalitarian ideal in education, it would be one of releasing people from the working class and making middle-class virtues universal.

The key point this time is that education necessarily subverts, weakens and eventually destroys one culture in order to replace it with another. Feminists have no doubt of the desirability of destroying the culture which encourages girls to underrate themselves. Even populist education movements have no doubt of the desirability of destroying the culture which encourages the working class to accept an underpriviledged position. They are cultures against which it is right to bias our education. Are there equally no doubts about the desirability of subverting the culture of an ethnic minority? It seems there is very little choice. If the minority group is totally subject to the economic, social and legal ways of the host country, it will necessarily be disadvantaged if it eschews the education which provides the most likely way of getting on equal terms. It might be difficult for schools to try to establish a positive attitude towards further education in children whose home and neighbourhood culture is suggesting something other, but that is what they must be committed to doing, and it is a deliberate attack on the value system of a social group, just as it is in the case of the working class. Why do we hesitate? Perhaps some feel less justified because with, say West Indians, it feels more like *outside* interference than when the same is done with poor white urban communities; but that is only to say how much greater is the alienation. Perhaps for others it is because they are less sure than our grandfathers of the intrinsic superiority of our culture over those of the New Commonwealth, the Old Empire. Could we, then, change our culture to one which eliminates the basic inequalities which in their turn make the education on offer so unattractive to certain ethnic groups — much as we are proposing in the case of women? In principle the answer may be 'Yes'; in practice there are a number of differences between the case of the ethnic groups and that of women. The first is that women constitute half the population, whereas the immigrant ethnic groups are very small in number. Secondly, the ethnic groups come from several discrete cultures, whereas the women's movement is an attempt to unite women to a common cause. Thirdly, women have always been involved in and fashioned by our culture; however unfair it has been, it is not alien. Fourthly, on the whole, the demand from ethnic minorities is for fair treatment within the current society, not, as with women, for a radically altered society.

An attractive compromise is to aim for an education system which alters only one aspect of a culture — that of not valuing the education on offer — whilst leaving the rest intact. But one might doubt if such a thing is possible, given the deep, complex and not always obvious connections between those social interactions which in sum amount to a culture. An ethnic minority group, then, is in a peculiar position: perhaps spirited in its attempt to resist the incursion of an alien education, but more in need of operating within the mores of the dominant society than the working class, for they can influence it less; perhaps having a contribution to make to a new common culture, but hopelessly outnumbered.

So with the three groups — women, the working class and ethnic minorities — who seemingly have similar problems, different situations seem likely to prevail. With women we change the purpose of education, with the working class and with ethnic minorities we change anything except the purpose, that of inducting them into the dominant society. The difference between the last two hinges on the desirability of changing the culture of those on the receiving end — are we releasing people from a cramping social environment or destroying a rich variation in human society?

There is a parallel ethical problem on an international scale, also touched upon in this book, when a society exports its culture to another land. Is 'educating' the Auca Indians of the Amazon Basin justified? Their culture too is inevitably destroyed by it. The question seems to pivot on the matter of dependency. If there is any justification for destroying the culture of an immigrant ethnic minority it is because that is the only means by which they might prosper in the host society. Their disadvantage is relative to and lies in their relationship with others in the society upon which they are wholly dependent. If it is true that the Auca Indians could continue to live independently of the western economic system, then the perception of their state as disadvantaged becomes less certain and the introduction of a Western biased education a morally doubtful proposition. What of countries already economically linked with other cultures? Here there is another kind of dilemma. Some people, in Nigeria for instance, argue for an indigenous education being offered by the universities as a means of redressing the bias towards an English culture which ironically bequeathed the idea of the universities in question. At the same time, however, they would wish for those people who are products of those institutions to shine on the international stage of scholarship, technology and business. We may wish that the philosophy, scholarship and science which infuse national education programmes, international trade, multinational business and intercontinental warfare owed as much to African, native American, and Asian cultures as they do to European, but at present they do not. Consequently an education indigenous to any other but a European culture cannot prepare people to compete in the 'international' world of scholarship and Big Science as it is today. The science education spawned by the European Enlightenment attacks the magical explanations of natural events both of the Auca Indians and of English children without side. That is not to say there are no other international movements or that we are not moving towards a common world culture; that is exactly the implication of the 'Global Village'; but even an education to a truly 'international' culture would destroy local cultures.

All this points to the complexity of posing such a question as 'Is Higher Education Fair?' with respect to our own country. Part of the problem is that the concept of fairness itself is one of the ideas developed and spread by our Western education system. It is part of our culture. However, it is a concept not always adequate for resolving some choices. Alan Little points to conflicts between being fair to individuals and fair to disadvantaged groups, also to the arbitrariness of perceiving provision for one group to be at the expense of provision for another. Yet a resolution of such dilemmas becomes more pressing if our universities, polytechnics and colleges are to become more exclusive. Will the cuts disproportionately affect those categories of people already under-represented in higher education? We must also ask the eventual cost to us all of these biases in our system.

This, finally, is the justification for the title of the book. Together, the papers presented here amount to a detailed and uniquely comprehensive analysis of the extent to which higher education involves members of our society. In so doing, it must pose the ethical questions: what kind of society do we want; what do we consider to be a just education system and exactly what do we mean by asking 'Is Higher Education Fair?'

David Warren Piper
London 1981

BIAS IS OF THE ESSENCE

Tyrrell Burgess

Higher education is exclusive. In 1980 some 113,000 eighteen-year-olds entered universities and colleges to begin courses which fall under the conventional definitions of higher education. Of the 793,000 not doing so, a small number had wished to go but had been positively excluded, either because they had not the minimum qualifications or because places were offered instead to better qualified applicants. A far greater number were effectively excluded because their previous education had denied them the chance or even the ambition to consider higher education. In an important international study of admissions to higher education nearly twenty years ago, Frank Bowles characterized the 'European' system as one in which selection began early in secondary education and was confirmed by an examination at the end of compulsory schooling which eliminated large numbers (Bowles 1963). Since then, the selection process popularly known as the eleven plus has been much mitigated, to be replaced by a gradual winnowing in the early years of secondary school. The effect of public examinations at sixteen is still to exclude from consideration for higher education most of the secondary school population. Even in a more open system there will of course always be individuals, perhaps large numbers, who do not wish to pursue academic life further. They are often said to be excluded, not by any barriers put in their way but by their understanding of their own best interests.

No one doubts the exclusiveness of higher education. Indeed in the English or European tradition, such exclusiveness is inseparable from the idea of higher education itself. An egregious example of this may be found on the first page of Sir Charles Carter's latest book: '. . . no one would consider a twelve session course in lampshade making for bored suburban housewives to be "higher education" ' (Carter 1980). Most people, inside and outside education, would however regard the exclusiveness as 'academic' and in intention neutral. They would argue that in admitting people to higher education there is no desire to exclude on any but objective academic grounds. There is no intention to discriminate except in educational terms. If there are too few places, then the better qualified will be admitted.

It has long been recognized that, whatever the intention, the effects of academic exclusiveness are not in other respects neutral. Those in higher education do not display the same characteristics as the adult population as a whole. They are overwhelmingly young, and even among the young they are preponderantly white middle-class men. It is possible to characterize those in higher education in such a way that groups of various kinds and sizes are revealed to be 'under-represented'. On the evidence of those who do get to higher education, there are effective biases against age, class, disability, some areas of origin, language, religion, race and sex. The instance of such biases is detailed in the chapters which follow. For example, Bill Williamson points out that children from the upper social stratum of our society are five times more likely to go to university than those from the lower stratum. Alan Little considers the position of ethnic groups and points out that, whereas 5 per cent of all school-leavers go on to a full-time degree course, the figures for West Indians and Asians are 1 per cent and 3 per cent respectively. Dale Spender, in discussing sexual inequality, quotes the remarkable fact that women are so poorly represented amongst the senior staff of universities as to make up only 2.3 per cent of professors. Even the student body is predominantly male, with women making up but 36.8 per cent of undergraduates and less than 30 per cent of postgraduates.

The chapters in this book do more than investigate instances of bias. They also seek to examine how such biases occur, often with a view to putting things right. Remedies are sought in changes in admissions processes, in school education, in attitudes and values, in socio-economic circumstances and even in cultural traditions. No doubt there is much which can be done outside higher education itself. Much can be learned by regarding universities and colleges as social institutions which have social consequences. But universities and colleges are pre-eminently educational institutions. If their practice has unintended or undesirable consequences it is to their educational practice that we must first turn. It is the argument of this chapter that biases in higher education are inherent, not accidental. They stem from the practice, and indeed the implied theory, of higher education institutions. They will remain unless the central activity of education is reformed. The purpose of this chapter is to set out the theory and practice of higher education and examine its consequences, to propose an alternative theory of knowledge and learning upon which the systematic biases of the system can be eliminated and to give one practical example based upon the theories proposed.

It is important to begin by realizing that 'higher education' is recognizably similar, not only throughout Britian but throughout the world. There are of course many evident diversities. Higher education is differently organized in different countries. In some the variety of provision is very great: higher education may form part of a tertiary system of post-school education or may be recognizably isolated and distinct. Countries differ in their proportion of specialist professional institutions alongside universities or colleges offering a liberal and general education. The balance between full-time and part-time students differs too. There may be important differences in the degree of state control. The institutions of higher education may also differ. A university may have a hundred thousand students on a dozen campuses or a thousand students on one. They may be more or less committed to a 'collegiate' system. They may or may not emphasize residence as part of their educational experience.

Britain contains an unusual degree of diversity in higher education. It has two systems of funding and control. It has very ancient and very modern institutions. Some institutions offer only postgraduate study: others offer a range from below first-degree level to well above it. There is a large variety of modes of attendance, from full-time to evening only.

These differences give rise to interest and study: there is a small but flourishing discipline of comparative higher education. What these studies tend to reveal, however, is that the differences, though important and interesting, are relatively superficial. In their central activities, of teaching and research, institutions of higher education conform. The point was put by an anonymous school-leaver, invited by his former headmaster to admire his old school's new building. He said: 'It could all be of marble, Sir, but it would still be a bloody school' (Newsom 1963). Or as Frank Bowles more soberly put it, in his discussion of two systems of admission to higher education: 'Both systems deal with the common body of the world's knowledge and both teach in the way men have always taught' (Bowles 1962).

Methods of teaching are not only consistent from place to place all over the world, but have been so since Aristotle. Students in higher education attend lectures, seminars or tutorials. They read books, write essays for their teachers' judgement, watch demonstrations. They may carry out 'experiments': that is, go through prescribed procedures in order to see for themselves some established process of work. They may get to do project work. In relatively rich places, the students may get a lot of individual attention: elsewhere they are dealt with very much in groups. In large institutions there may be a wide choice of subjects and of teachers; in smaller places there may be no choice at all. Usually, but not always, the higher the level, the more independence the student may have. Usually, though unnecessarily, arts students have more independence than science students. Throughout, the object of all these activities is to cover a set amount of knowledge (the course, curriculum, syllabus) and then convince the examiners that one has done so.

These methods derive from the way in which academic life is organized. Its normal form is the subject department headed by a professor, grouped sometimes in 'faculties' of allied departments. The dominance of the subject department is more recent than most people think, and it has been more resistant to change than academics believe. It derives from reforms both in Europe and the United States in the late nineteenth century. The consequence was well put by J. R. Gass in a preface to an OECD study of 'interdisciplinarity' (OECD 1972). He said: 'The disciplines are not only a convenient breakdown of knowledge into its component parts, they are also the basis of the organization of the university into its autonomus fiefs, and of the professions engaged in teaching and research.' To meddle with the disciplines, he concluded, was to meddle with the whole social structure of the university.

This can be well understood by considering the ways in which successful academics describe academic organization. This is how the vice-chancellor of a British university interpreted his university's charter in a book designed to explain universities to the public (Aitken 1966): 'The Charter declares . . . the university . . . "shall be both a teaching and an examining university, and shall further the prosecution of original research in all its branches". The branches of research, which are the branches of knowledge, determine the organization of academic study.'

In his university, like so many others, academic organization is divided broadly into faculties (of science and engineering; arts; medicine and dentistry; commerce and social science; and law) and then subdivided into departments. With their constituent departments the faculties form the framework of teaching and research 'and therefore of academic administration'. Organizationally a department is subordinate to a faculty and a faculty to the university senate. This subordination may be embodied in regulations. For example, 'the pattern of courses leading to a degree is often devised in a department, but requires the approval of the faculty and of the senate, whereas the content and the method of teaching of a subject course are left to be decided by the head of the department, in consultation with his departmental staff.' The teaching activities of a department are co-ordinated by the faculty, since a given student may be taught in more departments than one. The examining activities of a department are regulated by the faculty and the senate, in the interests of 'reasonably uniform standards'.

Sir Robert also offers this interesting contrast: 'Even problems of the timetabling of classes sometimes have to come to the Senate to be settled. By contrast, the research activities of a department are almost entirely its own affair; they are determined by the interests and ideas of the head of the department, and his staff (with his approval). . . .' Could even fiefdom go further? The central activity of research is independent: there is horsetrading over timetables.

Most teaching and research programmes can fit into and be administered in this framework, says the vice-chancellor, but a few *refuse to conform* with it (his italics). The solution is the extra-faculty department. Administrative problems also appear with degree courses taught in departments in more than one faculty: they are met either by cross-membership of the faculties concerned or by the establishment of joint boards or committees.

Departments are headed by professors to whom their staffs are responsible. Larger departments may have two or more professors, each responsible for teaching and research in a division of the subject, each with his academic staff. Departments not only grow, they divide. Sometimes a completely new department is formed, its subject forming a separate new degree programme. Sometimes new departments, separate for their administration and postgraduate work, remain associated in a 'school' for undergraduate teaching. There are also 'personal professorships' — for professors without portfolio, so to speak. All professors, in Sir Robert's university, were members of the senate.

It is by these means that academic life is based upon the establishment of a number of subjects, each with an organized body of knowledge and a 'structure' of its own. Upon these subjects is erected an academic bureaucracy through which the academic institution is organized. Attempts to break away from it, towards 'interdisciplinarity' with 'new maps of learning' in the British universities founded in the 1960s, towards increasing student choice through 'modules' and 'options', 'majors' and 'units', have failed before the resilience of the subject department.

This resilience accounts for the persistence of the dominant tradition of higher education the world over. I have elsewhere (Burgess 1977) called this the 'autonomous' tradition, and I contrast it with another, weaker, 'service' tradition. The first sees higher education as an activity with its own values and purposes, affecting the rest of society obliquely and as a kind of bonus. The second explicitly expects education to serve individuals and society and defends it in these terms.

The autonomous tradition is aloof, academic, conservative and exclusive. People and institutions acting in this tradition and with this view of their purpose think it right to hold themselves apart, ready if necessary to resist the demands of society, the whims of government, the fashions of public opinion, the importunities of actual or potential students. Many of us are glad that they do so. In totalitarian countries their stand may be heroic: educational institutions are often the first to be attacked by tyrannical governments. We can be glad of them in democracies too. Democratic governments can err. Popular demand may be foolish. Both can be arbitrary, unjust and capricious. A democratic society is a plural society, one in which criticism is welcome and alternatives possible. What is more, democracies recognize that there can be no certainty where human knowledge and understanding will next be advanced. Many of the greatest advances have been made against political oppression, popular indifference or worse. The creations of the human mind themselves achieve a kind of autonomy, imposing their own problems, and it is right that there should be people devoted to following the disciplines and solving the problems. This is particularly true in areas where most people see little promise: you never know when a discipline may be urgently needed.

This aloofness is expressed in academic attitudes. Defenders of an autonomous tradition claim to be concerned with the preservation, extension and dissemination of knowledge — for its own sake. They speak of pursuing truth or excellence. They will, they say, follow the truth, wherever it may lead. However described, the activity is self-justifying. At least, it is not justified in terms outside itself, like meeting the needs of society. Academics derive their justification from a discipline or body of knowledge.

As we have seen, autonomous institutions are by their nature conservative. It is true that within them advances may be made at the frontiers of knowledge, though they are by no means the only places where such advances are made. On the whole, however, they are resistant of new disciplines. Science, technology, art have all had their battles for recognition as disciplines. It is hard to get new matter into undergraduate courses or to drop old matter. Interdisciplinary courses always fail. This conservatism is defensible. It derives from the conviction that knowledge advances painfully by imposing order where previously there was chaos. Intellectual order is thus precious and vulnerable. Neglect of this may involve us all simply in attempts to teach chaos.

There is a very important consequence of all this for students and for the concerns expressed in this book. Autonomous institutions have to be exclusive. Given that what they do is self-justifying, they can responsibly accept only those who might 'benefit' from what they are doing. This effectively excludes most people. The exclusion may also be defended on the ground of maintaining standards, but since entry requirements are variable, this defence often rings hollow. Of course it is now widely recognized that exclusiveness, though ostensibly academic, is effectively social. The processes of selection, which in many countries begin in the schools, ensure that middle-class youngsters are over-represented in higher education, and working-class youngsters under-represented. In many countries the discrepancy is gross. The under-representation of other groups in higher education is documented elsewhere in this book. This is an inevitable consequence of the autonomous tradition and its expression in academic organization and educational practice.

Perhaps the point can be made clearer by contrast with the service tradition which is responsive, vocational, innovating and open. Institutions in this tradition do not think it right to hold themselves apart from society: rather that they should respond to its needs. They seek to place the knowledge that they have at the service of society. Indeed they believe that human knowledge advances as much through the solution of practical problems as through pure thought. It is important not to underestimate or vulgarize the service tradition. In seeking to serve it confronts very serious difficulties. In the first place there is the question of service to whom? Is it the student who is to be served, society as a whole, the government? There are many different interests — which is to be paramount? Can the institution serve more than one? The autonomous tradition settles this by asserting the priority of the discipline. The service tradition lays itself open instead to having serious human and political arguments. Clearly, different interests are not always compatible. For example, the interest of an employer in further education may be that his workers should do their jobs better; the interest of the employee, by contrast, may be to get a better job. Neither may be very well aware of what society, as interpreted by an elected government, may require or want.

Second, it is not merely a paradox to assert that one of the services which educational institutions should render to a society is a serious and direct criticism of it. There are few countries where this is explicitly recognized: the United States is the only place I know where a formally constituted committee has actually done so (Carnegie 1973). But criticism is vital to a democratic society, and a service institution is failing if it does not offer it.

All this raises the question of accountability. The challenge for service institutions is to work out forms of government which will enable them to do their work, which includes criticism, while responding to the society around them. It is not too much to say that this is one of the most serious problems democratic societies have to face, not only in education, but in all forms of social and political life.

Service institutions do not, on the whole, seek to claim that they are pursuing knowledge for its own sake. They are engaged explicitly in professional and vocational education — often in 'mere' vocational training. They attract resources because there are actual or potential students to be enrolled. Their 'research' is normally directed to some external problem, often in the form of consultancy. Apart from this they are typically teaching institution, devoted to helping students towards some qualification.

There are many people who would feel that to call service institutions innovating is to be at best fanciful. But it is in their nature to be so: they must accommodate growth, must accept new kinds of students, offer them new kinds of courses, create new structures of study, pioneer new forms of governance, recruit new kinds of staff, and so on. An OECD symposium on innovation in higher education (Burgess and Pratt 1971) revealed that not only in Britain, but in many diverse systems, where institutions were prepared to accept the service view of purpose, they were indeed innovating in all these ways.

Thus it is that service institutions have to be open. They cannot exclude students on the grounds that the latter are not properly prepared. Typically they accept 'maturity' or some such idea as an alternative to academic qualification as an entry requirement. Their students are as a consequence very diverse in themselves; they follow courses at many levels and by many different modes of study. In many countries they are the traditional route to high qualification for working-class people and their children. If systematic biases are to be eliminated in higher education, it will be necessary to extend the service tradition.

In reality the pressures are in the opposite direction. I have elsewhere discussed the process which I have called 'academic drift' (Burgess and Pratt 1970; Pratt and Burgess 1974). This is a world-wide tendency for institutions founded explicitly in the service tradition to seek to become more and more autonomous. Thus we see that in England the polytechnics (like the colleges of advanced technology before them) have sought to resolve dilemmas of accountability through reducing public control, have chafed at external academic validation, have emphasized a commitment to research, have established subject departments and faculties, have transferred 'inappropriate' courses elsewhere, have rejected students they would have previously taken. This is academic drift at work. A consequence is that outside education, in politics and administration, people simply fail to see any difference between universities and polytechnics. Disillusionment is expressed that the polytechnics are not doing what they were meant to do, that any distinctiveness they might once have claimed has now disappeared. A similar frustration can be seen among those who expected that the abolition of selection at eleven would enable secondary schools more effectively to meet the needs of every kind of adolescent. Instead they find, against all the hopes of the reformers of the 1920s, that most secondary schools have been content to offer to all the narrow range of values, experience and performance which formerly characterized the academic grammar schools.

There are many who explain 'academic drift' in institutional terms. They argue, for example, that it is natural for new or emerging institutions to ape those with established prestige. For a long time it was held that pay and conditions of service in 'autonomous' institutions were better than those in 'service' ones. There is of course also the general institutional point that any institution, however explicit the purpose for which it was founded, soon comes to have purposes of its own and indeed to act in ways which were not foreseen or intended. It is the institutions which are responsible day to day for what happens. Their staffs have their own goals. There may be directives and regulations, there may be a powerful board of governors or trustees, there may be all manner of devices for implementing the original policy — but these must in the end be powerless against the minute-by-minute, hour-by-hour, day-by-day activity of those actually in the institutions.

Their chief object (like that of everyone else) is the good life. In unequal systems, the less favoured tend to interpret this (sometimes wrongly) in terms of the situation of the fortunate. Universities explicitly have status in the eyes of government and of the public. This 'autonomous' status is thought to derive from various attributes of external and internal organization. Technical colleges thus strive to take on these attributes, generally without considering whether or not they are apt to themselves and their 'service' tradition — whether, in other words, arrangements which serve one purpose can reasonably be expected to serve another. It is quite common for instituions which have drifted academically to be genuinely astonished to find how they have changed: they can be heard asserting, all over the world, that they did not mean it.

All these pressures towards academic drift have very great force, and I have argued elsewhere that every institutional means possible should be used if there is to be any real attempt to prevent it. But I do not believe that this would ever be enough. We are dealing, after all, not just with *any* institutions but with educational institutions, and I believe that institutional changes will fail unless they are based upon and reflect educational changes. The autonomous tradition rests upon assumptions about knowledge, learning and education which are accepted without question throughout education and society. The prestige of universities and sixth forms derives from the convention that they know what they are doing. It seems only the plainest common sense that those who have spent a lifetime in the study of a subject, who have become specialist and expert in it, should be those who can say not only what the subject is and what are its characteristic insights and techniques, but can also introduce to its mysteries the less educated and less expert. There is a phrase used by academics which is in my experience unquestioned as a statement of what they do — that is the preservation, extension and dissemination of knowledge. If one talks to teachers of vocational skills one finds that their expressions are different, but their purpose is the same. And for all the accompanying claims about developing the individual which are uttered by teachers in both universities and colleges, it is clear that they mostly expect to do so through instruction in various branches of knowledge. If this view of knowledge is right, we are condemned, I believe, to the dominance of the autonomous tradition and we must reconcile ourselves to permanent biases in higher education.

Fortunately we do not have to accept this view of knowledge at all. The autonomous tradition in education, so far from being soundly based, rests in my view on assumptions about knowledge which are quite simply mistaken and on grounds which are intellectually and practically worthless.

It may be thought that the claim that our universities and colleges rest on intellectually worthless foundations is a bold claim to make. The possibility of making it arises from the discrepancy between known theories of learning and the practice of teaching. This is not the place to discuss the various competing and often incompatible theories of learning derived from the habits of those pigeons, rats and circus apes that have had the misfortune to be captured by learning theorists. It is enough to recognize that whatever the differences between these theories, they all have one characteristic in common. They hold that learning takes place through the activity of the learner. Educational practice, however, implicitly assumes that learning takes place through the activity of the teacher. Teachers have and control subjects, disciplines and bodies of knowledge, and the taught do not. Teachers present their material and the taught acquire and then reproduce it. Unfortunately this almost universal practice among teachers flies in the face of what is almost universally agreed about learning. Teaching and learning are in our current practice largely disconnected. Indeed there appear to be two kinds of need in the world, the need to learn and the need to teach. These two needs are at war: the one is incompatible with the other. In other words, where our educational institutions fail, the failure is at heart an eductional one. It is because they fail in education that they are so disappointing to individuals and to society.

This conclusion requires some explanation. To put it mildly, university and college teachers are not on the whole stupid. Nor do people go into teaching because they are filled with ill will or loathe their fellow men.

Teachers do what they do because they believe it to be right, and many of them show great humanity and ingenuity in mitigating in practice the worst effects of their implicitly held theories and beliefs.

Why is it then that teachers think it right, indeed accept without question, that they should act in ways that neglect or even oppose what they know about learning? The answer, I think, is partly that theories of learning are unsatisfactory and unconvincing and partly that teachers, like most people, have an implicit view of knowledge on which their practice depends but which chimes ill with theories of learning. What we need in short is a theory which better explains how people learn which is consistent with a theory of knowledge.

Most people have what one might describe as an accumulative view of knowledge. It seems obvious that more is known now than was known a hundred years ago. Over the centuries bodies of knowledge have been built up through the accumulation of facts. In recent centuries men have come to believe that a particular kind of knowledge, scientific knowledge, is an especially secure and reliable kind. It began with the physical sciences, but other sciences have aspired to the same kind of security. It was and is believed that what gives scientific knowledge its characteristic quality and security is its method. On this view, scientists base their activity upon observation — carefully controlled and measured observation. They record their findings, publish them and accumulate data. From this they may formulate hypotheses which fit the facts and explain the causal relations between them. They then seek evidence to support the hypothesis, and if the latter is thus verified they have established another law or theory. Science, on this view, is the accumulation of certainties based on observation and experimental evidence: numberless observations lead to a hypothesis which when verified is established as a law. This method of basing laws on accumulated observations is known as induction, and has for centuries been seen as the hallmark of science.

Of course the idea of induction has itself caused problems. It was David Hume who first spotted the logical difficulty which gave philosophers a good deal of trouble. The difficulty is that numberless confirming observations cannot give us any assurance that the next observation will be the same. Bertrand Russell in particular was worried that the rationality of science depended on a principle — induction — which could not itself be rationally defended.

It is the argument of this chapter that the organization and practice of higher education, both academically and institutionally, rests upon an implicit acceptance of induction; in other words upon a fallacy. It is impossible to speak, as academics do, of the preservation, extension and dissemination of knowledg unless one has in mind the gradual accumulation of certainties. The whole area of the preservation of knowledge is alien to scientific method: what we should be seeking to do is destroy our present theories. The organization of subject departments is defensible if they are small groups working on the problems of the subject, but not if they are (as they are) bureaucracies for the issue of established bodies of fact. It is accepted that one needs to have a first degree before one can do research: as if to say to the students, when you know enough you can start to think. The whole activity of teaching, in lectures, seminars, tutorials or what you will, is explicable only on the basis that knowledge exists and can be imparted. The presence of courses, syllabuses and curricula assumes that knowledge is somehow fixed and independent. It is this that leads to the claim that the theory and practice of higher education rests implicitly upon a foundation — induction — which is discredited. If we can deal with the problem of induction we can begin to rebuild higher education.

The boldest solution to the problem of induction has been offered by Karl Popper, who says bluntly: '. . . there is no induction, because universal theories are not deducible from singular statements. But they may be refuted by singular statements, since they may clash with descriptions of observable facts' (Popper 1976). For Popper the logic of scientific discovery is as follows: scientific discussions, he says, start with a problem (P_1), to which we offer a tentative theory (TT) or solution, hypothesis or conjecture. The theory is then criticized, to try to eliminate error (EE) — whereupon the theory and its critical revision give rise to new problems (P_2). As Popper puts it, 'science begins with problems and ends with problems'. But it does not begin and end with the same problems: P_2 is always different from P_1 — which is why we can speak of scientific progress. Popper sets this theory out as a schema or formula the importance of which has been overlooked by people who feel that if something is clear it must be trivial. This is it: $P_1 \longrightarrow TT \longrightarrow EE \longrightarrow P_2$.

Each step in this formulation, and its place in the sequence, has important consequences. It asserts, for example, the primacy of problems. The beginning of an inquiry is *not* the attempt to solve a problem (the tentative theory comes second, not first): it is the problem itself, and it is important to work as hard as possible on the formulation of problems before searching for solutions. This is because success in the latter often depends upon success in the former. An enormous amount of time and energy is wasted in the world by people who jump straight into solutions, and concentrate upon the difficulties of these — without pausing to consider whether they are apt for the problem formulated or even without formulating a problem at all. It is also misleading to talk of 'identifying' problems, as if the problems were sitting there waiting for us. They are not. Problem-formulation is a creative activity.

Nor should one be misled by the word 'tentative'. A theory is tentative because it has to be tested: it does not have to be half-hearted. Indeed, the bolder and more definite it is the better it can be tested. What we need are theories with a high informative content, because the more information they contrain the more likely they are to be false — but if they survive our best efforts to falsify them, they have enabled us to make a correspondingly large progress in understanding. The best theories are the most daring leaps of imagination, and science, like art, is an expression of the human spirit.

Error elimination is the process of expressing our theories in ways which can be tested. And the object of the test is to falsify the theory. This step is nearly as often neglected as the first — or is widely misunderstood. Neglect resides in the uncritical acceptance of theories, and in the unwillingness to consider what would falsify them. Misunderstanding arises because people think that the object of tests (or experiments) is to confirm a theory. But no amount of confirmation can make a theory more secure, and our knowledge remains as it was. But one falsification can destroy a theory — and our knowledge advances. We are ready to formulate the new problems.

With the introduction of falsifiability we reach Popper's criterion which demarcates science from non-science. This is itself one of those bold leaps of imagination whose consequences are only now being slowly realized. For example, it means that all knowledge, including scientific knowledge, is provisional, and always will be. We cannot prove that what we know is true, and it may turn out to be false. The best we can do is to justify our preference for one theory rather than another. Disciplines, even scientific disciplines, are not bodies of established fact: they are changing all the time, and not by the accumulation of new certainties. Of course, we assume the truth of our existing knowledge for practical purposes and are quite right to do so; but we must be ready for it to be superseded. What Popper has done is to replace the notion of certainty in science, and in all human knowledge, with the idea of progress. We cannot be sure that we have the truth: we can, however, systematically eliminate error. The way we eliminate error is by testing. In particular, observations are not used as a basis of a theory, but are derived from a theory and are used to test it. He says 'that observations, and even more so observation statements and statements of experimental results, are always *interpretations* of the facts observed; that they are *interpretations in the light of theories*' (Popper 1959).

What is interesting about Popper's theory of knowledge is that it is consistent with his theory of learning: indeed it is the same theory. Learning of any kind, not just discovery at the frontiers of knowledge, takes place through the formulation of problems and through trial and error in solving these problems.

What we have, in fact, is a continuum of learning, whose logic is the same, from the new-born babe to the research worker on the frontiers of knowledge. Each is engaged in the formulation of problems, in solving them and in testing the solutions. Most people will formulate problems that have been formulated many times before. Their proposed solutions will be familiar; their tests commonplace. But they will *learn* by this activity. They will not learn better or faster if we parcel up received solutions to problems formulated by others: indeed this is an anti-learning process. Moreover it inhibits the possibility of progress, because it is always possible that someone will formulate a common problem differently, will propose a different solution or a more effective test.

At the other end of the continuum are those people engaged on formulating problems which have remained unformulated in the past, who are leading the attack upon ignorance at its strongest. They may indeed be working in a discipline, upon the problems of the discipline, though it is a commonplace of scientific discovery that the successful formulation of problems may involve breaking through the limits of a discipline. The leap of imagination required of them may be enormous. But the nature of their activity is not arcane. We are all learners: in logic we are equals. It is my view that a higher education which is organized on the basis of the logic of learning will be more effective than one where every activity flies in the face of it.

There is something more, however, to be said about problems and their formulation. In Popper's schema of the logic of discovery he uses, interchangeably and often all together, a number of words for the second term of his schema — theory, solution, hypothesis, conjecture. This practice presumably derives from his impatience with discussions of meaning, which he regards as trivial. He does not wish understanding to be limited by definitions. What is more, it is part of what he is arguing that theories are solutions to problems, and solutions — even to practical problems — are theories. What is more, it is important to remember that the *logic* of the process is the same whatever the problems which are being tackled and at whatever level. I believe, however, that it is important to distinguish different kinds of problems. Indeed a failure to make this distinction vitiates much of our social as well as our educational practice. Let me give some examples. There are problems of what is the case, which we can call scientific problems. There are problems of how to get from one state of affairs to another, which we can call engineering problems (to use the examples of one engineer: how to get from one side of a river to another or from bread to toast). There are formal problems — those of mathematics, for example, or chess. There are philosophical problems, which include ethical and aesthetic problems.

Most people are concerned with the second of these kinds of problems, the engineering or practical problems. They need to know how to get from one state of affairs to another. Their problems concern their homes, families, jobs, incomes and leisure. They typically want to change their circumstances. In this they often believe that education will be a help.

Unfortunately they find that educators are preoccupied with the other kinds of problems and will fill them up with ready made scientific, formal and philosophical solutions. The courses offered presuppose that a grasp of these solutions must precede the tackling of practical problems. The whole activity of higher education, its teaching methods, its organized courses and its administered structure, assumes that knowledge is independent of problems. Few people ever ask, to what problem is this degree course a solution? If they do, the answer is seldom other than the problem of getting a degree. The examinations at the end of these courses test little more than the accumulation and manipulation of knowledge. The problems they pose are seldom more serious than the problem of passing the examination. Nor does the ideal of a community of scholars survive in practice the division between the teachers and the taught — the one with the duty to know and impart, the other with the duty to accept and to learn.

Of course there have been many people with this sense of unease about the practice of education. More important, there have been many teachers who have either instinctively or after worrying thought tried to organize learning rather than teaching. They have encouraged 'discovery methods', project work and independent learning. But they have been under attack, partly because these methods still sit uneasily in the rest of the system (how, for instance, does one examine such work?) and partly because they have been unable to give as coherent an intellectual account of themselves as is claimed by traditional academics. This insecurity is no longer justified. It is the traditional academic practice which needs to be defended.

In short, the consequences of the logic of learning for the practice of education are shattering. In the first place, what is important is not a particular fact or even a particular ordered collection of facts, but *method*. It is method rather than information which gives mastery, and it is method which must be the chief business of education. Nor is there any need to insist upon a particular field of human interest in which scientific method can be understood: an educator can use any interest of the student as a vehicle.

Second, it is clear that existing subject disciplines are ways of organizing knowledge from particular points of view. They were so organized to solve the problems of their practitioners. But these problems may no longer actually be those even of existing practitioners, let alone those of students and potential students. The presentation of knowledge as bodies of organized facts is a way of ensuring its unhelpfulness to most people.

Third, the provisional nature of knowledge suggests caution in regarding education as involving the accumulation of it. This is recognized increasingly as educators and their students find that it is possible, indeed normal, for the knowledge painfully acquired to become quickly out of date. Unfortunately the educators' solution is to offer 'refresher' or 'up-dating' courses, so that the students can have their obsolete knowledge replaced by some more — which will itself become obsolete in turn. There can be no sense in this process.

Fourth, since criticism is of the essence of the method, education must offer opportunities for students to be critical and to use criticism. It cannot, even (indeed especially) for the sake of instruction, ask the students to accept the greater knowledge, experience, wisdom of the teacher.

This implies, fifth, that it is the students who must take the initiative in planning their own education. There can be little justification for the prior imposition of curricula and syllabuses. Such curricula must necessarily presuppose purposes which may not be the students'.

Sixth, in testing the efficacy of the education provided we shall need to examine what it is the student can *do*, rather than what he knows. The latter always was a somewhat arbitrary proceeding, since even if the most successful undergraduate were to know all that an undergraduate *could* know — his knowledge would still be infinitesimal. Since we can know so little (and since what we know is provisional) we can at least learn how to do something — and what we can most sensibly do is tackle our own problems.

Most important, perhaps, this view of education cannot exclude people on the ground that they do not know enough, or have not had so many years previous education, or do not show an aptitude for a subject. These educational arrogances have a place only in a superseded view of knowledge.

We are in short face to face with the chance of a creative revolution in education. For almost all its history and in almost every place education has tended towards the autonomous. It has done so for what have been thought to be good 'educational' reasons. It is now clear that these reasons are not good: education can and should tend towards service and towards accommodating everyone. It can do so by accepting the logic of learning: by organizing education explicitly round the formulation of problems, the proposal of solutions and the testing of these solutions.

Nothing short of this offers a hope of eliminating biases in higher education against specific groups of people. We have a theory of learning which enables us to start with the people themselves and the problems which concern them. When we make people and their problems the centre of attention in higher education we can avoid biases against any of them. Until we do so the biases will remain.

There remains the question of whether this can be done. I wish to advance the bold claim that my colleagues and I in the School for Independent Study at North East London Polytechnic have shown that the organization of learning as described above is a practical possibility. The school offers programmes leading to a diploma of higher education and a degree. The method in each case is by independent study. In other words, we ask students themselves to plan their own programmes of higher education, not by choosing as in a cafeteria, from existing courses, modules, units or other packages, but by thinking seriously about themselves, their futures and what an educational programme might do for them. We ask them to consider when they arrive, what are the qualities, skills, knowledge and experience which they bring to the programme at the beginning. We ask them to say, tentatively at first for planning purposes, where they wish to be at the end of the programme and we encourage them to consider the problem of getting from where they are to where they want to be. The educational programme they then devise, with our help, is the educational solution to this problem.

Of course this experience is limited. The programme started in 1974 with an intake of a hundred students a year. But the school has taken on most of the organizational problems that such a programme creates. It has, for example, convinced the Council for National Academic Awards that they should validate the diploma and the degree so that the qualifications of its students have the same national standing as those of any other degree or diploma course. It has been able to give our students access to the accumulated knowledge and skills of colleagues in the polytechnic through a system of individual tuition and specialist interest. It has begun to develop the role of a personal tutor in such a programme of higher education. And it has managed to incorporate into the students' experience the kind of collaboration with peers which is absent in most other courses. I have no doubt that what the school tries to do could be done better (though it has not been done better yet). It must be done better and more widely if biases in higher education are to be eliminated.

CLASS BIAS

Bill Williamson

'He holds that dictated mental work on uncongenial subjects is overwork which injures the brain permanently. So we are not university graduates; but we are university men nevertheless. If a man is known to have been at Oxford or Cambridge nobody asks whether he has a degree or not' (George Bernard Shaw, *Buoyant Billions*). Secondborn explains why his father insisted on his leaving university without taking a degree.

All societies provide specialized institutions to pass on knowledge which is considered particularly vital to a way of life. What is regarded as knowledge deserving specialized understanding and training varies, of course, between cultures, as do the operative principles governing which people should have access to it. In Max Weber's view the character of a system of education is always dependent on the form of political domination within which it is found and, therefore, ultimately on the *life conduct* of a *decisive stratum* (Weber 1970). Specifically, he claims, what determines the 'pedagogy of cultivation' is the decisive stratum's 'ideal of cultivation'. If, as in the case of Japan, the decisive stratum were a warrior group, education would aim to form a 'stylized knight and courtier'. If a priestly stratum, education would aim to produce a scribe or intellectual. In the case of the Chinese literati, a genteel group of lay officials steeped in classical texts (that is, in the written word) dominated education and cultural life in China although they were both subordinate to the ruler and distinct from religious functionaries and military leaders. In the Europe of the middle ages and throughout the Islamic world, the control of higher learning was in the hands of a priestly or scholarly class distinct from secular rulers. This was not the case in China, with quite fundamental consequences for the development of conceptions of the scholar and of the qualities the scholar possessed. Mediaeval theologians in both Christian and Islamic universities generated a rational and dialectical theology, and certificates of competence were striven for. This again was not so in China. Weber notes: '. . . that the problems that have been basic to all Occidental philosophy have remained unknown in Chinese philosophy. With the greatest practical matter of factness, the intellectual tools remained in the form of parables, reminding us of the means of expression of Indian chieftains rather than of rational argumentation' (Weber 1970, p.433). This clearly was not an education which had any technical or functional relevance to the work the literati were expected to do. But it was indispensible as a way of legitimating their power and authority.

The point of these remarks is not, however, to open up a debate about whether the role of education, and higher education in particular is a technical-functional one or merely legitimatory (Collins 1971). Rather it is to inject from the outset a relativizing note into the discussion of the main theme — class bias — to underline heavily the need for an historical and comparative perspective on this question. At a minimum such a relativizing approach helps to render strange some of the principles which govern who should have access to high status knowledge in society. But far more importantly it invites questions about the degree of variation which exists among different societies about those principles and therefore questions about what aspects of the social structure of different societies are decisive in influencing the social shape of higher education. The example of the literati only suggests that kind of analysis which could, in principle, be carried out, in this case looking at the ideal of cultivation held by a dominant group and institutionalized in the practice of higher learning.

This theme will be taken up later, one of the key arguments of this paper being that the question of class bias cannot be discussed as if it were in some way concerned only with the social characteristics of those who apply to higher education: a problem, therefore, of the school system or of different patterns of child socialization. It is also a question of the form of higher education itself, its ethos, organization and pedagogy and social function, and to cast light on these questions we, too, need to know what the ideals of cultivation of the 'decisive strata' of our own societies are and in what ways they have changed.

QUESTIONS OF CLASS

The question of how higher education displays a social class bias is not, of course, a single question nor one that has a simple answer. It is complex and must be broken down into the many subsidiary questions which are implied within it. Nor are these questions just empirical ones: ie about quantities or trends for which, in principle, there is an answer if only the data were available. They are, in fact, conceptual too, since answers to them presuppose some further theoretical elaboration about the nature of class inequalities and the way in which these can be related to the structure and functioning of higher education.

I want to suggest in this chapter that the choice to be made in using the concept of social class is between the notion of class as a *category* and class as a *relationship*. My own preference, as will become clear, is for the latter, although the empirical complexities of using it in this way are enormous. Most of the time, however, particularly in the field of the sociology of education, or at least within the political arithmetic tradition within the sociology of education (Karabel and Halsey 1977), class is used as a categorical concept referring to groups of people with certain socio-economic characteristics which they share and in terms of which they are distinguished from other groups. It matters not at all here whether the people themselves conceive of themselves as part of a group, for this concept of class makes no reference to questions of identity, or consciousness, or feelings of solidarity. This, as I shall argue, is a serious omission. The advantages are that used in this way the concept can be operationalized; it can be given precise indicators.

Within the class-as-category tradition of research the typical questions asked are. How closely related are the social class distribution of the population of society and the social class distribution of the student body in higher education? How have such distributions changed over time? (Kelsall, Pool and Kuhn 1972; Halsey 1977.) The logic of such questions leads us quite naturally to more precise formulations. What are the relative chances of people from different social classes winning the opportunity of higher education? Have relative life chances been affected by such variables as demographic and occupational change? And the next step is to explore a multitude of relationships. Do educational life chances vary according to sex or region? Do people from different social class backgrounds have different preferences for higher education? How are inequalities in higher education related to inequalities in the system of secondary education? At each step the logic of the form of questioning leads to a closer specification of the problem. How far, for example, do different procedures of admission to higher education affect the opportunities of people from different social class backgrounds? Do different structures of higher education influence class participation rates? (Neave 1976.) In what way does the nature of the courses offered in higher education affect the social class distribution of students across different courses? (Burgess 1977.) To what extent is the demand for higher education a reflection of the distribution of income in society?

And with each more precise definition of the problem the question of what kind of social policies would be successful in achieving greater equality of opportunity becomes more complex. It is indeed hardly surprising that in the course of the last two to three decades, throughout the world, but particularly for our purposes in Western Europe, the search for greater equality of opportunity has been focused on policies of expansion, and of diversification (both of institutions and in the types of courses which are offered), and change reflected in the way in which higher education can be made more accountable to a wider range of interests in society as a whole. Policy debates are, of course, polarized between those who believe that 'piecemeal social engineering' — to use Karl Popper's term — can bring about significant social change and those who would prescribe a much more fundamental challenge to the whole institutional structure of higher education as part of a larger radical change in society itself. What is at issue, fundamentally, is how higher education functions in relation to the societies in which it exists. With respect to the question of class bias, the problem is one of choosing in which sense the term is to be used, a choice which also has particular consequences for how the structure of society itself is to be pictured. Both sets of questions are, in the end, intractably theoretical and neither can be dodged in the interests of some spurious notion of objectivity.

Tawney once noted that 'Life is a swallow, and theory a snail' (1931, p.78). This was in the context of a discussion of the inadequate ways in which class inequality had been conceived in political science. His point was to show that without a proper understanding of how inequality was an aspect of economic and social relations, little could be done to challenge it. And in Tawney's view, it was only through a fundamental challenge to inequality that the creative and liberating forces of a society could be really unleashed. Class inequality for him was not just a question of the distribution of property or income, it was the mark of a society which justified the attainment of ends which by any measure of civilization were not worth attaining. Against those who might define the necessity of inequality as a defence of excellence and high standards — an argument very pertinent to the theme of this chapter — Tawney had this to say:

'If civilization is not the product of the kitchen garden, neither is it an exotic to be grown in a hothouse. Its flowers may be delicate, but its trunk must be robust, and the height to which it grows depends on the hold of its roots on the surrounding soil.' (1931, p.83)

And in a comment not directly levelled at higher education but certainly embracing it, he noted:

'A cloistered and secluded refinement, intolerant of the heat and dust of creative effort, is the note, not of civilization, but of the epochs which have despaired of it — which have seen, in one form or another, the triumph of the barbarian, and have sought compensation for defeat in writing cultured footnotes to the masterpieces they are incapable of producing.' (1931, p.83)

I mention Tawney to underline two points. The first is that to gain any understanding of a tradition of higher education (or, for that matter, any social institution) it is vital to go beyond the terms in which it understands itself. Conventional notions of ability, excellence, scholarship or 'the good mind' have to be relativized, to be seen in context and connected up with the self-imagery of the group which uses them. The second, rather obviously, is that questions of class cannot really be discussed in an atmosphere of disinterested objectivity for the questions themselves arise out of a larger political problematic and a conflict over different political ends. This is not always evident, but it is always the case. Class distinction, after all, only becomes an issue when men can conceive of a society without it or wish to defend a society based on it.

With these preliminary points in mind, I turn now to a review of some of the evidence which exists to describe patterns of class bias in higher education. In doing so I have deliberately tried to inject a comparative perspective into the discussion. This is not just in order to relativize the problems and render the familiar strange. It is also to open up questions about how, quite apart from national variations in higher education which are attributable to the unique tradition of individual states, some common features of capitalist society itself exert a consistent pressure on higher education to develop and function in particular ways. Class inequality can then be seen to be a necessary property of this kind of society.

AN EMPIRICAL OVERVIEW

Tawney's point about life overtaking theory has a parallel in the way in which theory can overtake data. One of the greatest problems in studying the way in which class background affects educational opportunities is that there are very few data available. A great deal of official data is, of course, collected, but not in ways which illuminate the theoretical questions posed by social scientists. An account of this problem has to rely, therefore, on a diverse body of data drawn from offical sources, particularly social surveys and academic studies, not all of which are compatible with one another. Available data on social class biases in higher education can be discussed conveniently under four main headings or contexts. These are: (a) in the context of the overall expansion of higher education during the past twenty years; (b) in the light of the social class composition of students in higher education; (c) according to the pattern of enrolment in higher education by people from different backgrounds; and (d) in the light of social class differences in educational attainment of school students. Organizing the data like that is a convenient way of illustrating the kind of results which might be obtained by using the concept of class in the categorical sense discussed earlier. Following on from this account of the data, I shall examine some of these results in terms appropriate to the class-as-relationship perspective.

During the 1960s and early 1970s, throughout the developed world, higher education enrolments expanded enormously. This was a period of economic growth and of increasing public expenditure on education. The expansion of enrolments was the outcome, as Guy Neave has suggested, of four elements (1976). These were: the arrival of the postwar population 'bulge', the need throughout the western economies for highly trained manpower, the needs of the education system itself for more trained personnel, and, finally, though not exhaustively, growing demands for higher education from social groups previously excluded from this level.

During the 1960s, all over Europe and also in the United States and Japan, such pressures were coped with through the expansion of the higher education system although the rate of expansion began to fall near the end of the decade and has continued to do so during the 1970s. The number of students in third level education has, however, continued to increase. Table 1 makes this clear.

During the two decades of expansion the percentage of students from each post-school age group enrolling in higher education also increased, although with considerable variation among different countries. Table 2 illustrates this.

In nearly all cases the rate of expansion in the proportion of the 17-18 year-old group is greater than that of the 20-21 year-old group. It is depressing to note that in the UK the proportion of older age groups enrolled in higher education is one of the lowest in Europe.

TABLE 1
Trends in the number of students in third level education: EEC 1974-78
(1970/71 = 100)

	1973/74	1977/78
Federal Republic of Germany	136.9	158.5
France	113.1	126.5
Italy	123.3	146.1
Netherlands	113.8	146.9
Belgium	119.0	139.5
Luxembourg	118.3	135.8
United Kingdom	108.3	114.2
Ireland	113.1	140.4
Denmark	131.1	159.3
Europe	120.8	139.0

Source Eurostat (1980) *Education and Training 1970/71 - 1977/78* Statistical Office of the European Communities
Definition drawn from ISCED (International Standard Classification of Education). Third level comprises universities and all other types of higher education.

Such data do not, of course, illustrate in any way the consequences of expansion of the relative chances of students from different class backgrounds gaining access to higher education. They indicate only a general growth of opportunities. But within that growth the opportunities for students from a working-class background have, in fact, widened. The social class composition of the student body in higher education is given in Table 3.
    Neave says of these data that they show 'the extent to which the monopoly of upper-class entrants in higher education has, over the decade of the 1960s, gradually been reduced, though it still remains by far and away the most important single numerical grouping in all higher education systems with the exception of Germany and Yugoslavia.' (Neave 1976, p.78)
    The expansion of educational opportunities has been at the heart of 'liberal' theories of how to bring about greater opportunities for the least privileged in society (Halsey, Heath and Ridge 1980). Whether the

judgement that such expansion failed to equalize opportunities significantly in secondary education applies with equal force to higher education is not something which can be inferred from data on the growth of opportunities as such. It has been maintained, however, 'that inequality, far from diminishing with the expansion of higher education and higher educational expenditure, has in many countries increased for it is the non-manual classes which have exploited the extra opportunities' (Embling 1974, p.37). Some measure of the relative life chances of different groups is needed and this, of course, is the second of the contexts within which expansion must be examined.

TABLE 2

Percentage enrolment of students by selected age groups: EEC 1970/71 - 1977/78

	1970/71		1977/78	
	17-18 yrs	20-21 yrs	17-18 yrs	20-21 yrs
Germany	23.7	12.7	35.7	16.5
France	31.6	12.2	54.5	15.8
Italy	38.1*	20.6*	42.2+	23.1+
Netherlands	41.3	14.7	–	–
Belgium	52.7	21.0	63.4	24.7
Luxembourg	29.2	14.0	37.7	14.8
UK	26.1	12.8	31.5	14.0
Ireland	20.1	6.1	26.2	8.8
Denmark	30.9+	18.0+	29.8++	18.0+

* figures for 1972/73   + figures for 1975/76   ++ figure for 1976/77

Source Eurostat (1980) *Education and Training 1970/71 - 1977/78* Statistical Office of the European Communities, Table 1/7, p.186

Data collected by the OECD allows some assessment to be made of relative life chances of different social groups. Table 4 sets out some of the results.

The figures for the United States for the comparable period are 8:1 and 3:1 (Levin 1976). What they reveal, as the OECD report tries to make clear, is that while the relative advantages of upper stratum youth have declined, the process is a slow one and uneven. Two pieces of evidence from England and Wales emphasize this point. Between 1967 and 1977 the number of home entrance university students increased from 55,900 to 77,800. During the same period the number of applicants for places increased from 790,000 to 831,000. The percentage of total applicants gaining entry was 7.0 per cent in 1967 and 9.3 per cent in 1977. But when these proportions are broken down by social class there is a clear variation. Just over a quarter of applicants from social class group 1 gained entrance in 1967 and this figure rose to one-third ten years later. This compares with 3.1 per cent of social class 4. The figures are presented in Table 5.

TABLE 3
Social class background of students in higher education: by country

		Social class group					
		A	B	C	D	E	Others
England &	1961	61.0	13.0	–	–	26.0	–
Wales	1970	46.0	27.0	–	–	27.0	–
France	1960	55.2	34.4	5.8	–	4.6	–
	1974	42.5	39.2	6.4	–	4.9	–
Germany	1961	34.2	29.0	3.6	14.7	5.4	–
	1972	24.7	34.4	5.9	19.7	12.5	2.3
Netherlands	1961	42.0	...47.0...		–	8.5	–
	1970	37.0	...49.0...		–	14.0	–
Norway	1964	33.6	11.1	12.0	–	23.9	–
	1971	40.2	13.0	8.6	–	21.5	16.6
Yugoslavia	1960	...40.1...				20.5	
	1970	21.5	28.8	20.2	–	20.5	9.4

Source Neave 1976, p.79

Further evidence of the relative life chances of different groups over a longer time scale comes from a recent and different kind of study from the University of Oxford social mobility study and was carried out by A.H. Halsey and colleagues (1980). Based on the family and educational biographies of 10,000 men living in England and Wales in 1972, this study examined the different experience of education of four different age cohorts from the early part of the centry to the late 1940s and early 1950s. Using the technique of cohort analysis and expressing the data in a way which uses logarithmic scales to indicate the differences between different social groups, the data from this study are presented in Table 6.

What the figures indicate is that while the fastest rate of growth in opportunities for higher education has been for people with a working-class background, the relative opportunites for such groups have remained remarkably stable since the period of the First World War. The expansion of the system of universities in Britain since the 1960s has clearly benefited those who were already privileged more so than those who were not.

TABLE 4
Relative chances of upper stratum and lower stratum youth studying at a university

England &	1966	8:1	
Wales	1970	5:1	
France	1959	84:1	
	1968	28:1	
Germany	1961	58:1	
	1970	12:1	
Netherlands	1961	56:1	
	1970	26:1	
Sweden	1960	9:1	
	1968	5:1	
Yugoslavia	1960	6:1	
	1969	3.5:1	

Source   OECD 1974, p.31

TABLE 5
Percentage of university entrants: by social class 1967-1977

	Social class				
	1	2	3	4	All
1967	25.9	15.9	9.1	3.1	7.0
1970	28.7	17.3	11.0	3.7	8.4
1973	31.5	17.3	10.4	3.6	8.7
1977	33.0	17.5	10.9	3.7	9.3

Source   Recalculated from Edwards and Roberts 1980, Table 6, p.26

Britain, of course, is not unique in having had this pattern of change. Data from West Germany for a long time span are also available. They are set out in Table 7. Again, while the greatest proportionate increase in access to universities has been from working-class groups, white collar workers, officials and clerical workers (*Angestellte, Beamte*) still dominate the entrance figures. See Table 7.

TABLE 6
Attendance at university: by birth cohort

Father's social class	Percentages			
	1913-22	1923-32	1933-42	1943-52
I, II	7.2	15.9	23.7	26.4
	208*	258	233	214
III, IV, V	1.9	4.0	4.1	8.0
	75	120	58	95
VI, VII, VIII	0.9	1.2	2.3	3.1
	0	0	0	0
All	1.8	3.4	5.4	8.5
N.	(1846)	(1897)	(1856)	(2246)

* log distances

Source   Halsey, Heath and Ridge 1980

Manual workers constitute just less than half the employed population but in almost forty years new university students from the group rose from 2.1 per cent to only 14.9 per cent. This opens up the question of how far expansion alone can reduce social inequalities of opportunity in higher education. I shall return to this in the last section of the chapter.

The third context in which class inequalities need to be discussed is the distribution of students across different types of institution. This is important, for while all over Europe universities have expanded, so too has the non-university sector of higher education. Indeed, for most European countries since 1975 it is the non-university sector which has grown the fastest (Neave 1976; OECD 1974). This sector includes institutions such as the polytechnics in Britain, the IUTs in France, and the district colleges in Norway. Similarly, it is worth noting that part-time enrolments have increased greatly too (OECD 1974). The question arises whether the social class composition of the student body in non-university higher education is different from that in the universities.

TABLE 7
Historical survey: university attendance by status and sex since 1928: West Germany

Occupational group	Employed (males over 45 yrs) 1925	Students in the winter term					Employed (males; married; over 45) 1967	New entrants to university in winter term 1975/76
		1928/29	1951/52	1959/69	1967/68			
Manual workers	43.5	2.1	4.1	5.2	6.9	43.3	14.9
White collar workers	20.0	12.2	23.0	28.4	31.9	22.2	36.6
Civil servants	36.5	47.1	38.0	34.8	30.4	9.0	22.6
Self-employed	36.5	38.6	34.9	31.6	30.8	25.6	22.8
Total in 1000s	11 758	98.1	109.7	172.3	215.9	5 614	91.3
% women	x	11.6	16.2	21.7	23.5	x	37.4

Source Adapted from Ballerstedt and Glatzer 1979

There is evidence, in the words of the OECD report (1974), that 'Short-cycle higher education . . . tends to facilitate access to higher education for students who, because of their social origin, were previously excluded' (1974, p.32). The report gives the figures shown in Table 8.

TABLE 8
Percentages of lower stratum students

		Universities	Short-cycle higher education
England &	1961	26.0	37.9 (other than universities)
Wales	1970		36.0 (5 polytechnics)
France	1968	11.9	24.2 (IUT)
USA	1966	11.0	18.0 (two year establishments)
Yugoslavia	1970	17.0	22.0 (Vise Skole)
Canada	1968		
Ontario		26.7	40.0 (CCAT)
Quebec		24.9	38.3 (CEGEP)

Source OECD 1974

There is evidence that within this expansion of the non-university sector, certainly in Britain, there is a clear social class bias in the level of courses for which students are enrolled, with students from higher socio-economic groups being more likely to be enrolled on full-time degree courses than other students (Whitburn, Mealing and Cox 1976). It has also been suggested that the apparent improvement in higher education opportunities for working-class students has occurred in less prestigious institutions (Levin 1976) and that in the case of France there has been a systematic downgrading of the status of higher education institutions in the face of increased participation; one writer has described this as the 'junior-collegization of the French University' (Patterson 1976-77). I shall return to this point a little later for an explanation of it opens up issues which go well beyond the kind of questions raised by the class-as-category perspective which has hitherto dominated work in this field.

It is necessary to turn now to the final context of the data, the character of social class differences in school attainment which some take to be the underlying reason for the kind of results set out above. Jack Embling, for example, has written concerning class bias in Britain that 'it is in any case not at the point of entry into higher education that the trouble lies . . .' (1974, p.36). The root source of the problem, he believes, is in the way in which able working-class children leave secondary school preferring not to press on to higher education. This view is widely held and of long standing. Kelsall,

Poole and Kuhn (1972) in their study of university graduates in 1960 located the atypical characteristics of working-class graduates in their family and educational background. The critical factor, they believed, in explaining why some working-class pupils stayed on at school to aim for higher education and why some did not, was parental encouragement. This subtle variable of class affects decision-making. What such an explanation does is locate the problem in an aspect of the family or school experience of different groups of children. A similar explanatory strategy is outlined by Halsey, Heath and Ridge (1980), although the variables selected as being the important ones are different, and concern inequalities among students from different backgrounds in their access to selective schools and sixth forms.

Explanations of this type have to be taken very seriously for they raise the question of how far changes in secondary schooling might encourage able working-class students to stay on and seek higher education. Or, put differently, they beg the question of the extent to which ability is wasted when able children do not decide to develop their talents in higher education. If, for instance, it is accepted that the so-called 'pool of ability' is much larger than had been supposed (see Robbins Report 1963, Appendix 1; Halsey, Ridge and Heath 1980), it has been estimated by Halsey and his colleagues that throughout the 1970s an additional 7000 boys each year could have gained advanced level passes had they remained at school long enough and that during the 1960s the wastage rate was even higher, at something like 30,000 (1980, p.201). The wastage of ability has been truly colossal. The conclusions of this study are directly relevant to debates about the level of real demand for places in higher education and the urgent problems of cutbacks in expenditure on higher education. In Britain, certainly, it is a strongly held view that a numerical reduction in the 18-year-old age group is what justifies cutting the present level of expenditure on higher education. If the figures given above are correct then this is a wholly unwarranted assumption. This point has been made very forcefully by Edwards and Roberts who have argued that if the real demand or at least, potential demand for students were carefully measured, then it would be seen that among working-class people there is a great unfulfilled promise. They say:

> 'The dynamic of past development has been the valuation attached to higher education by sections of the population who already had a high perception of its nature and a high confidence in their ability to participate if they chose. The main internal inertia to a rapid advance in demand for higher education has been the failure to develop any real perception of its nature and possibility among the majority of the population.' (1980, p.37)

It follows, therefore, that 'the primary problem for education is not in higher education itself so much as in the provision of primary and secondary inspiration, facilities and a high dedicated level of teaching' of the sort already available to the highly educated classes rather than to those who need them most (1980, p.38).

This is an interesting argument for it locates social class differences in the demand for places in higher education not in differences of socio-economic status as such, or even, for that matter, in the actual supply of places, but in the much more subtle notion of the 'cultural accessibility' of higher education, a matter essentially of social class perceptions. This argument would explain why some working-class students value higher education and others do not, why some perceive it as being something in principle available to them and others do not.

In this way the argument put forward by Edwards and Roberts can be seen to be a variant of what my colleagues, a few years ago, described as the 'class-culture paradigm' of explaining class differences in educational attainment (Byrne, Williamson and Fletcher 1975). The main feature of this perspective is that it seeks to reduce the concept of class to a matter of life-style, attitude and belief: in short, to the cultural characteristics of different groups in society. Focused ultimately on the interests, aptitudes and motivation of children from different social groups this perspective tends to ignore the structural position of different groups with respect to the control and funding of education and to the structure of the social division of labour. It concentrates more on the socialization of different children than on their different relationships to the wider structure of opportunity in society. The general criticism that can be levelled at it is that, as a result of the still restricted notion of social class used in the analysis, it confuses symptom and cause. Nonetheless it is a very important and powerful paper. And even if its conclusions can be questioned, it still raises a key problem of the meaning to working-class people of higher education.

In what follows I want to elaborate this theme using what I understand as a relational concept of social class. My main point will be that higher education, and the universities in particular which have historically dominated it, do play a decisive role in structuring demand for places and that many aspects of the social inequalities which are traceable in the decision-making of school pupils have their roots in higher education itself and in the logic of the relationship between higher education and society. What this means is that the relative life chances for higher education of different social groups cannot be discussed apart from the form, control and social significance of higher education itself. This perspective invites questions about which groups, in Max Weber's terms, constitute and have constituted the decisive strata in society and which, therefore, have been able to shape the pattern of higher education. And to explore this it is essential to think historically and comparatively to uncover how the past exerts its influence on the present.

A MODEL OF PROCESS

In societies of the western capitalist type, a number of mechanisms can be identified which ensure that social hierarchies are transformed into academic ones (Bourdieu and Passeron 1977). These mechanisms are complex, inter-

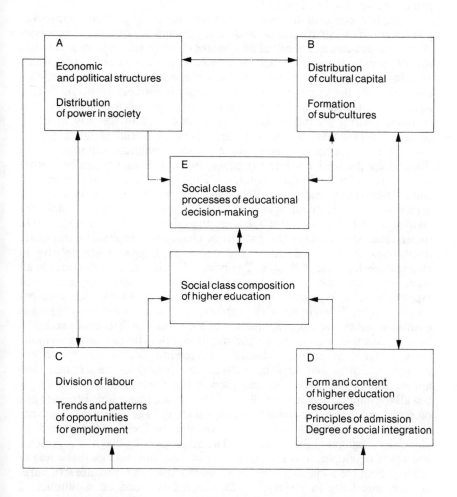

CLASS AND HIGHER EDUCATION A model of processes

connected social processes in their own right and each has distinctive variants in different societies. For convenience, and to simplify grossly, three principle ones can be identified.

The first concerns the social determinants of differential educational attainment in secondary schools and, as a consequence of that, of processes of decision-making as a result of which some children leave school and others remain, aiming thereby to reach higher education. The second is that which explains the form and content of higher education in modern societies together with the operative principles regulating access to it. As I have already pointed out, higher education cannot be separated off as if it occupied neutral ground — it is deeply implicated in the way in which schools function and the social distance between it and students from a working-class background is a critical factor explaining variation in the demand for the service it offers (Boudon 1974). This aspect can be further discussed in terms of the dominant idea of higher education which exists in a culture (see Halsey and Trow 1971). Since higher education is increasingly geared in to social structures of modern societies and increasingly under the control of central government agencies, the third concerns the necessity to understand what governs the pattern of change in universities and other institutions of higher education and which social groups are decisive in shaping the direction of change. The potent principle of class operates in all three contexts. This can be illustrated in the following diagram which represents a simple heuristic model of what influences educational decision-making among different social class groups. The focus on decision-making is useful and deliberate. Any explanation of social class differences in access to higher education must embrace the way in which different people actually think about their actions. Mechanistic accounts of the correspondence between education and, say, the needs of the economy (of the sort that have appeared in recent marxist writing (Bowles and Gintis 1976)) would simply beg all the important questions. But equally, an approach which focuses just on social processes of individual decision-making begs important questions about the structural linkages of education and the social structure and, in particular, changes in that structure. The accompanying diagram represents one way of developing a relational concept of class and through that a way of talking about the social mechanisms in education which reproduce structures of class inequality in society.   This model is based on a number of assumptions which cannot be elaborated fully here. Boldly stated they are as follows.

a   The differences of aptitude, attitude and opportunity thought to separate those who are believed to be capable of higher education from those who are not are rooted in the economic and political structure of societies. This is represented in the link between box A and box B.

b   The structure of the labour market for which students are prepared is what sets the real value of educational qualifications and, therefore, though never in a wholly rational way, the demand for them. The form of the division of labour is an artefact of the distribution of power in society for it is determined by the relative capacity of different groups to monopolize access to high status occupations and press claims for differential rewards of income, authority and prestige (cf Collins 1977). This link is suggested in the box A to box C relation.

c   The form, content and admissions policies of higher education institutions reflect the 'ideal of cultivation' of the dominant political groups, although these, at least in modern industrial societies, are under constant challenge. This is suggested in the box B, box D link.

d   The curricular range and content of higher education reflects the strength of different external demands based on assessments of the needs of the division of labour in society. There is therefore a constant pressure for change as the social class structure of society itself changes. This is the link between box C and box D.

e   Social class processes of educational decision-making cannot be separated off from the way in which social structures have constrained the opportunities available to people (boxes A, C, D), the secondary school experience of different groups (box B) and their perception both of the value of higher education and its accessibility.

f   Finally, variations in the class profiles of higher education among societies of the same structural type (in this case western capitalist societies) reflect historical variations in the speed and process of industrialization, patterns of social class formation reflecting the unique traditions of particular societies and state policies.

These arguments are elaborated in my *Education, Social Structure and Development* (1979). In what follows I wish to illustrate the implications of these propositions.

Statements about social structure only make sense if they can be translated into the behaviour of people; and in this case they have to be translated into how people make decisions about their education. These decisions are prepresented in box E of the model. It is these processes that have to be explained if the social class profile of students is to be understood. These problems have been a principle focus of an enormous body of research. And it is a research field in which there are many different frames of reference and research techniques. The two principle approaches are those concerned with the general problem of the social determinants of educability and, more recently, particularly from within the marxist tradition, a concern with the way in which social selection in education is an inevitable and necessary aspect of the social division of labour in a capitalist society. The first approach is well represented in Britain with the work of such writers as Douglas (1964) and Banks and Finlayson (1973) who wrote about the importance of home background as a major determinant of educability. In France the work of Girard (1964) on the cultural atmosphere of the family as a predictor of success at school is also typical of this approach. The writings of Bernstein on language codes could be seen in this light, too, for a principle claim running through it is that the child's use of language is a consequence of processes of communication and control within the family (See Brandis and Henderson 1970; Bernstein 1971-75). Much of this work has become part of the professional folklore of teachers and has been summarized by several writers (Williamson 1978; Tyler 1977; Marceau 1977; Husen 1979).

The second approach has several variants. In France there is the work of the marxist-structuralists, Bourdieu and Passeron (1977), with its emphasis on the way a capitalist society distributes cultural capital unequally among different classes and in that way ensures the reproduction of structures of inequality. For Althusser (1971) the role of education as a state apparatus in a capitalist society is to reproduce the conditions of capitalist production. American work by Bowles and Gintis (1976) on the 'correspondence principle' works within the same neo-marxian perspective suggesting that, contrary to their ideological claims to promote opportunities for all, schools reproduce a capitalist division of labour by preparing children for their fate in the labour market.

Education appears from this viewpoint to be a subtle process of adjusting expectations to the realities of the labour market and a way of legitimating structures of inequality. Those possessing educational certificates are considered worthy of high status employment; those without have only themselves to blame, given that all had an equal chance (Bourdieu 1974). And educational selection from this approach, though not exclusively in this approach, is seen much more as a process of self-elimination than as failure at critical hurdles in the school career (see Bourdieu 1974; Halsey, Heath and Ridge 1980).

Apart from criticisms that the first approach, ie that concerned with educability, does not fully take into account the way children of different backgrounds are disadvantaged by the poor resources available to them (Byrne, Williamson and Fletcher 1975), that their inability to respond to schooling has been falsely conceived (Labov 1970; Ginsburg 1972), or that, in any case, the principle determinants of adult inequality have not got much to do with either ability or schooling, but flow from economic inequalities (Jencks et al 1972), the most fundamental flaw, arguably, is the absence of a sense of history, for this leads to a neglect of how attitudes and behaviour are rooted in the social structures and the past experiences of different social classes. E.P. Thompson noted once:

'If we stop history at a given point, then there are no classes but simply a multitude of individuals with a multitude of experiences. But if we watch these men over an adequate period of social change, we observe patterns in their relationships, their ideas, and their institutions.' (1968, p.11)

With respect to the theme of this chapter the question which must then be asked concerns the meaning of higher education to different social groups and how that meaning has changed through time. It is, of course, an enormously complex question involving the history of higher education throughout Europe. It is only in the twentieth century that the mass of the ordinary people in a European society had any hope of higher education. In both Britain and Germany of the nineteenth century not only were the masses excluded from universities but so, too, were commercial and industrial groups (Briggs 1969; Ringer 1969). The decisive strata in Britain were a land-based bourgeoisie and aristocracy prepared to educate their sons for the Anglican ministry. In Germany they were a caste of officials and professional men and protestant theologians, an aristocracy of education whose ideal of cultivation traced all the way back to classical Greece (Ringer 1969). The requirement for the further education of labourers and of the growing number of technicians and engineers was everywhere met outside the university. And when the expansion of the universities and of higher education did begin to take place from the 1890s onwards, the academic models which predominated were those of the elite instititutions of an earlier age. One major consequence of this — a movement, as Raymond Williams once pointed out, reflecting the desire of successful industrialists that their sons should move into the now largely irrelevant class of gentry (1965, p.164) — was that the development was foreclosed of a higher education relevant to the needs of workers and capable of embracing developments in science and technology. The point I want to stress is the exclusion for financial, social and cultural reasons of working-class people from higher education in the universities. The corollary of this was that a demand for such education from this section of society was never cultivated; working-class people were never encouraged to see higher education as something available to them.

But growing middle-class demands for higher education had an important consequence for working-class opportunities. The extension of the examination system and of competitive entry into the civil service, to mention only two developments, had a considerable impact on the shape of the curriculum in the public school system and, later, in the grammar school. A curriculum shaped by the universities and aimed at entrance to them can be seen in retrospect to be something which served to increase the social distance from secondary education of working-class people, a gap which they began to bridge after the second world war but which still remains a wide one as much of the data presented earlier shows. Seen in this light the apparent unwillingness of some working-class people to seek out higher education is a direct consequence of their systematic exclusion from it over a long period of time.

If these brief comments underline both the need for an historical perspective and the limitations of too narrow a focus on the concept of educability, they also indicate, I think, that a crude correspondence theory of the role of higher education in the economy would also be misleading. The direct relevance of higher education to the needs of the economy has everywhere been small although there are examples where the links were strong as in the German Technische Hochschulen or the French Grandes Ecoles. This, of course, is hardly true at all of most European societies in the twentieth century but the links are still by no means direct.

This leads to the second of the three mechanisms which need examination, ie those governing the principles regulating access to higher education, as well as to the form and content of the institutions themselves (box D). Both, I think, have to be thought of in terms of the changing relationships between different social class groups over time.

And both issues can be thought of as part of a larger problem: the dominant idea of higher education and which groups have a right to it. In Britain, as Halsey and Trow have shown, 'the English idea' of the university, centred on Oxford and Cambridge, has a 'stubborn resilience' (1971, p.72). In their analysis six criteria express the traditional ideal: antiquity, cosmopolitanism, selectivity, 'education', domesticity and intimacy. And each one exerts a powerful influence on higher education in this country and each finds powerful support among the academic staff of the universities. To give three examples: the idea of antiquity has ensured that the new universities of Britain in the 1960s were established in ancient locations. The idea of a university of Scunthorpe — once suggested by Professor Armytage — would strike many academics as ludicrous (Halsey and Trow 1971, p.76). Secondly, British academics have clung tenaciously to the idea of rigorous selection of students, fearful that an open-door policy would lower standards. The consequence, of course, is hostility in Britain to the idea of the mass university or even, for that matter, of the large multi-university of the sort which exists in the United States. Finally, although much more contentiously, universities in Britain, in contrast to the polytechnics which were deliberately set up for the purpose, have been traditionally suspicious of being involved directly in training rather than education. And even in the polytechnics and in those universities which were formerly colleges of advanced technology, there has been a process of academic drift to emulate the model of the university (Burgess 1977; Neave 1979). In this way, the universities institutionalized the ideal of becoming cultured and of the public self-image of the groups which have traditionally had access to them and who, from positions of power in the civil service and parliament and the professions, continue to support them by recruiting their graduates to prestigious positions in the labour market (see Stanworth and Giddens 1974).

The idea of the university also pervades patterns of teaching and learning (Burgess 1977). In the English tradition the stress is on the development of the critical understanding of individuals in specialized yet hierarchically arranged subjects and on giving individual students a great deal of autonomy (see Bernstein 1971). In Germany the Humboldt notions of freedom to learn (*Lernfreiheit*) and freedom to teach (*Lehrfreiheit*) justify a very loose link between teachers and taught which necessarily confers advantages on students from academic backgrounds, just as in England the pedagogy of the public school facilitates an easy transfer to the university and thus confers a marked advantage on the already privileged in coping with a university education. In both societies the dominant model of the educated man reflects the public self-image of the bourgeois groups which have historically dominated the system.

This is not to deny, of course, that principles of access to prestigious higher education vary considerably. The distinction between sponsored and contest mobility (Turner 1971) or between the relatively open access of Germany, France and the USA and the restricted pattern of Britain, identifies two very different systems (Hopper 1971). The price of open access, however, seems to be high drop-out rates with students from a working-class background suffering most. In Britain drop-out rates are very low in comparison to many European states (Halsey and Trow 1971).

The final theme is change. During the 1960s, as I have shown, higher education throughout the western world expanded and within that development educatonal life chances for working-class people improved. The significance of the qualifications gained did not, however, remain static. Levin (1976a) has suggested that working-class students gained access largely to institutions of low status. It has further been suggested that 'qualification inflation' eroded the value of academic degrees and diplomas (OECD 1977a; Dore 1976). It is necessary to speculate, therefore, what the possibilities are for the next few years as higher education contracts. From the class-as-relationship perspective this is an important question and one which suggests connections between changes in the economic organization of society and in state policies on educational life chances.

It is, of course, too large an issue to be taken up here, but all over the western world there is an economic crisis. Growth seems a distant goal and its benefits less attractive. Some see it as a crisis of legitimization in societies of the western capitalist type (Habermas 1975). Others as a crisis of recapitalization (Miller 1978a). The elements of the crisis include low growth rates, tight controls of public expenditure, inflation and high unemployment. In education the crisis shows itself in falling enrolments, reduced resources for teaching and research, low staff morale and reduced opportunities for promotion. All these factors, ironically, make systems of higher education less rather than more able to cope with changing circumstances. The fall in enrolments is particularly interesting since it is not explicable by demographic variables (OECD 1977; Edwards and Roberts 1980). The reasons are not at all clear, although it has been suggested that the downward trend is mainly explained by qualified school-leavers seeking employment rather than further education (OECD 1977).

None of these developments augur well for improving the participation of students from working-class backgrounds in higher education as that is, at least at the moment, understood. The feedback implied in the model described earlier between changes in the economy, the structure of higher education and the decisions of school students is something which clearly needs further research and beyond that, imaginative efforts to change the way it currently operates.

Change involves choices, in this case of new models of higher education. It is indeed the case that the university is incapable of attracting and holding more than about 25 per cent of an age group or expanding beyond that without being utterly transformed (see Halsey and Trow, p.464). The question of what other institutions can replace or supplement them becomes urgent. Answers range from short-cycle higher education — the 'aggregative model' of shorter duration programmes of study with a stronger vocational relevance (OECD 1977) — to the notion of 'permanent education' (Scheffknecht 1978), with all that that implies in terms of paid study leave for workers. Within the university sector new structures have been conceived: eg the comprehensive university in Germany (Gesamthochschule) or the Instituts Universitaires de Technologie (IUTs) in France. Many of these developments have been reviewed by Guy Neave who attempted to estimate their impact on equality of opportunity. His general conclusion was that new structures — and, in particular the Open University in the UK — 'are apt to realize greater educational opportunity' (1976, p.118), but that there is a greater danger that *institutional reproduction* will create in higher education the tertiary differentiation between academic, technical and vocational education which throughout Europe has been gradually eroded in secondary schools. Without a strong commitment on the part of governments to the ideal of equality of opportunity and the massive growth of a dense network of educational facilities both part-time and full-time, available to a wider constituency of people who would not be distinguished by arbitrary criteria such as age, sex and social class, then administrative reforms or organizational changes alone will not suffice.

Such change, of course, would transform completely the models of higher education institutionalized in universities and through that, the hopes and aspirations of a growing group of people for status symbols of their new-found social importance. The pressure on systems of higher education to change, to become much more responsive to manpower needs, and to adapt their curricula to changing technologies, reflects changes in economic organization and social structure where social mobility depends more than ever on educational certification. White collar workers, technical workers, professionals and semi-professional are the groups which have benefited most from the expansion of higher education. Is it realistic to expect that they will settle for something less in the future? I ask this without knowing the answer but suspecting that whatever happens to higher education in the coming few years, those who have historically had little access to it will be those less likely to be consulted about how it should change or to benefit from the changes which will take place. And that is a question of class and of class relations refracted through the funding, form and control of higher education.

Perhaps, in the end, what is needed most is an imaginative new conception of what higher learning could be. I began with George Bernard Shaw and will end with him. Shaw understood universities as 'shops for selling class limitations' (*Man and Superman*) and believed that a university community should be a community of adults, 'not that of a rowdy rabble of half emancipated school children and unemancipated pedants' (*Misalliance*). Quoting Kipling approvingly he asked, 'What do they know of Plato that only Plato know?' And against the proposal to set up a special college for working men — Ruskin College — Shaw, in a letter to Charles Beard, said that a working man should avoid the place. 'He will learn nothing there that he cannot learn anywhere else, except the social tone, which will be as detrimental to him as a workman as it is useful to a gentleman, and the false perspective by which those dons who represent the survival at a university of the members least fit for the world, appear eminent to men too young to know what eminence at full pitch means' (Laurence 1972, p.87).

At a minimum, to develop such a conception we have to think outside the terms in which higher education is currently conceived. And that, too, is an aspect of class.

GEOGRAPHICAL BIAS

John Richardson

DIMENSIONS OF EQUALITY

As will be obvious from other chapters in this book, the concept of equal educational opportunity is not a unitary notion. Rather, there are several distinct factors or dimensions of equality and inequality which must be carefully separated in any discussion of possible sources of bias in higher education. Levin (1976b) identified four important criteria in evaluating the extent to which a nation's educational system provided a significant equalizing influence: the equality of educational access; the equality of educational participation; the equality of educational results; and the equality of educational effects upon life chances. In the case of social class, for example, there is considerable evidence that Western systems of higher education fail to promote equality on all four standards of measurement. (Much of this evidence is discussed in Bill Williamson's chapter in this volume.) However, research to date on geographical biases has been limited to studies of educational access and educational participation. There is virtually no evidence to show that geographical variations in the results or effects of higher education cannot be attributed purely to variations in access or participation. So, although there is an obvious need for future research in this direction, I shall not discuss here biases in the results or the effects of higher education.

There has been much research on geographical biases in the extent of participation in higher education. Of the four criteria which were proposed by Levin, this is obviously the one which is most amenable to quantification and comparison across education systems. It would appear to be directly dependent upon variations in the degree of access to higher education, and this has also been widely studied in different ways. However, the concept of educational access must itself be analysed or decomposed into at least three major dimensions: the equality of educational provision; the equality of educational selection for admission into the educational system; and the equality of educational demand amongst the total population of potential candidates for admission into the educational system. My discussion of geographical biases will focus upon each of these three factors as possible sources of variation in the extent of participation in systems of higher education.

Inequalities of educational participation based upon geographical characteristics probably occur in all educational systems. However, the manner in which one attempts to understand the source of these inequalities will depend upon the geographical scale or level of analysis which one adopts. Different researchers have studied variations amongst localities or neighbourhoods, amongst regions or provinces of an individual country, and amongst countries or nations themselves. Some writers do not clearly distinguish between these different sorts of investigation, but it is obvious that in principle the effective sources of inequity may vary from one geographical level to another. They will also depend upon the level of government which is responsible for the provision of education. In some systems of higher education, the responsibility for the provision of relevant institutions rests with a local authority (for example, the polytechnics in England and Wales); in some systems, that responsibility rests with a regional government (for example, the universities in the Federal Republic of Germany); and, in other systems, the responsibility rests with the national government (for example, the universities in the United Kingdom). Finally, it is interesting to consider the concept of the 'community' served by the relevant institutions: does a specific college or university regard itself as being responsible to a particular neighbourhood, with a definite 'catchment area' or 'hinterland', or does it regard itself as having a regional or even a national role (Keeble 1968; Sheffield 1969; Locke 1978)?

LOCAL VARIATIONS IN EDUCATIONAL PARTICIPATION

There is a vast amount of evidence to show that the nature of the community or neighbourhood in which an individual resides will influence the likelihood of that person's entering higher education. Most of this evidence has been obtained in the United States and in Canada, though there have been a few European studies as well (see, for instance, Conference of Ministers of European Member States of UNESCO 1968, pp.74-77). There are three major conclusions from this research. First, participation in higher education is greater amongst the inhabitants of metropolitan centres and large towns, and in general there is a direct relationship between community size and educational participation (Pike 1970, pp.72-73). Second, and a fortiori, participation in higher education is greater in urban communities than in rural ones (Folter and Nam 1967; Bereday 1973, pp.48-49). Third, participation in higher education is greater amongst the inhabitants of communities which have relevant institutions in their immediate vicinity (Beezer and Hjelm 1961; Pipher 1962; Willingham 1970; California State Postsecondary Education Commission 1978).

Provision

Obviously, these findings are not independent of one another, since colleges and universities tend to be established in the vicinity of large metropolitan centres and towns. The arguments in favour of having geographically centralized institutions of higher education are largely educational and administrative in nature; the arguments against such institutions are largely financial and sociological ones (Willingham 1971). Whatever one decides in attempting to resolve these conflicting arguments, it must be accepted that the predominantly urban and cosmopolitan setting of most institutions of higher education is likely in itself to constitute a major disincentive to potential students from other types of community.

The geographical distribution of relevant institutions affects the extent of participation in higher education in several different ways. In its most direct manner, the lack of provision of colleges and universities constitutes a 'distance barrier' to higher education, in the sense that a potential student is unable to commute to such an institution from his normal place of residence (Crossland 1971). In the case of the United States, for example, Willingham (1971) has calculated that 'educational opportunity for three-fifths of the population is inhibited by the simple fact that they do not happen to live near an accessible college'. This problem can be tackled either by encouraging the establishment of local colleges serving specific communities, or by the extensive provision of adequate accommodation for students at geographically centralized institutions.

On the other hand, even for those students who have geographical access to a college or university, the monetary costs of commuting to the institution might constitute part of a 'financial barrier' to higher education, in the sense that the potential student is simply unable to afford to pursue a course of study. A detailed account of the financial barriers affecting participation rates in Canadian higher education has been given by Pike (1970, pp.97-114), and most of his remarks are of general applicability. Obviously, the financial costs of higher education discriminate against potential students from the poorer sections of society. In their study of three German universities, Boning and Roeloffs (1970, p.58) suggested that 'children of lower income groups tend to go to the nearest university, or not to go at all if none is near'. This problem can be tackled by systems of student grants and scholarships, and by subsidized accommodation. Another proposal is that students who are geographically or financially unable to attend courses at traditional institutions should be assisted by distant-learning techniques (Jensen 1980). In the United Kingdom, the Open University is an obvious example of this sort of approach, and its methods have been taken up in several other countries.

Most researchers do not seem to consider that commuting costs are an important part of the financial burden involved in participating in higher education. Nevertheless, the geographical distance and financial demands might tend to encourage uncertainties on the part of potential students as to whether participation in higher education might be a legitimate part of their own personal development. The effects of geographical factors upon the demand for higher education will be discussed presently, but it is important to make one point concerning their effects in minority groups. It might be thought that the better provision of institutions of higher education in large metropolitan centres would tend to counteract other sources of bias operating against urban minority groups. In the United States, for example, it is true that blacks, Chicanos, and Puerto Ricans are somewhat more likely to live near a college or university than whites (Willingham 1971). Nevertheless, the geographical proximity of such institutions is unlikely to remove their cultural distance or their alien quality for such groups (Knoell 1970). Indeed, for many minorities, the geographical distance of colleges and universities is likely to enhance the perceived remoteness of higher education (Willingham 1971).

Selection
At first sight, biases in educational selection would not appear to be an important source of local variations in participation in higher education. There is not normally any explicit selection based upon a candidate's place of residence, though Bereday (1973, p.48) mentions that students who are not inhabitants of Moscow cannot qualify for admission to the university unless they have secured a place in a dormitory or a room in the city. Nevertheless, it is clear that access to higher education depends upon the results of primary and secondary education. In terms of the criteria proposed by Levin (1976), the possibility of being admitted to an institution of higher education is one of the obvious 'life chances' affected by inequalities in the provision of adequate relevant education at the primary and secondary levels. Specifically, as Embling (1974, p.40) has pointed out, the crucial factor is access to the traditional academic secondary school, whose function has always been to prepare candidates for college and university. The provision of this sort of school is clearly subject to geographical variation; Bereday (1973, pp.48-49) cites as examples the advantages of children attending urban schools in Japan and Sweden.

The sources of inequality in primary and secondary education have been extensively researched, and it would be well beyond the objectives of this paper to discuss them in any detail. An elegant account of these biases within the Canadian system of education has been given by Pike (1970, pp.81-95). It is obvious that they tend to operate against children from rural communities, from lower social classes, and from ethnic minorities, and probably against many other groups as well. They can only be removed by radical developments in primary and secondary education, and are thus beyond the direct control of those responsible for selecting students for higher education. However, they can be alleviated by positive discrimination on the part of admissions authorities in favour of such groups. For instance, admission to universities in Yugoslavia is systematically biased in favour of candidates from rural areas (Muradbegovic 1978). In the absence of such procedures, it is nevertheless reasonable to expect selectors in higher education to be aware of the inequities which result from the assumption that all of the candidates who submit themselves for admission to colleges and universities have had equal access to traditional academic secondary education.

Demand
Just as there is considerable evidence for an effect of the type of community in which an individual resides upon his participation in higher education, so too there is clear support for the idea that the nature of the community or neighbourhood affects an individual's demand for higher education. First, there is a direct relationship between community size and aspirations to participate in higher education, with individuals from large urban communities manifesting the greatest demand, and with individuals from rural communities manifesting the least demand. Numerous studies carried out during the 1950s and 1960s in the United States are mentioned by Sewell (1964). Second, it would also appear that aspirations to participate in higher education are directly related to the presence of a relevant institution in the immediate vicinity of an individual's school or place of residence. This relationship is manifested both in terms of whether the individual plans to attend a college or university, and in terms of whether he is prevented from or delayed in taking up a place at the institution concerned (Pipher 1962).

Sociological analyses have shown that these local inequalities in the demand for higher education are largely attributable to correlated variations in family socio-economic status (Sewell 1964; Siemens 1965; Sewell and Armer 1966). This suggests that financial considerations may be of major importance. Certainly, as was suggested above, the cost of participating in higher education may amount to a 'financial barrier' or at least a strong disincentive to potential students from poorer families, and this would go some way towards explaining why individuals from rural communities or from deprived urban neighbourhoods show less demand for higher education. One might then try to remove this sort of barrier by encouraging systems of grants, scholarships, or loans for potential students. Distant-learning techniques might also alleviate the problem, but they need to be provided at relatively low cost; indeed, it will be interesting to note whether the increasing costs of Open University courses will discourage potential students from the poorer sections of society.

Nevertheless, geographical location and socio-economic status affect the demand for higher education in a more profound manner by influencing an individual's perceptions of higher education as a legitimate and desirable goal both in this own personal development and in that of his children. The attitudes and expectations of a potential student's parents, teachers, and peers are significant influences upon his motivation and aspirations at all levels of the educational system, and certainly upon his decision whether to continue at school at the end of the period of compulsory education and upon his intention to apply for admission to college or university. Pike (1970, pp.72-73) has characterized the effects of the type of community upon the demand for higher education in the following manner:
'A university community is likely to be a community where local school

facilities are relatively good, where job opportunities are varied and plentiful, and one in which there are a goodly number of parents who have themselves attained a high level of education. Thus, young people living in a university community may attend university in relatively large numbers not simply because the institution is situated nearby, but because their aspirations and expectations are subject to the influence of these other community-related variables. . . .

'In addition, one cannot entirely ignore the argument pursued by some sociologists that a concomitant of the rural and small town environment is a set of values, beliefs and ways of doing things — ie a *subculture* — which adversely affects access to higher education. . . .'

On the other hand, Pike accepts that the major differences in educational behaviour which are assumed to result from variations in the attitudes, beliefs, and values of individual communities may well result from variations in the socio-economic composition of those communities. This is directly implied by the sociological analyses of aspirations for admission to higher education mentioned earlier. There is considerable evidence on the effects of social class upon the motivation to enter higher education (some of which is mentioned by Bill Williamson in his paper), and Pike (pp.115-125) presents an interesting account of the relevance of this research to variations in participation in the Canadian system of higher education. He also points out that variations in both motivation and participation in different geographical communities are probably also related to their ethnic composition (see also Alan Little's chapter in this volume).

The problems involved in dealing with these sorts of barriers to higher education are clearly much less tractable than some of the others which have been mentioned in this chapter, and they raise both moral and political issues of considerable importance. There are at least two questions of specific relevance to educationalists. First, how is it possible to work towards universal access to higher education without encouraging universal attendance; that is, how do we respect a person's right *not* to attend college or university (Willingham 1971)? Second, if we do not wish participation in higher education to be dependent upon 'artificial' factors such as geographical location, do we try to change the attitudes and values prevalent in those communities which are under-represented, and thus enforce an urban middle-class subculture upon those communities; or do we try to make our colleges and universities equally 'relevant' to the diverse and possibly conflicting subcultures which our society contains (Pike 1970, pp.120-121)?

REGIONAL VARIATIONS IN EDUCATIONAL PARTICIPATION
Not surprisingly, the extent of participation in higher education across different geographical regions depends upon the predominant nature of the communities or neighbourhoods which constitute those regions. Such geographical variations depend specifically upon the social and economic characteristics of the regions involved, and upon whether they are relatively

urban or relatively rural. They tend to be especially pronounced in larger countries where there are substantial social and economic disparities between different regions and provinces, and also where higher education is the responsibility of a relatively autonomous regional government. Nevertheless, similar disparities appear to operate equally in smaller countries such as the United Kingdom, and Bereday (1973, pp.48-49) suggests that regional inequities in higher education are typical of mass education countries.

The obvious example of a country with diverse socio-economic conditions and regional government is the United States. It is well known that participation in higher education varies considerably in different parts of this country. Specifically, there appear to be relatively high enrolments at all levels of higher education in New England and on the Pacific Coast (Embling 1974, p.34). A second example is Canada, which has received an equally detailed analysis. Pike (1970, pp.14-18, 203, 205) has presented information on the participation rates at Canadian universities, both by province of residence and by province of university attendance, as well as at other institutions of higher education by province of residence. Sheffield (1978) has provided more up-to-date statistics covering all aspects of further and higher education, but unfortunately these appear to relate only to the province of attendance. University participation rates tend to be highest among the residents of Quebec, the Prairie Provinces, and British Columbia, and lowest among the residents of Newfoundland, the Maritime Provinces, Ontario, and especially the Yukon and Northwest Territories.

Rather less information is available concerning educational participation across the regions and provinces of European countries. Relevant statistics for the universities in the United Kingdom are provided in the *Statistical Supplements* published by the Universities Central Council on Admissions. These tend to show lower participation in university education among residents of the North, and higher participation among residents of the South East, both in absolute terms and in relation to the number of individuals in the appropriate age group. Embling (1974, p.39) has indicated that similar discrepancies occur between the various regions of France, with the lowest participation rates in Haute-Normandie and the Loire, and the highest participation rates in the Paris region and the Mediterranean areas. Bereday (1973, p.49) has also pointed out that the Paris region contains only 2 per cent of the population of France, but 38 per cent of all of the country's students.

Provision

It appears to be generally true that regional variations in the degree of participation in higher education are related to concomitant variations in the provision of relevant institutions. This has been noted in the case of the United States (Embling 1974, p.34), and also in the case of Sweden (Bereday 1973, p.48-49). This relationship is especially apparent in the case of Canada, where most of the relevant institutions are located near the southern frontier and on the eastern coast, and where there are no colleges or universities at all in the Yukon and Northwest Territories (Sheffield 1978). In turn, the provision of institutions of higher education depends upon the economic resources of a particular region or province, and this will be reflected in the level of urbanization of the region. Such disparities between the different parts of a country will affect the provision of institutions, staff, and student grants and scholarships in a fairly direct manner (Pike 1970, pp.141-152). One would also expect these geographical variations in the provision of higher education to be correlated with the social-class structure of different regions, but there appears to be little evidence on this point.

Once again, the lack of provision of colleges and universities in a particular region constitutes a 'distance barrier' to higher education. Although Willingham (1971) had calculated that two-fifths of the population of the United States lived within commuting distance of an accessible college, he also showed that this proportion varied among the four main census regions of the country, between one-third in the Midwest and one-half in the South and West. Willingham argues that careful regional planning is necessary to reduce these geographical variations in the accessibility of higher education. One might think that an obvious way to overcome such regional biases would be to increase the number of institutions in the more remote and sparsely populated areas of a country. Bereday (1973, pp.48-49) mentions that the new universities in the United Kingdom were deliberately scattered on a regional basis, and he gives as other examples new provincial institutions at Trondheim and Tromsø in Norway and at Oulu in Finland. However, in most countries where the provision of higher education is the responsibility of a national government, universities tend to see themselves as having a national, rather than a regional, role. As a result, even institutions in relatively remote regions tend to recruit students nationally rather than regionally; indeed, they tend to draw the majority of their students from those areas of the country which have traditionally had the highest levels of participation in higher education (Keeble 1968; Bereday 1973, pp.48-49). Obviously, these tend to be middle-class students from the dominant cultural groups.

Similarly, one might expect that regional disparities in the provision of higher education could be counteracted by encouraging student mobility towards regions with relatively better provision of colleges and universities. As with local variations in the provision of higher education, student mobility could be encouraged by systems of grants and scholarships, and by adequate subsidized accommodation at geographically centralized institutions. In Canada, for instance, residents of the Yukon and Northwest Territories are assisted in attending courses at institutions in the provinces or at the University of Alaska. Once again, however, such schemes tend to enhance the greater mobility of middle-class students at the expense of children from lower income groups.

Thus, neither the regional provision of colleges and universities nor scholarship schemes for students from rural regions appears to be sufficient to remedy inequalities of access to higher education among different geographical areas. This suggests that regional variations in the provision of institutions of higher education are not the major determinant of differences in the degree of participation among geographical regions. The source of such biases must therefore be sought in the selection procedures employed in higher education and in the factors influencing the demand for higher education among the total population of potential candidates for admission into higher education.

Selection

In principle, regional biases in educational selection might take one of two different forms. First, institutions in different geographical regions might adopt varying selection criteria, which would produce unequal access to higher education related to the intended region of university or college attendance. Depending upon the possibility of student mobility among different regions, these sorts of biases would produce a variety of indirect effects upon regional patterns of participation in higher education. It is relatively easy to obtain information upon the admissions requirements of colleges and universities in the United Kingdom, but there has been no research on the possible effects of differences in such requirements upon the geographical distribution of successful candidates. Second, a particular institution might adopt varying selection criteria for candidates from different geographical regions, which would produce unequal access to higher education related to the actual region of residence. As in the case of local variations in access to higher education, there is not normally any explicit selection based upon a candidate's place of residence. Bereday (1973, p.48) mentions that some American universities attempt to recruit according to geographical quotas in an attempt to achieve a more uniform distribution of students across national regions. On the other hand, Pike (1970, pp.17-18) comments that the provincial government of New Brunswick has used financial controls to try to restrict the admission of students from other Canadian provinces. As he remarks, 'But when a province combines a low university participation rate for its own residents with a large intake of students from other provinces, some restriction may seem, for a number of reasons, to be an unfortunate necessity.'

Nevertheless, it must once again be remembered that the possibility of being admitted to an institution of higher education is one of the obvious 'life chances' affected by inequalities in the provision of adequate relevant education at the primary and secondary levels. In particular, the provision of a traditional academic secondary school is subject to obvious regional variation in most countries, and this is correlated with the social and economic characteristics of the different regions concerned. Keeble (1968) showed that the following indicators were all directly related to one another as properties of different geographical regions in England and Wales: the proportion of school pupils receiving sixth-form education; the proportion of high income families; and the proportion of children educated at independent schools. Moreover, Pike (1970, pp.21-27) found that geographical variations in the extent of participation in higher education were directly related to differences in the proportion of high-school pupils staying on to take their matriculation across the various provinces of Canada. It is clearly wrong to assume that the region in which a potential student resides is unrelated to the quality of his secondary education, and thus to the likelihood of his being admitted to higher education.

Demand
The factors which were specified above are also obviously related to a potential student's aspirations to enter higher education, for reasons which were discussed in considering local variations in the demand for higher education. The socio-economic composition of a geographical region affects a student's motivation at all levels of the educational system. In particular, potential students from the poorer regions of a country are less likely to regard entry into higher education as a desirable personal goal, especially if there is no relevant institution in their immediate vicinity.

These effects were explored by Keeble (1968) with specific reference to students admitted to Cambridge University. His analysis started from the observation that, although the university seemed to regard itself as having a 'national' role, the regional distribution of its students did not correspond to that of the population as a whole. Keeble showed that the same disparities were evident in the regional distribution of candidates applying for admission to the university, and he argued that the apparent bias in admissions was the product not of biases in the selection procedures, but of unequal demand for admission across different national regions. Three correlated factors explained most of these regional disparities in demand. First, the geographical distribution of candidates corresponded to regional variations in the proportion of school pupils receiving sixth-form education (cf Pike 1970, pp.21-27). Second, the geographical distribution of candidates corresponded to regional variations in the proportion of high-income families. Finally, the geographical distribution of candidates corresponded to regional variations in the proportion of children educated at independent schools. Private education in the United Kingdom has always been based upon traditional academic schooling as an explicit preparation for admission to university. Hence, Keeble's account demonstrates a clear relationship between regional variations in participation in higher education, regional variations in the demand for higher education, and the likelihood that a potential student will be a member of a community which identifies higher education as a legitimate and desirable personal goal.

NATIONAL VARIATIONS IN EDUCATIONAL PARTICIPATION
There exist obvious discrepancies among different countries in the extent of

participation in higher education. However, direct international comparisons are often difficult and sometimes meaningless, since there may be radical disparities between different countries in terms of their attitudes and beliefs concerning higher education. I shall restrict my discussion to a comparison of the member countries of the European Economic Community, since they share a similar cultural heritage, and have been subjected to similar social, political, and economic forces over the last twenty years. Nevertheless, even with this restriction, there still exist major differences among the various countries in terms of their understanding of the nature of higher education. Basic statistical evidence on the extent of participation in higher education in different countries is contained in the *Statistical Studies* published by the European Centre for Higher Education; Table 9 shows the participation rates for the member countries of the EEC in 1975.

Provision
Since there exist major differences in the very conception of higher education, it is only possible to make gross comparisons between different countries in terms of its provision. Traditionally, many countries in Western Europe have allowed free access to higher education for any student who successfully completes his secondary education. This is often marked by a formal proficiency examination, such as the Danish Examen Artium or the German Abitur. In several of these countries, the right to enroll at an institution of higher education is enshrined in national law. This may ensure good access to higher education, as in Belgium where over 90 per cent of school-leavers pass the relevant examination. On the other hand, the results of the examination may constitute a means of selecting candidates for higher education (see below). Nevertheless, until the 1970s, this relatively open admissions policy was only possible because of an adequate provision of institutions of higher education.

As is well known, the 1960s witnessed considerable expansion in all European countries in the numbers of students seeking admission to higher education. Initially, this was matched by an increased provision of relevant institutions, but in many areas the expansion of higher education did not keep pace with increased demand. Most European countries were therefore compelled to introduce quotas of places and formal selection procedures, at least in certain specific academic disciplines. Selection criteria which have been introduced include the results of school-leaving or entrance examinations, assessment by interview, consideration of employment experience, and also the outcome of random selection, possibly weighted by these various indicators. The introduction of such procedures suggests that the provision of higher education is no longer adequate in certain countries. However, it would appear that restrictions on access to higher education have been applied in roughly equal measure, and they do not in themselves constitute a source of geographical bias in educational participation. There are three notable exceptions to this general picture. Colleges and universities in the

TABLE 9
Numbers of students at universities and equivalent institutions in the member countries of the EEC (1975)

	Students			Population (x 1000)	Students per 10,000 population
	M	F	Total		
Belgium	55587	27773	83360	9846	85
Denmark	38236	21870	60106	5025	120
Federal Republic of Germany	553889	282113	836002	61682	136
France	425258	386000	811258	52913	153
Ireland	14804	10172	24976	3131	80
Italy	591796	376323	968119	55023	176
Luxembourg	127	68	195	360	5
Netherlands	90139	29995	120134	13599	88
United Kingdom	222112	110303	332415	59427	56

Source European Centre for Higher Education 1978

United Kingdom and in Ireland have always employed formal selection criteria in order to limit access to higher education, but the question whether the provision of relevant institutions in those countries is adequate or not is relative to the conception of higher education which one adopts. Finally, there is the extreme case of Luxembourg, which has no institutions presenting courses to first-degree level; students are required to study in other countries after completing their first year at the Luxembourg University Centre.

Discrepancies between different countries might be alleviated by encouraging the mobility of students on an international scale. The attitudes of the member countries of the EEC towards foreign students have usually been very liberal, but the actual numbers of students exchanged among the different countries has been rather limited (see Table 10). Obviously, international student mobility depends upon the specific admissions criteria used in order to evaluate foreign applicants, and these will be discussed later. A detailed analysis of student mobility between the various countries of Europe has been given by Masclet (1976).

Selection
National biases in educational selection may be divided into two types in the same manner as regional biases. First, different countries' institutions might adopt varying selection criteria, which would make for unequal access between intended countries of attendance. Obviously, there is a major difference in this respect between those European countries which have traditionally employed restrictive quotas and formal selection procedures, and those European countries which have traditionally guaranteed freedom of access. It should be added that the latter countries have usually been keen to extend their open admissions policy to foreign nationals, and, where restrictive quotas have had to be introduced, they have encouraged debate on the validity and propriety of the admissions criteria which have been proposed. However, relatively little is known about the implicit selection which occurs in these countries by virtue of inadequate provision of education at the secondary level: McIntosh (1978) points to the low secondary-school retention rates in European countries, and implies that considerable filtering-out of otherwise potential students occurs in secondary education.

The second type of national bias in educational selection occurs when a particular institution adopts varying selection criteria for foreign candidates, which would make for unequal access for different countries. Many European countries have tried to maintain the traditional liberal attitude towards foreign students which was mentioned above, and the Council of Europe has recommended that a quota of places should be held open for foreign students seeking admission to the institutions of higher education in each member country (Pedersen 1978). A notable instance is the Federal Republic of Germany, which submits foreign applicants to the same admissions procedures as German nationals, but which reserved 8 per cent of

TABLE 10
Numbers of students exchanged among all institutions of higher education in the member countries of the EEC (1975)

Country of origin	Host country							
	Belgium	Denmark	Germany	France	Ireland	Italy	Luxembourg	United Kingdom
Belgium		6	392	633	4	55	7	100
Denmark	13		208	159	1	13	1	68
Federal Republic of Germany	382	182		2022	17	227	1	672
France	463	96	2264		9	205	3	319
Ireland	14	9	54	120		6	0	580
Italy	576	13	817	1381	7		9	276
Luxembourg	555	1	654	764	0	6		59
Netherlands	774	30	1327	315	4	21	1	173
United Kingdom	139	112	1034	1776	354	124	2	
Total EEC students	2916	449	6750	7170	396	657	24	2247
All foreign students	9748	1958	47298	93750	1513	18921	47	49032

Source European Centre for Higher Education 1978

all places in higher education for such students. Other countries have promoted specific programmes to encourage student exchanges, an example being schemes operating between Belgian and Dutch universities. However, political and economic pressures have led certain countries to introduce restrictive quotas and discriminatory requirements for foreign students. Foreign applicants to British institutions of higher education obviously encounter difficulties in this direction. In 1976, the Belgian government instituted a quota of 5 per cent of the total student body and discriminatory tuition fees for foreign students from industrialized countries. In Italy foreign students coming from a country where access to higher education is subject to restrictive quotas must pass an examination in order to be admitted to a particular faculty.

However, there are certain other factors which constitute an implicit means of discriminating among potential students on the basis of their country of origin. An obvious case is that of language requirements. It may well be perfectly reasonable to require a certain standard of proficiency in the language of instruction, though an alternative would be to make attendance at a language course a formal part of the student's studies after admission. However, it has been acknowledged by Pedersen (1978) that language requirements are used as a means of regulating the admission of foreign students to Danish universities. It is certainly reasonable to demand that selectors appreciate the inequities produced by language requirements in terms of educational biases against potential students from different countries. Another implicit means of discrimination against foreign students is the acknowledgement of foreign diplomas and certificates as equivalent to home academic requirements. Although there exist international agreements on the equivalence of such qualifications between different countries, Pedersen (1978) has pointed out that these regulations do not entitle a foreign student to enroll at a specific university, only to apply for admission to that institution. Finally, the assumption that all candidates have enjoyed equal access to adequate relevant secondary education appears to give rise to inequities at the national level, as much as at the local or regional level.

It is clear that economic and political pressures on national governments over the last ten years or so have tended to increase, rather than to decrease national inequities in educational selection. As Pedersen (1978) has observed, higher education has come to be seen as an important element in the total social and economic development of national societies, and there is generally a lack of readiness to make it easy for foreigners to benefit from this national asset. Indeed, whereas the provision of higher education to students from other countries was regarded variously as an altruistic service to the international community or an effective method of cultural imperialism, it is coming to be regarded, at least in the United Kingdom, as a commodity to be exchanged in international trade.

Demand
There is very little comparative evidence on the demand for higher education,

and so it will be possible to make a few remarks by extrapolation from the discussions of local and regional variations in student demand. We have seen that geographical variations in demand are related to the attitudes, values, and beliefs prevalent in the potential student's community of residence, and that these are correlated with the socio-economic status of the community. To some extent it might be thought that the expansion in the demand for higher education which occurred in the 1960s might have tended to make such education more accessible to the mass of the population. Kogan (1979) has pointed out that there is indeed evidence that the increases in student numbers produced a more representative distribution of students in higher education as a whole. However, there is no evidence at all that such changes have affected the social distribution of students at universities: in all of the member countries of the EEC, university students continue to come from the higher social classes. This implies that increased access to higher education as a whole has not reduced inequities in its more selective and prestigious sectors.

These remarks apply chiefly to the socio-economic structure of the countries within the EEC. However, it is reasonable to suppose that the extent of the demand for higher education across different countries will depend upon the socio-economic characteristics of the regions or provinces which constitute those countries. As we have seen, these characteristics tend to influence, or at least to be associated with, variations among communities in terms of their attitudes towards higher education. At a national level, these attitudes are probably also influenced by the basic conception of higher education which is prevalent within that society, and by the specific role assigned to institutions of higher education within the political structure of that society. Presumably these national characteristics are partially responsible for the substantial differences in secondary-school retention rates which were pointed out by McIntosh (1978). Nevertheless, further research is urgently needed on the question of how such characteristics determine the provision of higher education and the demand for higher education in different countries.

GENERAL CONCLUSIONS

My discussion of geographical biases in higher education can be summarized fairly briefly. In general terms, the equality of educational participation is directly dependent upon the equality of access to the relevant educational system. The equality of access is determined by the equality of educational provision, the equality of educational selection for admission into the system, and the equality of educational demand amongst the total population of potential candidates for admission into the educational system. Geographical variations in provision, selection, and demand are the result of social, economic, and political factors operating at local, regional, and national levels. The principal determinant of geographical inequalities in the provision of higher education is the economic resources of different communities, regions, or countries. The principal determinant of geographical inequalities in selection for higher education is the provision of traditional academic secondary education among different geographical areas, as well as economic and political pressures operating to restrict access at an international level. Finally, the principal determinant of geographical inequalities in the demand for higher education is the attitude towards higher education as a legitimate and desirable personal goal prevailing among different communities, regions, and countries, and this is directly related to their socio-economic status.

RACE BIAS

Alan Little and Diana Robbins

INTRODUCTION

Black and brown British young people are markedly under-represented in higher education. This fact deserves an urgent response from the makers of social policy in the United Kingdom country for three reasons. Firstly, because of the waste of people and talents it represents. Secondly, because of the social consequences of 'benign neglect' which are already being experienced in areas of severe racial disadvantage. Thirdly, because it leads to a shortage of ethnic minority teachers in schools, colleges and universities, of doctors, civil servants, lawyers, social workers and other professionals. Black and brown people are needed in these professions not only for their professional contribution but also for their special qualifications in meeting special needs, and to encourage other minority young people to aim high.

During 1979, we completed a review of literature concerning the notion of transmitted deprivation in relation to ethnic minorities, and the use of 'affirmative action' as a policy of intervention. Most of the literature on affirmative action is American, and much of it derives from the academic debate about special admission programmes at institutions of higher education: the *de Funis* and *Bakke* cases, the first involving a law school admissions programme, and the second a medical school, were crucial in the development of case law relating to all kinds of programmes dependent on the Equal Protection Clause of the Constitution (subsequently, judgements in the *Weber* and *Fullilove* cases clarified and confirmed the constitutionality of these programmes). We show that the idea of 'special treatment' is not nearly as alien to British social policy as some commentators wish to pretend, and that affirmative action may be one of the policies necessary to correct the gross imbalance between black [1] and white students in higher education in the 80s.

SOLOMON'S JUDGEMENT

The precise numerical under-representation of black students in higher education is easier to observe than to prove. Comprehensive statistical information on the ethnic backgrounds of school children, college students, and teaching staff is not available. Numerous studies — most recently the first Report of the Rampton Committee (Rampton Committee 1981) — have deplored this. In order to document the extent of the academic under-achievement of some school children of West Indian origin, the Rampton

Committee asked the DES to include in its school-leavers survey of six LEAs (Local Education Authorities) for 1978/79 a question designed to establish the children's ethnicity. The results of this exercise need careful interpretation, as the committee was the first to acknowledge. Firstly, the LEAs were chosen because they included a high proportion of ethnic minority leavers (and, in fact, covered about half the total number for that year). But that also means that they represented some of the least advantaged areas in the country, given the concentration of ethnic minority families in inner cities; and it is important to compare the results for Asian and West Indian leavers with 'all maintained school-leavers in England' as well as 'all other leavers' (for the six LEAs) in order to make a real assessment of their relative success or failure. Secondly, while the committee grasped the nettle of disaggregation and showed important differences between the levels of achievement of Asian and West Indian pupils, it would be wrong to interpret these differences too simply: 'At this stage in our work we are not in a position to evaluate this information or to take into account the complex network of similarities and differences that would allow us to draw comparisons between the achievement of Asian and West Indian pupils' (Rampton Committee 1981).

Nonetheless, the figures provide an interesting starting-point for investigating these differences further. They show, for example, that while 2 per cent of West Indian leavers gained one or more 'A' level passes, 13 per cent of Asians did so compared with 12 per cent of all other leavers in the six LEAs, and 13 per cent of the total number of leavers in England. One per cent of West Indians went on to full-time degree courses in further education, compared with 5 per cent of Asians and 4 per cent of other leavers. And while 1 per cent of West Indians went to university, 3 per cent of Asians and of other leavers did so, compared with 5 per cent of all leavers in England. These figures do appear to show a consistent level of under-achievement for West Indian pupils, inviting immediate diagnosis and cure from policy makers. They do not, however, necessarily indicate that all is well for Asian school-leavers aspiring to higher education. Certainly they seem to be performing as well or better than 'other leavers' in these six disadvantaged areas (although in general less well than the average for the whole of England) according to the criteria chosen. But the figures need further unravelling: does the low percentage of Asian school-leavers going directly into employment (54 per cent compared with 74 per cent for all England) simply reflect their greater success in finding suitable further education courses? Why is the destination of so many (25 per cent as against 8 per cent of all England) unknown? And will the obvious faith of Asian school-leavers in the value of 'A' level courses (6 per cent following full-time FE 'A' level courses compared with 2 per cent for all England) be borne out by their future success?

We cannot tell exactly how ethnic minority children are achieving in school, how many go on to higher education, and whether the qualifications gained at school, university and college will have the same value for them in the job market as for their white counterparts. The recently published Schools Council project — *Multi-Ethnic Education: The Way Forward* by Little and Willey (1981) — provides up-to-date evidence of support in schools and LEAs for the statistical monitoring of performance, according to ethnic origin. The report is based on two surveys — one of all LEAs in England and Wales and the other of a sample of secondary schools, and of these a minority expressed reservations about collecting statistics: 'Authorities and schools favouring the collection of statistics emphasized that the information obtained must relate to educational needs, and that great care and sensitivity must be exercized in the method of collection. There was agreement that collection on the pre-1973 basis had yielded no information of educational value but that, as the Select Committee pointed out in their 1977 report *The West Indian Community*: ". . . the argument that the statistics were not satisfactory is not an argument that there should be no statistics . . .", replies from a majority of authorities and schools with a "high" or "medium" concentration of minority ethnic group pupils indicated support for the collection of statistics which would give an improved information base for assessing special needs and monitoring performance' (Little and Willey 1981).

The same lack of information about the ethnic composition of the student population of Great Britain, as of the school population, hinders identification of problem areas and policies to tackle them. Much more is known about both in the United States, where concern about obvious racial bias in the past has led to extensive monitoring of performance at school, college and job levels. A study of college education by Richard Freeman, published in 1976, was able to use 1970 census data, as well as data from a number of other empirical investigations, to demonstrate the relative achievements of educated black and white Americans: 'According to the empirical evidence:

1   Black graduates attained rough economic equality with white female graduates by the mid-1960s and young black male graduates attained equality in the late 1960s. However, while older black men made economic advances relative to whites, they continued to trail their white peers — the legacy of past discrimination.

2   Black youngsters and qualified personnel responded with extraordinary speed to the changed market situation, with the young enrolling in colleges and altering occupational plans rapidly in accordance with new economic opportunities. Perhaps because of generally low family incomes, black youngsters appear more attuned to monetary incentives than whites.

3   The economic gains of educated blacks were not reversed by the falling college job market. To the contrary, black college workers either maintained past or enjoyed continued advancement relative to whites in the depressed 1970s' (Freeman 1976).

While some of Richard Freeman's interpretations may be controversial, he is able to show very clearly from data collected on a national basis the impact of anti-discrimination policies in the 60s in schools, in college enrolment, in college employment, and in employment generally. 'The economic gains of college-trained black men reversed two traditional patterns of discrimination that had, rightfully, received considerable attention. First is the shocking fact that, as late as 1959, non-white college men earned markedly less than white high school men — second, for decades, discriminatory differentials between black and white men had increased with education, so that the more schooling a black had, the greater would be the gap between his income and that of a comparable white. Largely because of this, the rate of return for black investments in college was below that for white investments, which . . . could be expected to deter black youngsters from going on in their schooling.' And the policies which had so dramatically closed the gap between opportunities for white and black school-leavers and students in these years are summarized by Freeman as follows: '. . . black graduates did relatively well in the 1970s, generally continuing the advance in the market that began after the initiation of equal employment activity in the mid-1960s. Although the gains may have been marred by "tokenism" — the desire of companies to meet affirmative action goals by employing black graduates solely in "community relations" positions — there is no denying the extraordinary improvement in the economic status of black graduates, after decades of severe discrimination in high-level job markets' (Freeman 1976).

Evidence of continuing educational disadvantage among black school children in the US is considered further below; but the Freeman study is a useful example of how monitoring at various stages in the individual's career is necessary to determine the success of policies designed to eliminate disadvantage at one particular stage. To a great extent, however, discussion of the careers of black British graduates remains hypothetical. The under-representation of black and brown students in higher education needs urgent quantification and analysis on a national scale; but it has been observed, and measures to correct it cannot wait on comprehensive research. Once it is accepted that the only possible answer at present to How many? is 'Too few', the obvious next question is Why?

There are some answers here. 'We have met a group of West Indians,' wrote the Rampton Committee, '. . . currently studying in higher education, all of whom said that they had faced particular obstacles and difficulties in the course of their education which they had had to overcome to reach higher education' (Rampton Committee 1981). The committee planned to investigate these obstacles further, but the factors they identified as contributing to the under-achievement of West Indian children as a group in school must surely be their starting-point: racism, inadequate pre-school provision, an inappropriate curriculum, language difficulties, and weak parent/teacher contacts were among these. This is the last in a long series of studies which have pinpointed the demoralizing effects of racism — racial prejudice and discrimination, negative stereotyping and intimidation — on black British children (Little 1978). And it is these effects — the gap in opportunities created by past discrimination, the persistence of social structures based on discriminatory attitudes, and the day-to-day experience of prejudice — which are not removed by so-called 'colour-blind' policies.

Sheila Allen wrote in 1979: 'At the present time, it is clear that in general terms the colour of one's skin is an important and visible indicator of one's life chances' (Allen 1979). This is the point which differentiates those experiencing the range of 'obstacles and difficulties' which make up racial disadvantage from the rest of the disadvantaged population.

Ethnic minorities are not a homogeneous group — yet a number of factors combine to make them the victims of many similar problems. Inner-city areas, for example, are known to present multiple social problems — even if their definition is hard and their solution even harder. Edwards and Batley (1978) have described the background to studies of Birmingham, Liverpool and Lambeth undertaken between 1973 and 1977: 'The three "inner-area studies" . . . were part of the DOE "total approach" to the improvement of town environments generally and inner-city areas in particular.' They have criticized the confused and confusing definitions of urban stress and deprivation which lie behind the studies. But it has been observed that ". . . while the solutions to the problem of urban deprivation are elusive, the same does not follow for racial disadvantage.' This conclusion was reached in 1976 in a report to the Home Secretary by the (then) Community Relations Commission, which attempted to answer the question of the '. . . extent to which the needs of ethnic minority communities differ from those of the rest of the population in areas of urban deprivation . . .' (CRC 1977). The report was based on a review of the literature, including detailed analysis of the 1971 census data, and on interviews with 'policy-makers, practitioners and lay-persons'. From all these sources the study concluded that 'There was widespread recognition of the special issues relating to the disadvantage of ethnic minorities and it is clear that "racial disadvantage" is the product of a racially discriminatory society.' A second factor which made ethnic minorities 'special' was their relative concentration, which might make area-based policies of particular value in tackling racial disadvantage: 'In the tackling of urban deprivation, such a strategy is limited. Although one can define the 10 or 100 or 1000 most deprived neighbourhoods in the country, these will contain only a small proportion of the most disadvantaged population. On the other hand, an "area priority" strategy is likely to be highly effective in the combating of racial disadvantage, since 70% of ethnic minorities live in 10% of enumeration districts.'

Ethnic minority groups in Great Britain are not as heavily concentrated or as homogeneous as their American counterparts. Recent analysis (CSO 1979) of the pattern of births to New Commonwealth and Pakistani mothers has shown quite different detailed settlement patterns for different ethnic groups, and has demonstrated again the tendency for people of similar ethnic origins to cluster together. Even within London, the settlement patterns for citizens of West Indian origin were quite different from those for Pakistani and Bangladeshi residents. But overall, taking ethnic minorities *as a group*, they are heavily over-represented in inner-city areas. A study of Camden (Syson 1975) undertaken in 1975 for the Institute of Community Studies demonstrated that the ethnic minority population of that particular area was not necessarily over-represented below the poverty line — while one-parent families and the elderly, for example, were. Yet extensive data collected by Professor Peter Townsend (1979) shows that *as a group* non-white citizens are over-represented amongst those 'in poverty' (16 per cent of non-whites as opposed to 9 per cent of whites), and among those 'in or on the margins of poverty' (38 per cent of non-whites as opposed to 33 per cent of whites).[2]

Numbers of pieces of research as well as official reports have described the 'ethnic dimension' of urban deprivation, the special needs of ethnic minority groups and the special degree to which they experience disadvantage. The need for consideration of the '. . . special dimension of racial disadvantage' in framing an effective education policy for multi-racial areas has been documented (Little 1978), and the persistence of a basic pattern of discrimination and disadvantage in housing has been described (McKay 1977). Rutter and Madge (1976) summarized the research on ethnic minority groups and deprivation completed by 1976. They listed the possible causes of the educational disadvantages faced by children of New Commonwealth immigrant parents: '. . . such as large family size, poor living conditions, lack of play and conversation in early childhood, and less satisfactory schooling. London data suggest that children of West Indian parentage are three times as likely to suffer from multiple social disadvantage compared with indigenous children . . .' (CRC 1973). Evidence was adduced for a continuing high level of discrimination in employment in 1976, and a disturbingly high level of unemployment among young blacks; as well as the findings of all surveys, national and local, that a high proportion of black people, compared with the indigenous white population, live in poor quality housing: 'For many, overcrowding, multiple-occupancy and lack of basic household amenities characterize their home. . . . Intergenerational continuities and disadvantage in the housing situation of black people in Britain will depend much more on the extent of white prejudices and discrimination than on anything the families can do for themselves.'

The existence and extent of racial disadvantage and discrimination, defined by the Community Relations Commission as '. . . the disadvantages experienced by racial minorities which spring from racial prejudice, intolerance and unequal treatment in society . . .', were demonstrated in the course of a research project undertaken by Political and Economic Planning (PEP) between 1972 and 1975. The findings were presented in four reports between 1974 and 1976 (PEP 1974, 1975 and 1976); and two of these were covered in the review by Rutter and Madge. The overall findings of the project were finally brought together in one volume (Smith 1977), and present the most recent comprehensive picture of racial disadvantage in Great Britain.

The survey found, first, that '. . . the links between membership of a racial minority group and each particular form of deprivation were exceedingly strong.' Other groups could be identified — such as one-parent families — which were over-represented in disadvantaged categories, but the chances of multiple deprivation '. . . for Asians and West Indians . . . are very much higher . . . than for any other group' (Smith 1977). Secondly, the study showed that while the deprivations of ethnic minorities might be similar to those for the rest of the population (although experienced to a special degree) they might arise from different causes and need different remedies. Thirdly, while social mobility was common within the white class structure, the identification of blackness with low social status could become inescapable if it were not challenged.

More recent evidence of the crippling deprivations which the children of newcomers in general have to suffer has been provided by analysis of the data obtained in the follow-ups to the National Child Development Study by the National Children's Bureau. The data specifically concerned those immigrant families including a 16-year-old member. Analysis of the school performance, in reading and mathematics, of the 16-year-olds provided two general conclusions: 'Firstly, immigrants tend to have relatively poor attainment overall, but when children of similar financial and other material circumstances were compared most of the immigrant groups do as well as non-immigrants, the main exceptions being West Indians. Secondly, the poorer school performance is generally only found among first-generation immigrants, and to some extent is relatively short-term and language specific.' So there appear to be few differences in attainment between 'immigrant' and indigenous children which cannot be explained by these 'financial and other material' factors. In a second paper, Essen and Ghodsian (1980) looked more closely at the social and home circumstances of the children in the sample and described the burden of disadvantage carried by the children of newcomers: 'What emerges quite clearly from the above is the strikingly bad housing, employment and financial conditions of which the first-generation Asian and first- and second-generation West Indian and Irish 16-year-olds and their families live. The disadvantages shown in this report probably represent the minimum that these families endure.'

There has been no comprehensive study of racial disadvantage and discrimination since the passage of the 1976 Race Relations Act: and it is to be deplored that the 1981 census data will now provide no evidence of the impact which the act might have had on patterns of ethnic minority housing, income and employment. Meanwhile, the PEP reports provide stark evidence of the field in which the act was designed to operate; and evidence of its effectiveness will have to wait for the next PEP study.

The development of race relations legislation will be considered in greater detail below, but we should make clear here our contention that — whereas the earlier legislation was concerned with the absence of racial strife, with 'harmonious community relations' — subsequent measures, and in particular the 1976 Race Relations Act, have made explicit the disadvantage and discrimination faced by NCWP citizens of New Commonwealth and Pakistani origin, and have come closer to trying to deal with the attitudes and social conditions which may have been behind the possibility of social conflict in the early 60s. It is *these* policies which invite comparison with the United States, where their development has been paralleled by the feeling that 'something more' was necessary in order to achieve racial justice, beyond simple anti-discrimination measures.

Any comparison between discrimination and disadvantage among black groups in the United States and the UK invites the charge that the differences between their situations are as marked as the similarities. Ethnic minorities in Great Britain may have a common experience of discrimination and disadvantage, but represent a wide range of cultures, languages, skills and aspirations: taken as a group, they comprise something over 3 per cent of the population. In the US the minority population is remarkably homogeneous: black Americans (so defined in the census by self-identification) account for 90 per cent of the non-white population. And some 25 million black Americans — mainly and increasingly living in all-black areas — confront institutions designed to favour the remaining 200 million (Orfield 1978). The history of blacks in the States and the development of slavery is well known and well documented (Higginbotham 1978; Bell 1972). As late as 1857 — about 300 years after the first importation of black slaves into the New World — the judgement in the Dred Scott case stated clearly that blacks had no constitutional rights as citizens nor indeed as human beings: 'It becomes necessary therefore to determine who were citizens of the several states when the Constitution was adopted. . . . In the opinion of the Court, the legislation and histories of the times, and the language used in the Declaration of Independence show that neither the class of persons who had been imported as slaves, nor their descendents, whether they had become free or not, were then acknowledged as part of the people, nor intended to be included in the general words used in that memorable instrument' (Dred Scott v. Sandford 1857).[3] More than another century was to go by before the struggle to overcome generations of humiliation and subordination could be said to be gaining on institutionalized racism. In Great Britain, on the other hand, black people in the 50s settled as citizens with equal rights, who had recently fought fascism alongside white citizens, who had perhaps been actively recruited by British employers, and who regarded the United Kingdom as, in some sense, 'home'.

It is all the more significant, therefore, that legislation to overcome discrimination in Great Britain should have seemed politically and socially necessary so soon after the Civil Rights Act 1964 outlawing racial discrimination in the States was passed. We concede the point made by

Rutter and Madge (1976) that '. . . the history and social climate surrounding black-white relations are so different in the two nations that direct parallels can seldom be drawn.' Yet the evidence suggests that white racism has operated in both countries, that colour has been an important factor in the concentration of black groups among the most disadvantaged sectors of each society (Rex, date unknown; Kuper 1974), and that anti-discrimination law has been seen by policy makers both in Britain and the US as a mechanism firstly for defusing social conflict (Jones 1976; Newman et al 1978; for UK see Jones 1976), and secondly for breaking down patterns of disadvantage.

It has been observed that the limited American welfare state is contracting, and will continue to do so in the 80s; that '. . . the lessons of the liberal 1960s are being drawn to vindicate emerging conservation action. . . . An inhumane social programme is peddled as a realistic answer to American problems; the public is told that "lowered expectations" will mean fewer problems' (Miller 1978b). In the same article, Professor Miller records that the War on Poverty, the American dream of the 'great society', was meant to produce 'a truly democratic society with truly equal opportunity . . . easily and harmoniously.' There was only limited success, followed by black resentment at too little too late, and a white lower- and middle-class backlash. A number of pieces of research have traced the progress of equal opportunity for blacks since 1964, and it is generally agreed that substantial advances have been made. One study holds that civil rights legislation has brought about such fundamental changes in American society, and particularly in the labour market, that specifically racial barriers have long since ceased to be the issue (Wilson 1978). One analysis of the US National Longitudinal Survey by Richard Freeman published in *The Public Interest* suggested that black workers were markedly better off in the early postwar years. Two groups were held to have benefited most: the better-educated and more skilled, and those from more advantaged family backgrounds. Interestingly, the study also claims that black Americans were overcoming the transmission of racial disadvantage: 'Otis Dudley Duncan's analysis of the 1962 OCG (Occupational Change in a Generation) Survey showed that ". . . the Negro family (was) less able than the white to pass on to the next generation its socio-economic status". If you were black, it did not matter much what the status of your parents was; discrimination dominated your position in the labour market.' But '. . . 1973, the impact of parental socio-economic status on the education and labour market standing of blacks was similar to that of whites' (Freeman 1978). Such claims, as we have already indicated, are controversial, and other studies hold that such an analysis begs the question of the parental status in the first place; and point out the situation of middle-class blacks trapped in the ghetto: 'Studies of black economic mobility have observed the "low degree of occupational inheritance between high-status black fathers and their sons and the high degree of intergenerational downward mobility among blacks compared with whites" (Brigitte Mach Erbe: 'Race and Socioeconomic Segregation' American Sociological Review, December 1975)' (Orfield 1978). Similarly, a 1975 study produced evidence to show that '. . . whatever gains blacks have made, they have not won control over the sources of wealth which can be passed on from one generation to another' (Levitan, Johnston and Taggart 1975). The same study (Levitan et al.) sees the unique combination of social consensus, government commitment and economic expansion as leading to manifest absolute if not relative, gains for blacks, but cautions against the belief that 'the battle is won'. In the same way, an article by Barbara Carter and Dorothy Newman (1978) pointed to the fact that the Government Statistical Policy Division 'Social Indicators 1976' included only the most traditional measures of the American blacks' position, and failed to produce the necessary information about discrimination. Blackness itself was not recognized as a social indicator, as if the palpable gaps between blacks and whites in almost every area had no racial correlation: 'At the root of blacks' disfavoured position is a combination of inter-acting forces in the society. These include the cumulative effects on American institutions of generations of blatantly overt racial discrimination in every area of life; the continuing subtle practices of racial and economic discrimination; and the absence of national will or commitment to undertake the pragmatic practical, social and economic policies necessary to enforce those policies forthrightly.'

The over-representation of black Americans in every category of disadvantage in the 70s has been fully recounted. Even studies — like that mentioned above, by Richard Freeman (1978) — which emphasize the progress which has been made, particularly in the job market, do not deny that '. . . economic parity between most groups of blacks and whites has not been achieved, nor has the high incidence of poverty, unemployment and social ills in the black community been eliminated . . .'; and the conclusion is inescapable that 'For those who remain seriously disadvantaged, anti-bias activity is not enough.' [4]

Two comprehensive studies (Levitan et al. 1975; Newman et al. 1978) making use of the relatively extensive data on minorities available in the States have analysed the position reached by black Americans by the mid-1970s. Their main findings broadly indicate that blacks remain heavily under-represented among the rich, and over-represented among the very poor: they have a greater dependence on wages, are more vulnerable to economic conditions, and do less well under income security programmes. Substantial black/white differentials in the job market persist; in life expectancy and health care; in access to power and capital. As regards housing, 81 per cent of American households are in segregated neighbour-hoods; and within the ghetto blacks face poor services, discriminatory housing departments, absentee landlords, and less for their housing dollars. And at school things are little better. The cycle of 'poor schooling — low incomes: low income parents — poor schooling for children' has not been broken for blacks. *Years* at school for blacks have increased absolutely and relative to whites, but black *achievement* has not improved relative to whites. Desegregation of schools appears to lead to small IQ gains, but other policies — equalization of resources and reform of methods — have not produced significant results. In 1972 a slightly greater proportion of black children were 'behind' in school than in 1968 despite compensatory programmes. The faith which both black and white Americans have in education as a method of advancement may be misplaced. 'Credentialism' in the States has produced the best-educated unemployed in the world — disproportionately black.

This evidence of continuing discrimination and disadvantage among black Americans provided the impetus behind the three main inter-related methods of attack on their situation since the 60s: anti-discrimination law, black protest, and the 'War on Poverty'. All these are well researched. The study by Dorothy K. Newman (1978) and others describes *protest* as '. . . the cutting edge of progress', and is able to support this argument with evidence from each stage of the civil rights movement. Legislation in the States has centred around the Civil Rights Acts of 1964, and 1968, and the Voting Rights Act of 1965. But the position has been complicated and constantly modified by the influence of individual court judgements, which are fully covered in the book by Derrick Bell (1972). Agencies enforcing the Civil Rights effort since the 60s have proliferated. At the federal level, two divisions of the Department of Justice are involved in anti-discrimination: the Civil Rights Division which is the chief federal agency for enforcing civil rights law in the courts, and the Community Relations Service which promotes civil harmony through conciliation and technical assistance. The executive agencies comprise: the US Commission on Civil Rights, which is appointed by the President and collects useful volumes of evidence in monitoring civil rights policies; the Office of Federal Contract Compliance Programmes, within the Department of Labour, which promotes equal opportunity in employment and derives its power from the cancelling of contracts and the authority to bar an employer from competing for other government contracts; the Equal Employment Opportunity Commission, which overlaps to some extent with the OFCCP, but whose strength lies in the power to bring an employer to court. The Office of Civil Rights within the Department of Health, Education, and Welfare (US Commission on Civil Rights 1979) is primarily responsible for ensuring equal educational opportunity. The nine Regional Offices and State Advisory Committees are co-ordinated by the US Commission on Civil Rights, which by this means gains a unique insight into civil rights issues at a local level. Action against discrimination in federal housing programmes is the responsibility of the Department of Housing and Urban Development (McKay 1977).

The committee which reported under Mr. William van Straubenzee MP in 1973 on employment discrimination in Northern Ireland considered the US discrimination law and a useful summary of it is included in their report (Report and Recommendations of the Working Part on Discrimination in the Private Sector of Employment 1973). The legislation has clearly been used as a model elsewhere (Lester and Bindman 1972). In the same way, links between the US 'War on Poverty' in the 60s — the introduction of compensatory education programmes, health insurance, welfare and other benefits (Levitan et al. 1975) — and area-based position discrimination programmes in Great Britain have been demonstrated (Edwards and Batley 1978).

To a great extent, American research has seen a direct relationship between the effectiveness of the agencies and the situation of black people. In his study of affirmative action, Livingston (1979) writes: 'If equal opportunity requires at least roughly proportionate group results, the facts reveal how very unfair the game has been. What justice in the abstract seems to require, the plight of black Americans makes urgent.' On the other hand, opponents of affirmative action argue with Nathan Glazer that black progress is continuing at a reasonable rate supported by anti-discrimination legislation, without the 'something more' which discriminates against the white population and denigrates the black. Glazer's arguments are considered more fully below, but behind them lies the assumed success of early civil rights measures. He defends this position with studies such as those of Richard Freeman (1978) which suggested that '. . . national anti-discriminatory policies have successfully altered the job market for black workers,' while conceding that this '. . . should not be taken to mean that the equal employment effort should be weakened.' We have already mentioned Richard Freeman's (1976) work on the economic status of college-educated black workers. In summary, he finds '. . . extraordinary improvement in the status of black graduates, after decades of severe discrimination in high-level job markets,' and suggests that this is 'the result of affirmative action and related anti-discriminatory activity.' Other studies set out to contradict those whom they describe as the 'neo-conservative intellectuals who oppose further civil rights initiatives' (Orfield 1978). Among them, Dorothy Newman and her associates (1978) argue that the heart of black disadvantage lies in discrimination and ineffective machinery for dealing with it; they demonstrate the ineffectiveness of the machinery from the continuing high level of black disadvantage.

One study of employment discrimination (Marshall et al. 1979) tries to go further than this. By undertaking a small number of detailed case studies, Ray Marshall and his associates hoped to take into account all the variables influencing employment opportunities for blacks, and reach a clearer indication of the success or failure of anti-discrimination laws and agencies. They continually stress the need for something more, apart from law enforcement and conciliation: they identify this something more with '. . . outreach and affirmative action programmes'.

The debate about affirmative action, and 'positive', 'benign' and 'reverse' discrimination in the United States has been long, confused and bitter. The private actions undertaken by De Funis and Bakke against institutions of higher education demonstrate the constitutional, political and moral controversy which can arise from these degrees of preference. All these terms are used to describe the programmes framed by Government agencies and individual employers which try to do 'something more' for minorities, remove entrenched patterns of discrimination and ensure that equality of opportunity goes beyond the simple prohibition of overtly biased acts. The notions of indirect discrimination — the disadvantages suffered by minorities more as a result of '. . . institutional practices and patterns than of deliberate acts of prejudiced individuals' (Bindman and Grosz 1979) — and of affirmative action are closely linked in the States. It became increasingly clear during the 60s and early 70s that the disadvantages faced by black Americans — particularly in employment — would not be removed by ending individual acts of discrimination (Carter and Newman 1978). The landmark case of Griggs v. Duke Power Co. in 1971 laid the foundations for the subsequent attack on indirect discrimination because it dealt with the *effects* of employment practices rather than their intent or purpose. Job qualifications and tests used were held to be racially discriminatory and therefore contrary to Title VII of the Civil Rights Act if they produced adverse racial effects which could not be validated by the employer as accurate indicators of actual job performance.

One of the many paradoxes in this controversey is that the Griggs doctrine as well as the Equal Protection Clause of the Constitution[5] was subsequently extrapolated by the defenders of white candidates in their attacks on the racially exclusive, special admissions programmes to law or medical schools: 'When a racial classification was assessed by strict scrutiny criteria,[6] the classification typically was held unconstitutional' (Sindler 1978). But as Ronald Dworkin (1978) has shown, the US Supreme Court in the Bakke decision of 1978 was unable to resolve the ambiguous position of *'beneficial'* racial classifications. The technical, but important question of the appropriateness of strict scrutiny to all racial classifications was asked; but in the event begged the question of the constitutionality of affirmative action as opposed to quota programmes: 'The difference between a general racial classification that causes further disadvantage to those who have suffered from prejudice, and a classification framed to help them, is normally significant, and cannot be consistently denied by a constitutional law that does not exclude the use of race altogether.' The confusion — and it is widespread — about the meaning, the morality and the legality of affirmative action can be traced to its development as an equal opportunity policy.

The Civil Rights Act 1964 was concerned with individual rights, individually isolated: affirmative action is to do with group right — with the perception that black Americans as a group were disadvantaged in relation to whites, and that only some attempt to equalize results could remove unequal opportunites. Affirmative action came to be seen as an attempt to overthrow the American ideal meritocracy, and replace it by 'proportional equality of results' (Sindler 1978); and led to confusion and distress amongst those of the liberal establishment who opposed discrimination on the very grounds of the rights of the individual: 'I never felt in greater agony of tension between two passionate commitments, both of which I entertain and which are in conflict with each other,' declared Richard Lyman, President of Stanford University; 'I do not know what I would do if I were a Supreme Court Justice — I would hope for some Solomon's judgement that will help us have our cake and eat it' (Stanford Observer, quoted in Sindler 1978).

Sindler has commented that the plea for a 'Solomon's judgement' which would somehow reconcile the rights of the individual with the rights of the disadvantaged group was based on a misconception about the role of legislation in this kind of field: 'The exquisitely complicated problems presented by *Bakke* (and *De Funis*) can never be "settled" through case law, no matter how reasoned the Court's decision in *Bakke* or subsequent cases. Rather, they are enduring problems not amenable to full resolution at any one time but in process of partial and changing resolution at all times' (Sindler 1978). But this tension was nonetheless felt by the institutions where special admissions programmes were being developed, and to Lyman's 'two passionate commitments' some added a third — an overriding concern with maintaining academic standards. Earlier this year, the influential Harvard Law Review was involved in a controversial decision on editorial selection '. . . This year, by a narrow vote, the editors decided that meritorious was not the same as fair,' and that the under-representation of black and women students on the editorial board should be corrected by affirmative action. 'The claims of legal rigour and scholarship demand respect. Yet law is untypical . . . it is a discipline and storehouse of judgement but also a weapon for rich and poor.' For these reasons, the Review's note editor took the view that '. . . "absolute merit" is a will o' the wisp, and urged the review to lend its weight to breaking down the many barriers facing women and minority lawyers' (The Economist 1981).

Many studies (Gross 1977; Downing 1978; Glazer 1975, 1976; Sindler 1978) have traced the ways in which affirmative action programmes emerged in the late 60s. The phrase was first recorded in an Executive Order (10925 on 6 March 1961) issued by President Kennedy which called for 'affirmative steps' and 'positive measures' to achieve equal opportunity in federal employment, and required federal contractors or subcontractors to undertake 'affirmative action' to promote equal opportunity in their workforces. A Department of Labour monograph in 1965 (later to be called 'The Moynihan Report') foreshadowed the future debate by calling for a '. . . new and special effort . . .' to produce roughly equal group results and to avoid social conflict (Moynihan 1975). The formal position was amended and extended by subsequent Executive Orders: 11246 of September 1965 transferred responsibility for equal opportunity in the Federal Government Service to the Civil Service Commission, and among contractors to the Department of Labour; 11478 of August 1969, which *mandates* affirmative action in federal employment; and 12106 of December 1978, which transferred responsibilities for affirmative action programmes in federal departments from the Civil Service Commission to the EEOC. According to the Congressional Research Service (Downing 1978), affirmative action plans to promote equal employment opportunity — which *may* be undertaken by an employer, but *must* be by federal contractors or subscontractors — is designed to overcome 'under-utilization', which is defined by the Department of Labour as '. . . having fewer minorities or women in a particular job group than would reasonably be expected by their availability . . . . Generally the following are essential items in an affirmative action plan:

i　　utilization analysis of minority persons or women in the workforce . . . [ie to discover patterns of direct or indirect discrimination and disadvantage which have led to 'under-utilization' of blacks or women as a group];

ii　　establishment of numerical employment goals and timetables based on this . . . analysis . . . [ie the employer will see, say, a 50% under-utilization of women in the workforce from his analysis, and will commit himself to filling this gap with suitably qualified women applicants within a set period];

iii　affirmative outreach . . . (Marshall et al. 1979) [ie active recruitment of under-utilized groups];

iv　　provision of training opportunities for present employees with potentialities for upward mobility . . . ;

v　　abolition of segregation . . . ;

vi　　validation of tests used for employee selection to make sure that they do not screen out a disproportionate number of minority persons and women without accurately predicting subsequent job performance . . . ; [in fact, the operation of the Griggs doctrine under the aegis of the EEOC has made the validation of tests very difficult for an employer].'

All this was described succinctly by one US official quoted in the van Straubenzee Report (1973) as: '. . . anything that you have to do to get results . . . . Affirmative action is really designed to get employers to apply the same kind of imagination and ingenuity that they apply to any other phase of their operations.' This sounds reasonable enough, but is confusing as affirmative action has come to mean different things in different situations. Active, even militant monitoring by the EEOC and civil rights groups has made the distinction between quotas and 'numerical goals with timetables' very fine indeed, so that the line of appointing *only on merit* within an affirmative action programme may be hard to hold. Consensus over the Civil Rights Act of 1964 (Glazer 1975) as amended in 1972 has not stretched as far as busing to desegregate the schools, attempts to desegregate housing, [7] apparent preference in hiring, or special admissions programmes for professional schools.

The moral dilemma which affirmative action has presented to the

American liberal establishment is acute: how can consideration of group membership be appropriate in pursuing the rights of the individual? Glazer is right to underline the gravity of abandoning '. . . the individual and the individual's good [as] . . . the test of a good society . . .'; others take this as a measure of the importance of the policy's goal. But to a great extent the moral position adopted by American academic opinion towards affirmative action is closely related to (if not determined by) *the view taken of the situation of black Americans in the 70s.* 'The extent to which inequalities of group results make a hollow mockery of "equal opportunity" is further revealed in the data cited by Justice Marshall in his separate opinion in the Bakke case,' writes Livingston (1979), in defence of affirmative action:

'* The life expectancy of a black child is five years shorter than that of a white.
* The infant mortality rate among blacks is twice that of whites.
* Black women are three times more likely to die during childbirth.
* The proportion of blacks living below the poverty line is nearly four times that of whites.
* The unemployment rate for black adults is twice that of whites.
* Unemployment among black teenagers is nearly three times that of white teenagers.
* Black males with college degrees average only $110 per year more than white males with only a high school diploma.
* While blacks are 11.5% of the population, they constitute only 1.2% of the lawyers and judges, 2% of the physicians, 2.3% of the dentists, 1.1% of engineers, and 2.6% of college and university professors.'

The opposite point of view was expressed cogently and influentially by Glazer in a series of lectures in 1974. He purported to offer a third path to the American liberal '. . . between pointless homogenization and segregation, without affirmative action.' And the key to this was the progress made by blacks in the 60s and 70s. While admitting that it is much disputed, Glazer presents an optimistic view: discrimination in the labour market has collapsed, black incomes have rapidly gained on white, and greater security and higher status are both available to black citizens. Integration in housing is increasing in relation to rise in incomes and the good effects of desegregating the schools by unpopular and expensive busing programmes are not proved. The bad factors that do persist — this argument continues — like higher unemployment for blacks, an increase in the number of female-headed families, lower educatonal attainment — all these could have as much to do with the failure of the individual as with the effects of 'institutional racism': 'The popularity of the term shows that simple racism must be on the decline; but it is used to condemn all cases of differential representation.' Glazer (1975) shows how the 'problems' identified by others can perhaps be explained away, and 'solutions' invalidated. Unemployment may partly be due to the '. . . existence of attractive alternatives to working'. Desegregation of the schools by busing attacks the principle of neighbourhood schools. Desegregation reduces the concentration of black teachers as role models, has no proved educational effect, and may increase 'white flight'. There are two other reasons for housing segregation apart from discrimination — economics and culture.

But, as we have said, there are other data to be considered. Others would ask with Professors Pettigrew and Green how legitimate and 'democratic' was the original growth of the neighbourhoods Glazer discusses. Gary Orfield (1978) has shown that the alternative to desegregation involves choosing segregation '. . . and doing nothing is accepting segregation,' with a resulting nation of '. . . divided, angry and separate peoples'. And as regards housing, the economic argument simply begs the question of centuries of economic disadvantage, while the 'culture' one obscures the evidence that black Americans may like their neighbours and their ethnic identity but do not like the ghetto at all.

The evidence of racial disadvantage adduced by the other side of the argument has already been summarized above. Even if the individual failure argument has any force at all, they argue (Orfield 1978), there is plenty of room for improvement in the black's situation by policy initiatives. Barbara Carter and Dorothy Newman (1978) have summarized their case in favour of affirmative action as follows: 'At the root of the blacks' disfavoured position is a combination of interacting forces in the society . . . . [Policies to erase the effects of this combination] and commitment to enforce them are necessary if blacks are not to continue to be unduly disadvantaged by our traditional systems of privilege. Affirmative action is one of these pragmatic policies needed to erase subtle forms of discrimination, but, still in the late 1970s, it has been the subject of wide-ranging attacks to discredit it.'

Even when the facts of racial disadvantage are admitted, the debate is not settled. The arguments against the injustice and impracticality of thinly-disguised quotas, against proportional representation as socially divisive, against 'preference', on the grounds that it denigrates the real capacities of minorities, and against interfering with the rights of employers are all put forward as overriding *moral* considerations (Downing 1978). Ronald Dworkin (1977) has tried to settle the moral argument once and for all: he identifies a distinction between equality as a policy (that is, for example, a policy intended to equalize opportunity) and equality as a basic right which may in the short term be suspended in the interests of that policy. The right to treatment as an equal within society may not always involve absolutely equal treatment, if the overall gain to society is sufficiently important. But in general the proponents of affirmative action cling to a more pragmatic view (Orfield 1978): a negative ban on discrimination has not delivered the goods; minorities and women have been denied opportunities for so long that they now need not just opportunities, but compensation, even if only temporarily; discriminatory attitudes persist, and affirmative action is one way of cancelling out their effects; a distinction between goals and quotas can be maintained. This part of the argument holds that doing nothing more than prohibiting overt discrimination is to accept in perpetuity the disadvantaged position of black Americans in all its manifestations. The US Supreme Court has not clearly settled the legal debate, as indicated above. Three times, white individuals have complained to the court that special provisions for ethnic minorities discriminated against them and therefore violated the Equal Protection Clause of the Constitution, or Title VII of the Civil Rights Act, as unambiguously as past discriminatory acts against blacks. The De Funis case was settled in 1974 on a technicality: but it raised a lot of the important questions which have been debated ever since. When De Funis applied to Washington Law School in 1970, competition for places was very fierce and letting someone in had come to mean keeping someone else out. In recognition of the fact that black Americans were grossly under-represented amongst lawyers, several law schools operated voluntary 'special admissions' programmes designed to take years of disadvantage and humiliation into account. In the same way, medical schools introduced race-conscious programmes of admission in the 1970s; and it was one of these which Alan Bakke claimed discriminated against him when he was turned down by Davis Medical School, in preference for less-well qualified (although not necessarily under-qualifed) minority candidates. In fact, the universities had never claimed to be bound only by rigid adherence to 'merit' in selecting students. They had retained discretion to take into account other factors — parental connections with the school, athletic or musical ability, and disadvantaged background amongst them. Nevertheless, the case excited great interest as a test of whether 'reverse discrimination', or affirmative action in favour of minorities, which must — by virtue of the competition for places — discriminate against the majority, was constitutional. Americans, it is said (Sindler 1978), take it for granted that the Supreme Court will wisely settle difficult disputes of this kind: but in the event, a politically attractive compromise was reached in June 1978, which did not satisfy all constitutional doubts. Briefly, the majority opinion of the court decided that Bakke must be admitted, quotas were not to be used, but affirmative action and race-conscious provisions in admission programmes might legitimately be used to overcome patterns of past disadvantage. Subsequently, a third case — United Steelworkers of America v. Weber — was heard by the Supreme Court, and the decision in June last year was clear-cut. The court held that voluntary affirmative action plans, even those containing numerical goals, do not automatically violate the Civil Rights Act: 'The majority rejected the argument of a white worker, Brian F. Webber, that the training programme constituted illegal reverse discrimination against whites by reserving half the places for black workers' (New York Times 1979). Following this, the Carter administration told universities and colleges — many of which had suspended affirmative action plans after the ambiguous Bakke dicision — to press on with special admissions programmes. A circular issued by the Department of Health, Education and Welfare in October 1979 advised against quotas, but in favour of '. . .

numerical goals to achieve the racial and ethnic composition of the student body . . .' which they wanted. They might also use lower admissions criteria '. . . when traditional criteria are found to be inadequately preditive of university success' (The Guardian 1979). For the time being, at least, it seemed that the battle in favour of affirmative action had been won.

Three important distinctions have emerged in the American debate over affirmative action. The first is the moral one — between what is good for the individual and what is good for society; between equal treatment and treatment as an equal. This has been too large a pill for public opinion to swallow. But there is evidence that two others — between goals and quotas, and between 'compensation' and 'preference' — have gone down rather better. An investigation of American attitudes to race as measured by opinion polls since 1935 by Seymour Martin Lipset and William Schneider (1978) showed that Americans were *not* in favour of discrimination or disadvantage, but were overwhelmingly opposed to 'preferential treatment'. The confrontation between egalitarian and individualistic values — exemplified by the Bakke case — has posed a dilemma for all Americans. They appear to have resolved it by seeing a distinction between compensatory programmes with goals — making allowances and providing extra help for overcoming past deprivations — and preferential treatment, with quotas: 'Relatively few object to compensation in the form of special training programmes, head start efforts, financial aid programmes, community development funds and the like. But most Americans draw the line at *predetermining* the results of the competition.' It remains to be seen whether the current political judgement of what US public opinion will bear is the right one, or whether a 'white-ethnic' backlash — already seen by some — is bound to follow.

At first sight, the special admissions programmes of American colleges and universities seem unlikely to be appropriate or acceptable in the British context. Talk of affirmative action and numerical goals, or of special provision for special needs in relation to ethnic minority groups raises exactly the same cries of positive discrimination as have been heard in the States. It is instructive to ask why. The debate in the House of Commons in March 1979 on the Local Government Grants (Ethnic Groups) Bill (Hansard 1979) demonstrated this very well. Despite the fact that — as one Member pointed out — provisions similar to those in the bill giving special help to ethnic minorities had been accepted by governments and local authorities of all political complexions for thirteen years, the 'preferential treatment' proposed by the bill was denounced as illegitimate favouritism. The obvious charges against preference were all listed again. It was called inherently unjust. Without any consideration of the complex moral issues involved in group disadvantage which has informed the American debate, it was simply assumed that 'colour-blind', meritocratic policies would be more just. Special treatment was said to denigrate the capacities of blacks, without any explanation of why removing unfair obstacles from the path of minorities should imply some incapacity on their part. 'We worry conscientiously about undermining the dignity of minorities . . . . But what of the dignity and sense of self-worth of those who owe their positions in the professions to the preferential advantages whites have enjoyed in the past?' asked Livingston (1979). In a sense, he claims, condescension in the short-term is unavoidable: '. . . the only way to avoid the risk is to do nothing, to wait for the oppressed to claim their inheritance by force.' The third charge levelled in the Commons debate against special provision — that it would alienate the white population and produce a backlash — seems to point in the same direction: ignore racial disadvantage. But will it then go away? The recent essay by David Kirp (1979) on race and education in Britain, *Doing Good by Doing Little*, tries to suggest that it might. At all events the virtues of British inexplicitness in race relations policy are contrasted with the sledgehammer quality of American affirmative action. Doing good by stealth, and doing the right thing by doing very little indeed is an attractive programme in such a controversial field as this. But there are three obvious objections to it. Inexplicit policies are fundamentally undemocratic, and they are likely to conceal confused objectives leading to weak and ineffectual implementation. Thirdly, and most important, if they are the basis of British race relations policy in the past two or three decades, they are demonstrably ineffective in removing the disproportionate incidence of most kinds of disadvantage from amongst ethnic minority groups.

The main objection to Kirp's 'inexplicit' policies is the scale, persistence and social consequences of inequalities between racial groups. This is the key argument for explicit action in wider areas of social policy than immigration control and anti-discrimination, in the same way that it was the politically crucial argument for changes in immigration and anti-discrimination policies.

The need for the kind of affirmative action programme found in the States can be defended just as strongly and logically for Great Britain. Patterns of disadvantage and discrimination exist and are being passed on to the second generation of ethnic minority citizens: the present legislation and litigation are cumbersome, expensive and of unproved effectiveness. Simply ending discrimination will allow these patterns to crystallize; doing nothing *more*, to borrow Orfield's phraseology, may be to accept increasing segregation, continuing disadvantage and an unacceptable degree of polarization.

The need for special programmes exists, and precedents exist. Edwards and Batley (1978) have traced the development of the idea of area-based positive discrimination in Great Britain in the 60s, in parallel with the US War on Poverty. The Urban and Educational Priority Programmes, the Community Development Projects, the General Improvement Areas, the Housing Action Areas and the 'Six Cities' studies all bear witness to the political acceptability of deciding some *areas* needed more help than others.

The largest scheme of this kind — the Urban Programme — has been operating now for eleven years. It was specifically inspired by the especially disadvantaged situation of ethnic minorities in generally deprived areas, and as recently as 1975 the last government was describing it as an integral part of its attack on racial disadvantage. In education, it has been suggested to us by one of Her Majesty's Inspectors (a government inspector of education) concerned with educational disadvantage that the term 'positive discrimination' and much that has followed from it has long been an accepted feature in the service. Where it is used in relation to deprived and disadvantaged pupils it is now an almost neutral term, though it may become less so at a time of reducing resources. The Plowden Report gave it the seal of approval and there is little argument in educational circles that equality of opportunity means more and different from some, if equal access to educational chances is to be a reality for all. The debate for some years is about what the 'something extra and different' should be. In national terms the Rate Support Grant has been weighted in favour of urban areas, the Social Priority Schools have been established, an Urban Programme exists and Section 11 has been specifically directed at the needs that arise from the presence in the area of people of New Commonwealth and Pakistani origin. The concept of discriminating positively in favour of the disadvantaged is entrenched in the British educational system and many LEAs give priority within their resources to meeting special educational needs and trying to equalize educational chances.

As is clear from the preceding paragraph, the idea of providing for special needs, and therefore in some sense discriminating in favour of some groups (without the implication of it being *at the expense* of the rest) is not new in Great Britain. We would argue that the special nature and degree of racial disadvantage will not be removed by policies aimed at the disadvantaged generally. And the principle seems to have achieved limited acceptance by the education service which has been, and is, involved in a range of activities particularly aimed at meeting the specific needs of ethnic minority pupils. Patchy as it may be, Section 11 has directed money into the teaching of English as a Second Language (85 per cent of £43 million pounds in 1979) and many LEAs have added much more to that. In addition, there has been a build-up of specific advisory teams, additional teachers in schools and centres, in-service courses for teachers, teachers centres and the production of teaching materials. Thirdly, there are three sections in the Race Relations Act (and similar provisions appear in the Sex Discrimination Law) which introduce a further new element in British anti-discrimination legislation. Sections 35, 37 and 38 allow for the recognition of 'special needs' and special treatment to meet them. Education, training and welfare are all included in Section 35; 37 covers 'discriminatory training' by certain training bodies; and 38 'other discriminatory training' by employers. In this context 'discrimination' means ethnically-exclusive *positive* discrimination which recognizes special needs arising from the racial disadvantages faced by ethnic minorities as a group and accepts that simply ending discrimination would not lead automatically to equal opportunity. In this limited field, the provisions are analogous to the 'something more' which has become necessary in the United States once anti-discrimination law was seen to be inadequate.

Finally, there are the special access courses introduced by the Department of Education and Science in 1978 in seven LEAs and designed to prepare students for entry to higher education: 'They will be aimed at students who have valuable experience, but lack the qualifications required and who have special needs which cannot be met by existing educational arrangements' (DES 1978). The explicit purpose of these pilot courses was to fill the gap which still remained in black recruitment to the professions despite the much publicized need for black teachers, policemen, social workers and so on. How successful these courses can be in enabling ethnic minority students '. . . to undertake responsible careers which bring them into contact with the community,' remains to be seen, but the need for special provision has been accepted.

Juliet Cheetham (1981) wrote recently about the British concern to avoid 'separatism and possible artifical specialization,' in the context of social work training: the notion of positive discrimination for ethnic minorities receives only moderate theoretical support and almost no practical application; partly because of fears about a political backlash. In America the issues are plainer and less contentious and there has been a long tradition of specialist ethnic organizations.' Yet the arguments in favour of 'something more' to ensure that the ethnic composition of the population is broadly reflected in sixth forms, polytechnics, colleges, universities and in the professions are identical in both countries. A valuable detailed study of a University of California student Affirmative Action plan undertaken by two HMIs in 1979 (Melia and Kitching 1981) contrasts 'the systematic approach' to educational disadvantage in the States '. . . with that in the UK where few adequate statistics . . . are available,' and comments on the potential of the UC model plan for use in Britain. The under-representation of ethnic minorities in higher education is known, the need for black professionals fully accepted, the under-achievement of some black and brown British children is beginning to be understood, and policies to overcome the legacy of racial discrimination and disadvantage are being developed. There are no easy solutions to the problem of opening up higher education to a disadvantaged group without affecting the rights of the individual: there is no 'Solomon's judgement'. Lord Scarman commented in 1977 that we are on dangerous ground here, but that in a mature society we must accept that such measures are ultimately just as a means to the end of individual freedom. He spoke of the need '. . . to load the law in favour of deprived groups,' in periods of social development (Scarman 1977). We believe that the events of St Paul's, Bristol, of Brixton, and of other inner-city areas this year are symptomatic of such a period of development; and that the mechanisms needed to overturn the legacy of past neglect, injustice and misunderstanding may well include the affirmative action programme.

AGE BIAS

Alan Woodley

INTRODUCTION

A study of undergraduates in the years immediately following the Second World War would have revealed a fairly high average age. However, this was a temporary aberration caused by the influx into higher education of ex-members of the armed forces. A return to the status quo quickly followed, with the vast majority of entrants to higher education being drawn from among school-leavers. Some institutions, such as Birkbeck College and Ruskin College, continued to cater almost exclusively for 'adult' or 'mature' students and many dedicated individuals studied privately for an external degree of London University. Nevertheless it would be no great exaggeration to say that mature students had returned to their somewhat marginal position in British higher education.

During the late sixties and the seventies things began to change as the concept of 'education permanente' or 'lifelong learning' began to be taken up throughout Europe and North America. The reasons for the change are many and complex but a few should be mentioned here. Squires (1979) cites the high rate of cultural and technological change and the need for re-education during a person's life; disillusionment with the ability of the formal education system to increase upward social mobility; and doubts about the socializing effects of keeping young people in full-time education for so long. To these could be added the rise of 'credentialism' and the need for adults to gain qualifications in order to compete for jobs and promotion with the younger generation. Finally one must mention the self-preservation instincts of higher education. Faced with a decline in the number of eighteen-year-olds in the population they have turned to adults with open arms in what Richard Hoggart has referred to as 'a death bed repentance' (THES 1981).

Turning from causes to symptoms one can point to the creation of the Open University, special entry schemes for mature students, and the setting up of the Advisory Council for Adult and Continuing Education as evidence that the situation for adults wishing to enter higher education is improving. However, these are only outward signs of improvement. What we want to do in this chapter is draw upon available research evidence to examine what these changes have actually meant for adult students. Can higher education be described as 'fair' to adults?

THE RESEARCH LITERATURE
The National Institute for Adult Education has been working in recent years on a computer bank of research bibliography and this provides a useful entry into the research literature. Each research document receives a series of descriptor words which correlate to the ERIC system used in the United States and these descriptors may be used to retrieve relevant items. The bank now contains over three thousand items drawn both from this country and abroad and a review of its contents is available (Charnley, Osborn and Withnall 1980). Another good source of material is the register of research in progress in adult education which is held at the University of Manchester (Legge 1972-77).

Charnley et al. noted several deficiencies in the research, including the concentration on historical aspects of adult education, the apparently random selection of research topics with few signs of linkages or of overall coherence, and the restriction of studies to particular institutions. Another factor which they might have noted is the relative lack of attention paid to adults in higher education. To illustrate this point, a recent register of current educational research projects which contained 1992 entries was found to have only four projects concerning adults in higher education (NFER 1979).

Much of the research literature which is available concerns the Open University and its students (Kirkwood 1979; Mayor 1979) and there are also several studies based on conventional universities. There has been a small amount of work done in polytechnics and colleges of education but almost nothing on mature students taking advanced professional or vocational courses. These disparities will become apparent in the remaining sections, so it is worth commenting on the likely causes. The Open University, as a distance-teaching institution, has the need to monitor its own performance and, with its computerized student records and committed manpower in the Institute of Educational Technology, it has the facilities to do so. In conventional universities, as compared with polytechnics, there are academics with more research time, more postgraduates looking for convenient research topics, and more accessible statistics via the Universities Central Council for Admissions. Other work appears to have been done by beleagured administrators or Masters degree students struggling through despite the lack of data and resources.

Almost inevitably the research studies tend to focus on the researcher's home institution and in the main they are concerned with very basic questions such as how many mature students are there, what are their social characteristics and what progress do they make as students? Considerable attention has also been given to the special problems thought to be faced by older students. However, there have been very few studies relating directly to the subjective experiences of being a mature student. Some studies, such as Hopper and Osborn (1975), Tapper and Chamberlain (1971) and King (1980), have proceeded from a strong theoretical base but these are the exceptions.

STUDENT NUMBERS

Before proceeding it is important to note that the researcher is on dangerous ground when looking at questions of 'bias' or 'fairness' in higher education. Whereas everybody would agree that a coin was 'fair' if it came up heads fifty per cent of the time, and most people would agree that higher education was biased against women if they did not form half of the student population, nobody, I think, would make out a case that each age group should be represented proportionately (ie those aged forty-five and over form fifty per cent of the population aged over eighteen, therefore they should form fifty per cent of students in higher education). In the absence of any absolute criterion one can only make comparisons across time and across institutions to determine whether higher education is becoming more or less biased against older people and where this bias is located.

When trying to count the number of adult students in higher education by using official statistics, the researcher faces several problems:

i   How do you define adult? Is the relevant age twenty-one, twenty-three or twenty-five and do you use age on entry or current age?

ii   How do you define higher education? The Department of Education and Science (DES) includes all 'advanced' courses (ie those above 'A' levels) in its definition, whereas others might only include degree-level courses. Do you include postgraduate students?

iii   Some DES statistics refer to England and Wales only, some to Great Britain and some to the United Kingdom.

iv   Some statistics include overseas students and some exclude them. This is important as overseas students tend to be older on average.

v   By the time the detailed DES statistics are published they are several years out of date.

Plunging into this minefield, Table 11 shows that about one in six full-time students in higher education in the United Kingdom are aged twenty-five or over and about two out of every three part-time students. Overall, one in three students in higher education are aged twenty-five or over. This could be called the most optimistic view as it includes overseas students and postgraduates and uses the widest definition of higher education.

Wynne (1979) has made a commendable effort to disentangle the official statistics concerning adults in higher education and in Table 12 we draw on his work in an attempt to describe the distribution of adult students in more detail. To do this however, we have to go back to the academic year 1975-76 as all the figures are not available for later years. It should be noted that Table 12 refers only to England and Wales.

Table 12 shows where the bulk of older higher education students were in 1975-76. They were with the Open University or they were taking advanced but non-degree courses in the further education sector (categories j-m). In numerical terms the universities offered more places on full-time undergraduate courses to older students than did the further education sector, but the proportion of older students was much lower. The further education sector on the other hand, offered far more part-time undergraduate opportunities than the universities and it seems likely that, in total, the two sectors catered for an equal number of older undergraduates. The number of older students on initial teacher training courses was very high, both in relative and absolute terms. Although not singled out in Table 12, the Diploma in Higher Education courses appear to be catering for many older students. A study of selected courses showed that 84 per cent of the 1979 intake were aged over twenty-one at the time of entry (Davidson 1980).

TABLE 11
The percentage of students from the United Kingdom and from overseas in higher education aged twenty-five and over

	1976/77	1977/78	1978/79
Full-time students	17.5	17.5	17.7
Part-time students	62.6	59.5	66.0
All students	31.2	30.9	33.3

Source Social Trends 1981

We now wish to look at how the position of older students has changed over time and in Table 13 we show the initial entrants to full-time higher education in Great Britain between 1966 and 1980. During this period the intake of students aged twenty-one and over doubled in size and the proportion of the total intake grew from seventeen per cent to twenty-four per cent. However, it should be noted that the greater part of these increases took place in the first few years and progress since then has been much slower.

Figure 1 shows the number of men and women 'home' entrants to full-time higher education since 1966, broken down by type of course. The cut-backs in teacher training clearly affected older students and particularly women. The numbers going to university increased steadily but the greatest increase was amongst entrants to other advanced courses.

In the part-time degree area there has been no single trend. Between February 1971 and February 1980 the Open University increased its United Kingdom undergraduate population from twenty-four thousand to sixty-six thousand and it is expected to plateau at around this level (Open University 1981). In conventional universities, at Birkbeck and for privately registered students with the University of London the numbers have remained fairly steady. The number of part-time undergraduates in the further education

TABLE 12
The distribution of adult students in higher education in England and Wales (1975-76)

		All students	Aged 25 or over	Comments
a	Full-time/sandwich undergraduates in universities	175,931	11,173	Mature = 6.4% of total
b	Full-time/sandwich undergraduates in FE	60,992	7,443	Mature = 12.2% of total
c	Part-time undergraduates in universities[1]	492	Unknown but probably majority	Part-time = 0.3% of all degrees
d	Part-time undergraduates in FE	5,571	Unknown but probably majority	Part-time = 8.4% of all degrees
e	Birkbeck undergraduates	1,139	Unknown but probably majority	93% are part-time
f	Open University undergraduates	43,792	Approximately 40,000[2]	
g	Open University associate students	2,549	Approximately 2,000[2]	
h	Students on initial teacher training at colleges of education	82,369	15,548	Mature = 18.9% of total
i	External students in the UK registered 'privately' with the University of London	9,113	Unknown but probably majority	
j	Full-time students in FE on advanced but not degree courses	44,932	14,951	Mature = 33.3% of total
k	Sandwich students in FE on advanced but not degree courses	16,458	2,352	Mature = 14.3% of total
l	Part-time day students in FE on advanced but not degree courses	76,237	Approximately 30,000	Mature = 40% of total[2]
m	Part-time evening students in FE on advanced but not degree courses	33,166	Approximately 22,000	Mature = 60% of total[2]

[1] Excluding Birbeck and the Open University
[2] The proportion aged twenty-five and over was taken from 1976-77 figures as this data was not available for 1975-76

Source   Wynne 1979; DES Statistics of Education (Volume 3) 1976 sector has increased slowly but now forms a smaller proportion of the undergraduate population (Wynne 1979). The number of students taking advanced but non-degree courses on a part-time basis in the further education sector appears to be increasing still but it is not possible to determine whether the same is true for mature students. In the Associate Student area at the Open University the numbers have increased from 3000 in 1975 to 8000 in 1980.

TABLE 13
Initial entrants to full-time higher education in Great Britain (1966-1980)[1]

	Age		
	Under 21 ('000s)	21 and over ('000s)	21 and over as percentage of total
1966	87.6	17.7	16.8
1967	92.9	23.2	20.0
1968	97.4	27.7	22.1
1969	101.2	26.7	20.9
1970	102.6	27.3	21.0
1971	106.1	29.2	21.6
1972	106.9	28.1	20.8
1973	105.2	29.6	22.0
1974	105.5	30.5	22.4
1975	107.4	31.4	22.6
1976	107.2	33.0	23.5
1977	104.8	30.2	22.4
1978	105.3	32.4	23.5
1979	108.7	34.3	24.0
1980 (prov)	111.7	35.2	24.0

[1] Overseas candidates have been excluded. 'Higher education' includes all courses above 'A' level standard.

Source   DES Statistical Bulletin 12/80 September 1980

As well as variations between sectors there are also considerable variations within each sector. Wynne (1979) showed that whereas at Essex University in 1976 twenty-two per cent of new undergraduates were aged twenty-five or

FIGURE 1
Mature entrants to higher education

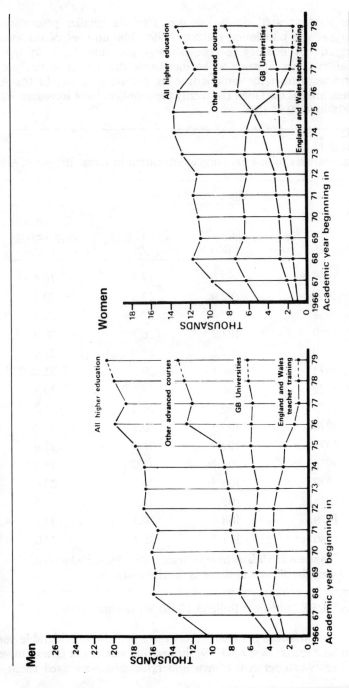

Source DES Statistical Bulletin 12/80 September 1980

over, the number fell to as low as three per cent for other universities such as Oxford, Exeter and Leicester. Whitburn, Mealing and Cox (1976) found the percentage of polytechnic degree students who were aged twenty-five or over varied from one per cent (Bristol) to twenty-six per cent (North East London).

Another possible way of determining the extent of bias against older people in British higher education would be to make comparisons with the situation in other countries. However, the problems such an approach present to the researcher would appear to be insurmountable. The lack of adequate statistics and the definitional problems mentioned earlier are multiplied when one begins to look at other countries, and their cultural differences add to these difficulties. For instance, the proportion of adults in higher education will be affected by the proportion of the population who enter directly from school and whether or not it is customary for students to work their way through college. A report from the Organisation for Economic Co-operation and Development (OECD 1977b) attempts to summarize participation rates in adult education in nine member countries but unfortunately the terms of reference tend to exclude higher education from consideration.

In summary, it would appear that the opportunities for adults to enter higher education have increased over the last decade, both in absolute and relative terms. However, there have been great variations between the different sectors and in some cases such as initial teacher training there has actually been a decline in the number of places available. Also, most of the adults in higher education are studying part-time or at a distance, modes of study which are generally considered to be the most difficult to follow.

BARRIERS TO ENTRY

Implicit in much that is written by supporters of education for adults is the assumption that there is a great deal of latent demand for higher education. They contend that there are large groups of older people who would be willing and able to benefit from higher education but who do not do so because they are unaware of the opportunities available or are prevented by certain other barriers. In this section we examine whether the research evidence supports this position.

Jones and Williams (1979) cite the report *Links to Learning* (ACACE 1979), which describes a number of innovations in educational information, advisory and counselling services, and the small numbers of admissions under special entry schemes, as evidence that there are far more openings for return to study than the public generally knows of. While intuitively appealing, such evidence is hardly conclusive. However, these views are supported by a study of awareness and beliefs about the Open University among the general public (Swift 1980). Overall awareness of the Open University had risen only to seventy per cent by 1980, varying from ninety-three per cent for social class groups AB to fifty-five per cent for the

DE groups. Furthermore many people were misinformed about the nature of the Open University. For example, only thirty-four per cent of the public had heard of the university *and* knew that no formal academic entry qualifications were needed. This is not to suggest that desire for higher education will always come when the opportunities are made known, but knowledge is clearly a pre-requisite.

Most well qualified school-leavers are guided smoothly, and often unthinkingly, into higher education. Adults on the other hand stand outside the system and, as Hopper and Osborn (1975) noted, what distinguishes those who return from those who do not is whether they have encountered various kinds of bridging factors. Such factors include participation in trade union activities, taking a WEA class, or a 'lucky chance encounter' with, say, a tutor or a student. These factors instil self-confidence, they teach study skills, they guide adults to 'the least regulation-ridden universities and the most welcoming' (Layard, King and Moser 1969). It seems highly likely that there are many more adults who are prevented from entering higher education by the absence of these bridging factors in their personal situations.

One approach to the problem of latent demand is to ask people directly what sort of courses, if any, they would like to take. A recent British study questioned adults about education and found that sixty-one per cent would like to take a course in something. However, the majority required evening or short day-time courses and only four per cent mentioned 'working for degree' as an important factor in their attending (ACACE 1981). In the United States only four per cent said that they would pursue a baccalaureate degree if they went back to college. Most of those surveyed would have preferred a shorter course in a community college or a vocational school (THES 1977). Whether such surveys tap public demand in any real sense is open to debate (McIntosh 1981). How many of the people who say that they would like to enter higher education would seriously contemplate doing so? How many who say 'no' would change their mind if, for instance, paid educational leave were available?

Some of the barriers faced by potential mature students can be discovered by looking at those who take some steps towards entering, but who default at some stage. For instance, a study of people who sent for details about the Open University but did not subsequently apply for entry revealed that the main barriers were the time required for study each week, the cost, attendance at summer school and the restricted range of subjects that were taught (Woodley and McIntosh 1976). In another study Open University undergraduates were asked why they had chosen to study with the OU rather than on a full-time course (McIntosh and Woodley 1978). Most said that they could not or did not wish to live on a student grant but several other factors were also important. Many enjoyed their jobs and did not wish to break their career. Some said there was no full-time course in their area and that they were unable to move due to their spouse's job. Others lacked the entry qualifications for a full-time course or could not get a grant as they had already had one.

We turn now to the admissions process itself to examine whether mature applicants find it more difficult to gain a place. Here the statistics produced by the UCCA enable us to look at the acceptance rates for different applicant age groups. Table 14 shows that in 1979 applicants aged under twenty stood much the best chance of being accepted. The acceptance rate declined between the ages of twenty and twenty-three and then picked up again to a limited extent in the higher age ranges. This pattern held true for men and women, but women aged over twenty were more successful than men in gaining a university place. The figures for earlier years suggest that the position may be improving for applicants aged over thirty.

TABLE 14
Percentage of home UCCA candidates accepted for entry: by age

	1973	1976	1979		
	All candidates	All candidates	All candidates	Men	Women
40 and over	39	37	45	43	48
30-39			46	39	52
25-29	40	44	40	37	44
24	41	39	38	36	41
23	36	43	35	33	38
22	37	38	36	33	42
21	37	41	36	36	38
20	48	48	45	46	45
19	55	60	58	58	58
18 and under	54	58	58	56	56
Total	52	56	54	53	55

Source   UCCA Statistical Supplement to the 11th, 14th and 17th Report

At the moment there is little research evidence to suggest whether older applicants are less successful because they are more likely to withdraw their application, because universities are less likely to offer them a place, or because they are less likely to achieve the pass grades demanded by a conditional offer of a place. One study of the Joint Matriculation Board's scheme for adult students who do not meet normal entry requirements showed that only thirty-eight per cent of such applicants were offered places

(Roderick, Bell, Turner and Wellings 1981). This is well below average and the researchers cite poorly presented applications, anxious performances at interviews, and hostility in certain university departments as possible reasons. They also mention that some older applicants turned down the offer of a place and among the reasons given were inability to obtain a grant, opposition from the applicant's spouse, and promotion at work.

The UCCA now publishes a table which cross-analyses accepted home candidates by age and entry qualifications (UCCA 1980). Table 15 shows that a considerable proportion of admitted adult students had not met the normal entry requirements and that this proportion increases with age. Further analysis of the UCCA figures reveals that the proportion of adults admitted without 'A' levels has increased over the last few years and that those adults admitted with 'A' levels tend to have fewer passes and lower grades.

TABLE 15
The entry qualifications of a sample of accepted home UCCA candidates in 1979: by age group

| | Age | | | |
	Under 21 n = 6940	21-25 n = 393	26-39 n = 244	40 and over n = 45
	%	%	%	%
GCE 'A' levels	92.6	66.2	45.5	31.1
Scottish qualifications	5.4	4.6	5.3	2.2
ONC/OND	1.2	3.1	5.7	2.2
HNC/HND	0.1	10.2	4.5	4.4
Degree	#	4.1	2.0	2.2
Other UK qualifications	#	6.6	32.0	53.3
Overseas qualifications	0.4	2.8	2.5	4.4
Unidentified qualifications	0.3	2.5	2.5	–

means less than 0.05%

Source   UCCA Statistical Supplement to the 17th Report

It has been suggested that older students are more likely to find it difficult to enter university because they tend to apply for popular subjects in the arts and social sciences. However, the UCCA statistics for 1979 show that students aged twenty-one and over also formed a significant proportion of the applicants for medicine, dentistry and health subjects and for engineering and technology (Table 16). The older applicant appears to be discriminated against by the admissions process in all subjects except education, and particularly in the case of the medicine, agriculture and engineering subject groups.

TABLE 16
The percentage of home candidates in each subject who were aged twenty-one or over in the proposed year of entry (1979)

		a) All candidates	b) Accepted candidates	$\frac{b}{a}$) $\times$ 100
Subject group				
I	Education	11	11	1.0
II	Medicine, dentistry and health	16	7	0.4
III	Engineering and technology	14	9	0.6
IV	Agriculture, forestry and veterinary science	8	4	0.5
V	Science	8	6	0.75
VI	Social, administrative and business studies	15	12	0.8
VII	Architecture and other professional and vocational studies	11	8	0.7
VIII & IX	Arts	12	10	0.8

Source   UCCA Statistical Supplement to the 17th Report

Applicants to the Open University undergraduate programme do not face the qualification barrier. Admission is open to everyone and selection for entry is on a 'first-come, first-served' basis, subject to certain course and regional quotas. The barriers which exist are the limited number of places available each year and the factors which cause almost a third of those offered a place to decline it. These factors include changes in personal circumstances such as pregnancy, changes at work leading to increased working hours, and the time and money involved in OU studies (Woodley 1978). However, over a quarter decline the place in favour of a course elsewhere and for a third of this group this is a course in higher education.

As noted earlier, teacher training has traditionally offered many opportunities to mature students. In Table 17 we show that, as with university students, the older the students the more likely they were to be admitted without the normal entry qualifications. The proportions admitted exceptionally increased between 1969 and 1975 despite the decline in the number of places during this period. Men were more likely to be admitted in this way in both years.

TABLE 17
The percentage of new entrants to teacher training courses who were admitted exceptionally

		Age					
		18-19	20-24	25-29	30-34	35-39	40 and over
1969	Total	1.0	4.1	12.9	13.9	12.0	18.4
	Male	2.0	4.5	17.2	21.4	16.5	19.1
	Female	0.7	3.6	10.1	11.3	11.0	18.2
1975	Total	0.9	6.4	17.7	16.7	16.4	23.7
	Male	1.5	6.2	19.0	27.4	27.1	31.2
	Female	0.7	6.6	17.1	14.6	14.5	20.9

Source DES Statistics of Education (Volume 4) 1969 and 1975

CHARACTERISTICS OF OLDER STUDENTS
Although we have shown that there are many thousands of older students in higher education, nothing has been said about who they are. In this section we look at age, sex and social class distribution to see whether higher education is biased towards certain types of older person.

In Table 18 we have taken those students who were aged twenty-one and over and then, when the figures were available, calculated the percentage who were twenty-five and over, thirty-five and over, and forty and over. The results show great differences between the various sectors, the extremes being the Open University with ninety-two per cent aged twenty-five and over and conventional universities with only eighteen per cent. Teacher training provided relatively more places for those in the higher age ranges than universities, but the six per cent for the forty and over group had stood at ten per cent in 1971. This suggests that this age group suffered disproportionately from the cut-backs in colleges of education. Few data are available for the upper age groups but it seems likely that the Open University is the main provider as ten per cent of its students were aged over fifty in 1977.

In Table 19 we look at the sex distribution of older students. It can be seen that in the case of university undergraduates there were proportionately fewer women in the twenty-one to twenty-nine age group than among younger students. However, there were proportionately more in the thirty and over age group. There were almost double the proportions of women in each age group in initial teacher training but broadly the same pattern was found. The figures suggest that women are more likely to re-enter full-time higher education in their thirties, presumably after bringing up children. They also suggest that expanded opportunities for twenty-one to twenty-nine year olds in these two sectors will lead to a lower overall proportion of female students. In the case of the Open University it is in the twenty-one to twenty-four age group that the highest figure for women is found, suggesting that many of the places are taken by young mothers.

TABLE 18
The percentage of students aged twenty-five and over, thirty and over, and forty and over in 1977[1]

	25 and over	30 and over	40 and over
University undergraduates	18	7	(2)[2]
Open University undergraduates	92	69	32
Initial teacher training	40	28	6
Advanced courses in FE:			
Full-time	43		
Sandwich	25	No data available	
Part-time day	54		
Evening only	72		

[1] Base = all students aged twenty-one and over
[2] Figure taken from Hopper and Osborn's study

Source   DES Statistics of Education (Volumes 3 and 4) 1977; Open University statistics

Several studies have examined the initial social class positions of adult students, as measured by father's occupation. Data drawn from universities, polytechnics and colleges of education all tend to show that there is little difference between adult and conventional entry students in terms of this variable (Swift and Acland 1967; Hopper and Osborn 1975; Whitburn et al. 1976; Taylor 1970). One exception was the University of Sussex where the ratio of middle class to working class was found to be fifty-five to forty-five among a sample of mature students, compared with a national under-graduate ratio of seventy-two to twenty-eight and seventy-eight to twenty-two for the university as a whole (Tapper and Chamberlain 1970). A study of Open University students has also shown that, whereas a high proportion of them had experienced inter- and intra-generational mobility, some fifty-two per cent had fathers in manual occupations (McIntosh and Woodley 1974).

TABLE 19
The porportion of women students in 1977: by age group

	18-20	21-24	25-29	30 and over
University undergraduates	38%	32%	26%	44%
Initial teacher training	82%	64%	50%	74%
Open University undergraduates	–	47%	41%	39%

Source   DES Statistics of Education (Volumes 3 and 4) 1977; Open University statistics

PERFORMANCE OF OLDER STUDENTS
Many researchers have looked at the relationship between age and performance in higher education. Harris (1940) in the United States found evidence to suggest that younger students tended to obtain better degree results. Similar findings have been made in Britain by Malleson (1959), Forster (1959), Howell (1962), Barnett and Lewis (1963), McCracken (1969) and Kapur (1972), in Australia by Flecker (1959) and Sanders (1961), in Canada by Fleming (1959), and in New Zealand by Small (1966). However, qualifications must be attached to these findings.

Most of the studies mentioned above were based on samples of students who were mainly aged between seventeen and twenty-one. As such, the results probably suggest that bright children admitted early to higher education fared better than those whose entry was delayed while they gained the necessary entry qualifications. This view is supported by Harris (1940) who discovered that the relationship between age and performance disappeared when he controlled for intelligence. Other studies have shown that those who gain the necessary qualifications and then delay entry for a year or two were more successful than those who entered directly from school (Thomas, Beeby and Oram 1939; Derbyshire Education Committee 1966; Orr 1974).

Where studies have involved samples containing large numbers of older students the results have indicated that the relationship between age and performance is not a linear one. Philips and Cullen (1955), for instance, found that those twenty-four years and over tended to do better than the eighteen and nineteen-year-old group. Sanders (1961) showed that the university success rate fell until the age of twenty or twenty-one, then from about twenty-two onwards the success rate began to rise again.

The problem with these two studies is that many of the older students were returning servicemen and as such were perhaps a typical mature-age students. They were often 'normal' entrants whose entry to university had been delayed by war and many had undergone some training in science or mathematics in the armed forces. Also, while Eaton (1980) cites nine American studies which confirm the academic superiority of veterans, there is some contradictory British evidence. Mountford (1957) found that ex-service students who entered Liverpool University between 1947 and 1949 were more likely to have to spend an extra year or more on their courses and more likely to fail to complete their course.

When assessing the performance of older students it is necessary to take into account the subject being studied. Sanders (1963) has indicated that the maturity associated with increasing age and experience seemed to be a positive predictor of success for some arts and social science courses. The general finding that older students do better in arts and social science and worse in science and maths is supported by Barnett, Holder and Lewis (1968), Fagin (1971), Sharon (1971) and Flecker (1959).

Walker's (1975) study of mature students at Warwick University represents the best British attempt to unravel the relationship between age and performance. He took two hundred and forty mature undergraduates who were admitted to the university between 1965 and 1971 and compared their progress with that of all undergraduates. This gave him a large group to work with and his methodology showed certain other refinements. Firstly, he excluded overseas students. Such students tend to be older than average and also to fare worse academically (Woodley 1979), thus distorting any age/performance relationship. Secondly, he used two measures of performance; the proportion leaving without obtaining a degree and the degree results of those taking final examinations. Finally he weighted the degree class obtained according to its rarity value in each faculty.

Walker found that eighteen per cent of the mature students left without a degree, which was not significantly different from the sixteen per cent for the total student population. This accords with the findings of Nisbet and Welsh (1972). In a study of two hundred and fifty-four mature age students at the University of Aberdeen, it was found that they had approximately the same failure and withdrawal rate as students straight from school.

The mature Warwick students who sat the final examination gained better degrees than other students. Furthermore the degree results of both the twenty-one to twenty-five and twenty-six to thirty age groups were significantly better than those of all students, and the degree results of students aged twenty-six to thirty were significantly better than those of all other mature students. The degree results of the over thirties appeared to be slightly worse but they were not significantly different from all students or from all other mature students as there were only thirty students among them.

Other important results emerged from Walker's study. There were no differences between male and female mature students in the proportions leaving without a degree or the degree class obtained. Mature students in the arts faculty gained significantly better degrees than other students. In social studies they fared somewhat better and in science somewhat worse, but in neither case was the difference significant. Walker also compared the performance of mature students who had the qualifications needed to satisfy the General Entrance Requirement (GER) with the performance of those who had not. Although the results did not achieve significance, those without the GER were less likely to leave without a degree and more likely to gain a good degree. This fits in with the results obtained in numerous other studies which are cited by Eaton (1980) and supports her contention that it is inappropriate to apply traditional admission criteria to the selection of mature-age students.

Very little research could be found into mature student performance in non-university higher education in Britain. However, Eaton and West (1980) provide a useful review of fifteen studies and reports from various types of tertiary institutions in Australia. The mature students studied varied in terms of entry qualifications and mode of study but the authors were able to conclude:

'. . . whatever their qualifications for entry, their performance can be described in one word: successful. As a body they tend to gain good marks, have excellent pass rates and acceptable attrition rates. In so far as comparisons can be made with normal students they perform as well, if not better.' (Eaton and West 1980)

At the Open University the experimental admission of students aged between eighteen and twenty led to a detailed consideration of the relationship between age and performance when using this particular mode of study (Woodley and McIntosh 1980). It was found that the first-year success rates for those aged between thirty and sixty were fairly constant, but below this the younger the students the less likely they were to gain a course credit. This relationship remained even when differences in previous educational qualifications were controlled for. Once the first-year hurdle had been surmounted success or failure on subsequent courses did not appear to be related to age.

PROBLEMS FACED BY OLDER STUDENTS

There have been many studies which have concentrated upon the problems faced by mature students in higher education and in this section we briefly summarize their findings.

Effects on Domestic Life

Nisbet and Welsh (1972) found that forty-two per cent of their sample of mature students at Aberdeen University had experienced strain in their domestic life as a result of taking up full-time study, and the figure rose to fifty-eight per cent for married students. The major source of strain was 'neglect of wife and family', followed by money problems.

In a study of mature chemistry students, forty-nine of the fifty-one married students noted effects on their social and domestic life brought about by a sudden and dramatic change in lifestyle (King 1980). Thirty-seven students described their marriages as being 'under strain' to varying degrees and during the course of the study eighteen marriages actually broke up. The effects on the non-student spouses were particularly disturbing, there being twelve nervous breakdowns and five suicide attempts, of which three were successful. As far as was known, there were no such incidents among the students themselves during the course of the study. From interviews with wives of mature students, King concluded that the following three phenomena were the main causes of strain:

— Jealousy of husband's female colleagues and increased possessiveness borne out of the fear of losing a loved one.
— Isolation from husband's world concurrent with a sudden reduction in her own social life and loss of previous friendship group.
— The higher education experience changes people and one member of a marriage is changing and the other is not.

Tapper and Chamberlain (1970) also found these types of problems and predicted that married mature-age students would almost invariably divorce their spouse during or soon after their study. However this view has not been supported by the very limited number of studies which have focused on the ramifications for the families of mature-age women returning to study (eg Katz 1976; Galler 1977; Berkove 1979; Hooper 1979). In some cases there were positive gains, and Kelly (1980) found considerable support for the view that one of the by-products of a mothers' return to college was a strengthening and deepening in father-child relationships, a change which was welcomed by both parents.

King studied only four female chemistry students of mature age but found relatively little domestic stress in the three cases where the husbands themselves were graduates. In Kelly's study the husbands were predominantly in managerial and professional occupations. It seems possible, therefore, that there is less domestic stress when women return to study because they are more likely to be catching up with their spouses rather than overtaking them. The husband of King's fourth student was a manual worker who expressed concern about his wife's rise in status and earings. He later committed suicide.

Returning to Study

King (1980) noted that many older students got into difficulties very early on in their first year. From interviews with these students it emerged that a key problem was their inability to gauge the level and depth of work required of them. They had shown great enthusiasm but in their anxiety had actually overworked. They tried to cover everything but learned nothing well. On the other hand there were also older students who failed their first year because they had succumbed to the relaxed university environment and had done too little work.

Lack of study skills was mentioned as a problem by almost one half of King's first-year sample. The older the students, the more likely were study skills to present difficulties, and they were found to be virtually exclusive to those students who had entered with qualifications other than 'A' levels. The majority of those with problems had taken or were taking a study skills course but on the whole they were critical of their usefulness to science students.

Another common problem seemed to be the conflict between the mature student's 'established everyday modes of thought and the specific, rather "unnatural" processes demanded by the various disciplines' (Challis 1976). These difficulties concerning re-orientation to the academic paradigm were also noted by Hopper and Osborn (1975).

Personal Adjustment

While most entrants to higher education are merely moving from one learning environment to another, the mature student is often faced with a profound change in lifestyle which requires a great degree of personal adjustment. Several studies mention the serious doubts felt by mature students about their ability to cope academically (Challis 1976; Cleugh 1972; Nisbet and Welsh 1972) and others note a general feeling of high anxiety and low self-image (Hopper and Obsborn 1975; King 1980). Tapper and Chamberlain (1970) refer to an identity crisis and Hopper and Osborn (1975) suggest that this involves a change of friends, lifestyle and conception of self. On the latter point, Cleugh (1972) suggests that all higher education leads to a re-assessment of self and self-image but that for the mature student, who has had more time to build up a self-image and come to terms with it, it is likely that an imposed re-assessment of this image is a more traumatic and stress-inducing experience.

King (1980) also detected that he called a 'crisis of re-orientation' among mature students which tended to occur in the early to middle part of the second year. He found that the students in his sample experienced difficulties in studying during this period and concluded that their problems were associated with a motivational shift (from 'extrinsic' to 'intrinsic'), a re-assessment of the value of higher education, a re-assessment of 'what's on offer' socially and academically with subsequent experimentation, and conflict between the real and imagined processes of higher education.

Decline in Ability

Many mature students feel that they will find it difficult to cope with higher education due to poorer memory and a decline in learning ability (Cleugh 1972). However, McLeish (1962) concludes from his review of the age factor in adult education that 'there is no mystical handicap which fetters adult education because of the age of adults'. Two classic studies which he considered were those of Thorndike (1928) and Sorenson (1930). Thorndike found that a decline in learning ability did occur but this was only a minor factor in success or failure. Capacity, interest, energy and time are the key determinants. Sorenson provided evidence to show that an observed decline in learning ability was more a function of absence from learning than of age itself.

Rogers (1977) suggests that the actual capacity of short-term memory may not change too much with age but recall may be more difficult for an older person because the 'scanning' stage is more easily disrupted by other activities. She also notes that the pace at which adults can learn declines and that the older a person is, the more likely he is to become confused and make mistakes if asked to learn something new under time pressure.

Marginality

Hopper and Osborn (1975) noted that most adult students encountered a set of difficulties after they entered higher education involving 'cross pressures, resocialisation and isolation.' They described the students as entering a 'marginal situation' within education. Aspects of this 'marginality' have now been explored in a number of studies.

Approximately one half of one sample of mature students said that they experienced some difficulties in establishing good relationships with younger students, a small proportion commenting on their immaturity and untidy appearance (Nisbet and Welsh 1972). Tapper and Chamberlain (1970) suggested that such problems were caused by differences not only in age but also in social class.

King (1980) explored the concept of isolation from other students in some depth. He found that mature students generally lived in non-student accommodation and participated much less in social events with other students. This clearly led to less contact with other students but the interesting point which emerged was that this was often a deliberate strategy. For these students there was a lot at stake and many of them had failed at school through being distracted. Therefore they could not risk being enticed away from their studies.

Challis (1976) actually found difficulties and resentment between mature students and younger students. Younger students thought they made 'silly statements' and displayed 'rigidity of thought.' They felt mature students talked too much in seminars and they particularly disliked the 'habitual references to personal experiences.' On a more general level they resented the fact that mature students held back from social activities and formed friendship groups among themselves. In this particular institution there were enough mature students for such a grouping to take place and where this happens the feelings of isolation are somewhat diminished (Hopper and Osborn 1975; King 1980).

Older students often had problems dealing with members of the teaching staff. In part this arose from the inconsistency between the status bestowed by their age and the status bestowed by their subordinate position of 'student' (Hopper and Osborn 1975). Such inconsistencies can also lead to problems for teachers and may lead them to treat mature students differently (David 1979).

Curriculum and Teaching Methods
The review of research into teaching methods in higher education by Beard and Bligh (1971) offers nothing on the subject of older students but evidence from elsewhere suggests that some teaching methods are more appropriate than others.

K night and McDonald (1978) conclude that adults returning to higher education must be given great help with basic skills and they must be given explicit instructions as to what to do. However, within this framework they should be given as much control of their learning as possible, they should be able to use their own life experience and they should be presented with relevant knowledge rather than knowledge for its own sake. Rogers (1977) suggests that lectures are the worst form of teaching for adults and that learning should take place through discussion and activity and should be self-paced.

The mature chemistry students studied by King (1980) disliked the following:

— The competitive environment fostered by the institution, which was too reminiscent of school.
— The inefficiency of the system employed to provide feedback on student progress.
— The practice of 'cue seeking' by younger students in an attempt to do well at exams.
— The assumption made by institutions that all their students had 'A' levels.
— Strategies such as class tests, grades and pep talks which were employed by institutions to motivate students to work.
— Practicals. They were too time-consuming and contrived and were frequently copied.

Some higher education institutions which cater exclusively for adults, such as the Open University, the University Without Walls and the Weekend College in Detroit (Feinstein 1979), have been able to design their teaching systems to meet the needs of adults, while others where adults form only a small proportion of the student body have not seen any need to make changes. However, it should not be assumed that all adults require the same curriculum and the same teaching methods. Elton (1975) found that some mature students, the exam-orientated 'Marthas', would be more suited to the Open University with its highly structured teaching materials whereas others, the education-for-its-own-sake 'Marys', would be more at home in a conventional university. The question of learning styles and study methods among adults on degree courses is being actively pursued by a research group at the Open University and a number of illuminating publications are already available (for example Morgan, Gibbs and Taylor 1980).

Part-time or Distance Study
Virtually all of the problems listed above are experienced by adults studying part-time or at a distance, even if not to the same extent. However, there are also many other problems to be faced. These include the difficulties of combining work and study, the lack of regular contact with students and tutors, practical difficulties such as attending study centres or summer school, and difficulty in sustaining motivation over the many years needed to gain a degree (Woodley and McIntosh 1980).

A point that emerges from most studies is the heterogeneity of mature students in terms of their personal characteristics and their educational routes to higher education. It follows, therefore, that one would not expect all mature students to experience the same sorts of problem or to the same degree. Tapper and Chamberlain (1970) were aware of this and divided mature students into seven ideal types on the basis of their family background and secondary schooling and suggested the sorts of problems each type was likely to encounter. Hopper and Osborn (1975) also realized that not all mature students would experience the stresses predicted by their original hypotheses and later excluded adult students in colleges of education, 'qualified' teachers pursuing career advancement, adult students re-entering the education system through the kinds of routes offered by the trade union movement, and older women in general. Some have concentrated on particular categories of mature student, such as women (Smith 1969), single mothers (Kassman 1978) and chemistry students (King 1980), and it seems likely that these more specialized studies will produce the most useful insights.

Before leaving this section we should also mention that several researchers have commented on the advantages which mature students have over their younger counterparts. Hopper and Osborn (1975), for instance, note that they have more experience of life and work to bring to their studies, they are likely to be more organized and systematic in their work and they are used to dealing with a wide range of people. They are also more likely to be highly motivated to succeed for they have all made a definite decision to enter higher education, their goals are clearer and they have more to lose as they have often 'burnt their boats' by giving up a career.

OUTCOMES FOR OLDER STUDENTS

Walker (1975) mentions that benefits can and should be measured in other ways besides final examination performance. Did mature students benefit as people more or less than younger students? Did they gain the jobs or higher degree places that they wanted? These are questions which could be asked when attempting to assess the fairness of higher education to older people but which have rarely been the subject of research.

The study of mature students at Aberdeen University was a retrospective one and respondents were asked in open-ended questions to give an account of their feelings during their time at university (Nisbet and Welsh 1972). Forty of the one hundred and seventy-seven respondents said they were disappointed to discover that university was not what they had expected it to be:

> 'They complained that it was ordinary, not the unique intellectual experience they had expected; that it was not a 'quiet place of learning'; and many said that all that was required of them was to memorise lecture notes, to regurgitate them at examinations and never to attempt to question a lecturer's views.' (Nisbet and Welsh 1972)

The results of a survey of outcomes for Open University graduates (Swift 1980) show that, despite the fact that more of the graduates had been orientated to personal rather than career benefits, four out of five had received benefit in terms of better pay, promotion, career change, improved job skills or ability to perform their work. Many had also gone on to take further professional training or postgraduate work. There were widespread personal benefits in terms of widened perspectives, more self-confidence and greater maturity, but there were also losses, such as the costs to family life and loss of time for hobbies.

The problem with both of these studies is that there are no control groups. Were younger students more or less disillusioned with Aberdeen University than mature students? What are the comparative costs and benefits for young and old graduates from conventional universities which would place the Open University results in context?

CONCLUSIONS

In this chapter we have drawn on the research literature to show that opportunities for adults in higher education have been increasing over the last decade. However, there is some evidence that many more adults are prevented from entering higher education and that those who do overcome the barriers to entry do not represent a cross-section of the adult population. It is also suspected that the recent cut-backs in higher education may have a disproportionate effect on older students as did the decline in teacher training places some years ago.

The most recent research on age and university performance would suggest that older students fare as well if not better than younger students on arts and social science courses but slightly worse on science courses. Reasons which have been suggested for their poor performance in science include poor mathematical ability, smaller numbers of older students resulting in greater marginality and the fact that greater life experience cannot be used to advantage on such courses (King 1980; Tapper and Chamberlain 1970). The performance of mature students in the upper age ranges has been neglected due to the small numbers involved.

The question we started out with was 'can higher education be described as "fair" to adults?' and, as we pointed out early on, such a question poses great problems for the supposedly value-free researcher. We have shown that adults encounter barriers to entry but so do young people. The main barrier which faces young people is that of entry qualifications yet this is often removed for older people, thus placing them in a privileged position. We have shown that adults experience certain problems within higher education but so too do many young students, and overall performance rates show very little difference.

A case for unfairness to adults can perhaps be made by pointing out that the great majority are studying on a part-time basis or at a distance. Such courses may produce additional study problems, they are less likely to attract student grants and they tend to have higher drop-out rates. However, this would only be unfair if it could be shown that they would rather be taking a full-time course.

At the moment institutions of higher education seem to be reaching out to mature students in order to survive. To achieve this they must be aware of the problems older people face and adapt their teaching and administrative systems accordingly. Most of the research evidence would point towards flexible part-time courses with few entry qualifications. In the long term we will no doubt return to a situation of competition for a limited number of places and then institutions must decide what proportion of mature students should be admitted. Some will argue that they should favour the young as they have longer productive lives and that those who are turned away will later become 'deprived' adults. The possible arguments in favour of more mature students would seem to be that they actually fare better in certain subjects; they have a good effect on younger students; they need to be numerous to avoid marginality; and they compensate for certain sex and class biases found among the younger students. As we have seen, research results can feed in to these arguments, both to prove and disprove commonly-held ideas on the subject.

As a full-time researcher, far be it from me to finish without the standard appeal for further research. There are clearly areas where little work has been done on mature students, especially in the polytechnics and the whole of the further education sector. However, the time will shortly come to move beyond the single institution study which merely counts and describes the mature students found there. What we need are more studies which illuminate the process of becoming and being a mature student, as in King's (1980) excellent study, studies which follow the progress of mature students both during and after a course, and studies which use adequate control groups for comparison. Also, as it is now recognized that mature students are an heterogeneous group, they should be treated as such, with studies concentrating on certain sub-groups. The results will almost certainly show that there is not one curriculum, teaching method or mode of study which is appropriate for or 'fair' to all older people.

SEX BIAS

Dale Spender

When women possess the same influence over the education of men as men have over the education of women, then perhaps it will be possible to state that there are no biases based on sex in higher education: currently, however, we inhabit a society dominated by men with the result that women's education is controlled and determined by men, which constitutes a considerable bias in favour of men and against women (Stock 1978, p.15).

Documenting, analysing, and protesting about this bias is not a new activity, particularly among women, but a centuries-old tradition: since the seventeenth century (at least) women have been protesting against male control of education and the way it has been used to construct and promote sexual inequality. Until relatively recently this protest frequently focused on the exclusion of women by men from the universities, but, unlike many contemporary educationalists who tend to confuse the underlying cause with some of its manifestations, the women who were engaged in this process were usually quite clear that the problem was one of male control and the exclusion of women from the universities but one of its outcomes.

Today there are educationalists who are prepared to assert that there *was* a bias against women but that it has long since disappeared. It would be difficult to deny the fact that 'In Britain women were excluded from all universities until they were admitted to all scientific courses at the newly-created University of Durham College of Science in Newcastle in 1871' (Rendel 1980, p.142), and difficult to deny that this exclusion constituted a bias; but it is also difficult to assert that the bias against women was eliminated once they were allowed to enter the halls of learning.

Many of the early pioneers of women's education would not have concluded that the battle had been won simply because men were prepared to admit women to their institutions on their terms, for to these women the fundamental problem was the prerogative of men to set the terms. They wanted to be free to introduce their own terms and they would not have been misled into believing they had achieved their aims when men permitted some women to attend some classes.

The charges that many of these women made against men could not easily have been interpreted as just a demand for entry which would be satisfied once women were permitted to partake of men's education. For example, Aphra Behn (1640-1689), caustic critic of male control of education, protested loud and long about the way in which men exercised their control against women, which encompassed excluding women from their institutions (Goreau 1980). Likewise, 'Sophia, a person of quality' (1739) accused men of controlling education in their own interest, and among the examples of male control that she cited was that of the exclusion of women.

Mary Wollstonecraft (1792), in what is still one of the most sustained and cogent arguments for women's educational rights, boldly demanded to know 'Who made man the exclusive judge if women partake with him the gift of reason?' (Kramnick 1978, p.87). In 1938 Virginia Woolf mounted a no less vigorous attack against male control of education in *Three Guineas* in which she presented the (voluntary) exclusion of women from universities as a *solution*, rather than as a problem. It was because men controlled education that she advised women to refrain from entering their institutions and proposed instead the formation of a 'Society of Outsiders' in which women would be free from the influence of men and therefore free to develop a form of education that met their own needs and was consistent with their own values (Woolf 1977, p.206).

When women assert today, as many of them do, that higher education is no less biased against women and in favour of men than it was in the time of Aphra Behn, 'Sophia', Mary Wollstonecraft or Virginia Woolf (Rich 1979; Smith 1978: Spender 1981 in press; Stock 1978) they are stating their case within a tradition in which it has been *male control* of education that has been perceived as the substance of this bias. There are grounds for claiming that such an assertion can be as readily substantiated today as it has been in the past, for in terms of the extent to which women have been able to enter the halls of power as distinct from the halls of learning, and to assume control of their own education (which is of course an unquestioned right of men) the gains have been very few.

In recent years women have once again taken up the old argument that universities are a male domain and that far from altering their central composition and character, the potential contribution of women has been contained by the creation of 'a woman's place' (Rita McWilliams-Tullberg (1975), for example, subtitled her book on women at Cambridge 'A men's university — though of a mixed type'). Men continue to retain control and to decree the form and substance of education of women as well as of men, despite the fact that they no longer exclude women in order to engage in such activities.

It cannot be stated with credibility that the admission of women to higher education has led to any significant change in the distribution of power for 'Though women's participation in the educational process at all levels has increased this century,' says Dorothy Smith (1978), it 'remains within marked boundaries' the most important of which is 'that which reserves to men control of the policy-making and decision-making apparatus in the education system' (p.287).

Rita McWilliams-Tullberg (1980) has analysed this distribution of power at Cambridge and she claims that before women were admitted to full membership of the university (in 1948) men ensured that the locus of power had been shifted so that it was beyond the reach of women members. For years what may have been perceived as an 'illogical arrangement' prevailed at Cambridge, where Emily Davies opened her college for women students in 1869, but where from 1870 till 1919 women were admitted to the institution and even examined (by private and informal arrangement) *without being granted degrees*. Such an arrangement appears not so illogical, however, when it is recognized that the recipients of degrees left college 'not merely with a feeling of affection for their alma mater but with a vote in the future administration of university affairs' and, says McWilliams-Tullberg, 'A refusal to share this power with women was one of the major reasons for denying them their degrees' (p.118).

The arguments against granting degrees to women were many and various but 'implicit in all of them was the view that women should not have any say in decision-making processes and therefore could never be admitted to full and equal membership with men in the university' (McWilliams-Tullberg 1980, p.138). More explicit was 'the fear of women's "interference" in men's affairs' and it was not unusual for Cambridge men to argue that 'If women took part in the government of Cambridge it would cease to be responsive to the wants of men' (p.134).

That women might be equally interested and equally justified in seeking to establish a form of education that was responsive to the needs of women was neither then nor now an issue treated seriously by the men who control the policy-making processes of higher education. Although women finally became full members at Cambridge in 1948 the power of men to preserve an education system responsive to the needs of men was reasonably well protected, for members no longer enjoyed the influence they had once possessed over university affairs: 'the voting rights of non-resident graduates had been reduced to a token and the number of women students at Cambridge was contained at a reassuringly low level' (McWilliams-Tullberg 1980, p.120).

A current analysis of the distribution of power within higher education reveals that it is still by and large concentrated in the hands of men and beyond the reach of most women. And this power is still used primarily — as it was three centuries ago — to promote a system of education that is responsive to the 'wants' of men, including the 'want' to appear superior to women.

WHERE WOMEN ARE THE POWER IS NOT

More than one hundred years after the admission of women students to universities it is an easy task to assess the extent to which they have entered the policy-making spheres, and it is unquestionably obvious that their gains have not been great, with 2.3 per cent of professors in Great Britain being women (unpublished current DES statistics). While the numbers of women increase the further they move from the spheres of influence, they are still small, with women comprising 6.4 per cent of readers and senior lecturers, 14.5 per cent of lecturers and assistant lecturers and 33.8 per cent of all other teaching posts (which include undertaking the work of lecturers and running classes on lecturers' syllabuses). In all, women comprise 13 per cent of the academic staff.

When it can be argued that technically all academic positions are available to women then this small proportion of women requires some explanation and even those who most ardently defend the claim that there are no barriers to women's entry are often forced to conclude that there is some factor responsible for women's relative 'absence'. Frequently this explanation is found to be in the behaviour of women, and not in the structure of the universities.

While this 'failure', or 'under-achievement', or 'deficiency' in women is discussed in more detail in later sections it must be noted here that those who have the power, have the power to provide the explanations, and it is precisely this power that women have historically identified as a major source of bias against women. When women are in a position to provide explanations (as I am here) then they are often very different from those which have found favour in male dominated institutions.

The explanation which has perhaps enjoyed the most favour in male dominated institutions is that women *choose* not to participate and even choose not to be promoted. That women choose not to enter powerful and prestigious positions, however, not only stands in direct contradiction to women's avowed goals over the centuries, but appears to be an explanation peculiar to women for it is rarely if ever proffered in relation to other disadvantaged groups and there is no reference in the literature to those of the working class or ethnic groups choosing *not* to take up academic positions.

As Margherita Rendel (1980) has said, there are many factors which 'cast doubt on the notion that women "choose" to participate in the academic professions in the ways in which they do' (p.156) but while attention focuses on women's *choice*, it is diverted from the structure and organization of higher education and society.

People do not simply 'appear' in university positions of influence: there is a highly structured route by which they enter and proceed, and what can prove to be significant choices are often made in the early stages when students of both sexes can choose to follow paths which at least move in the direction of higher education, or they can choose to move in other directions which can later effectively deprive them of the opportunity to enter universities. As admission is usually a preliminary requisite for advancement to a prestigious position within a university, the fact that boys more frequently than girls choose to become university students means that from the outset there are more men than women making themselves eligible for positions of power (current unpublished DES statistics indicate that women comprise 36.8 per cent of undergraduates in British universities and 28.6 per cent of postgraduates). This pattern of entry lends itself to the interpretation that women are 'under-achieving' in comparison to men.

Space does not permit the presentation of a detailed analysis of the fallacious — and political nature — of this assessment, but it must be pointed out that the education system as a whole is subject to male control and that females are just as much without influence in most schools (in which they make their 'choice' about university entry) as they are in universities. Kristin Tornes (1981) has stated that, like universities, schools have also been designed to meet the needs of males, which includes the preparation for a male-defined career, and that one result is that they are 'only partly relevant for the girls' future work' (p.15): and, adds Tornes, the girls know this.

The school socializes students 'to a certain use of time, achievements can be measured, tasks are presented within known premises, to be accomplished within set time limits,' says Tornes, and 'These are premises for work in the sphere of production, but highly doubtful as qualifications for reproductive work' (p.15). Girls are being nothing less than rational if they take into account the possibility of reproduction — and the demands it makes on women as society is presently organized — and nothing less than sensible, if they seek experience which is more consistent with their needs, as they too are currently socially constructed.

The present education system which has emerged under male control and which has its origins in the experience of men fails to accommodate the experience and expectations of women. It is not women who are the defecit model: it is not reduced aspiration or under-achievement that may prompt female students to choose paths that lead away from formal education, but a rational assessment of the relevance of educational institutions in relation to the demands that are and will be made on them as women in a male dominated society.

This is a bias against women in education, a bias structured through the entire system and which has particular implications for higher, as distinct from compulsory schooling. If women were in a position to influence their own education, *and* the education of men, then there are reasons for suspecting that they would accommodate some of the demands of reproduction in educational content and organization, and *they would also help to prepare males as well as females to meet these demands*. In her essay 'Towards a Woman-Centered University' Adrienne Rich (1979) suggests how higher education could look if women were free to decree and implement the policies that served their interests and values and it is perfectly possible that if such an institution were to be established tomorrow, it would *not* be women who failed to enter or who were explained in terms of reduced aspiration or under-achievement.

Men have designed their institutions to meet their own needs and where the needs of women are different from those of men it is not at all surprising that women should rejct the men's institutions. Only when women have their own control would it be possible to state that the bias against women had been removed and only when such a bias is removed would it be possible to make comparisons between women and men in terms of choice, aspiration, or achievement (unlike the present situation in which comparisons are made between advantaged and disadvantaged groups in favour of the advantaged).

At the moment, however, there are only the institutions of men, structured in men's interests, and within these institutions women — predictably — frequently find themselves disadvantaged in comparison to men. For example, women are often required to make their 'choices' about the future when they do not possess the vital information which is necessary as a basis for such choice. While boys are free to decide what they will do without reference to other individuals, girls have no such freedom: they cannot make plans until they know if and whom they are going to marry, what adaptations they will be required to make to their husband's work, where he will live, what his attitude will be to working wives, whether there will be work available in the area. Women are not independent agents, says Sandra Acker (1978): men make plans, but women can only make *contingency* plans:

> 'In a sense they plan to do everything — job, housework, children, leisure, community involvement . . . women have to prepare to adapt to the value system of a potential male, to be single if unavoidable, to work when necessary, to be childless if fate so decrees, to cope when children grow up, to manage after divorce or widowhood. What kind of career adapts to this range of contingencies? . . . (a) . . . women cannot really plan for the future given that her life in the decades ahead will be largely determined by a man she has not yet met, and children she has not yet had.' (Acker 1978, p.123)

Rita McWilliams-Tullberg (1980) has said that 'Time has shown men to be adept at handicapping female competitors' (p.140) and by structuring society and education to serve their interests men have handicapped women and ensured that it is women who must plan for a *range* of possibilities while they, singlemindedly, can concentrate on and develop *one*, if they so desire.

Women, then, if they choose to enter higher education at all, are more likely to opt for a form that they believe will allow the greatest flexibility, and traditionally, teaching and nursing have been popular choices, which in part explains the concentration of women in particular disciplines. Such a choice is, however, somewhat surprising for there is evidence which suggests that these are not the best professions for facilitating a combination of career and of the commitments women are expected to meet. They are two of the professions in which practitioners have little if any control over their time and conditions of work, and it is instead professions such as law, dentistry, medicine or engineering which afford the greatest flexibility (Brock-Utne 1981). But teaching and nursing are neither prestigious nor powerful areas, they are 'a nice job for a girl' and the question therefore arises as to the origin and purpose of this belief, and about the advice women receive.

It has become 'fashionable' to speak in terms of traditional and non-traditional careers and occupations in relation to women, and to advocate counselling females to enter non-traditional areas, as if the problem were simply one of women's incapacity to appreciate that they too were permitted entry to the scientific and technological establishment. The implication often is, that all that is required is the provision of some sympathetic and supportive advice designed to acquaint women with the fact that physics or engineering, for example, are open to them. Such superficial analyses and solutions are not only insulting to women, they also ignore the distribution of power in society and the academic world, and the way in which males have appropriated and defended that power.

Strategies such as counselling women to enter non-traditional areas will probably prove to be ineffective in modifying the distribution of women across disciplines, or the progress they make within them, but they could help to substantiate the thesis that there is something wrong with women who do not avail themselves of the opportunities that are technically available to them — in terms of entry and even promotion — even when they are specifically informed about and encouraged to enter these non-traditional areas.

In some respects 'non-traditional areas' is a euphemism for 'bastions of male power' and to suggest that the problem consists of women's inability to recognize that the area is open to them, rather than one of men protecting their power base, provides more insights about who generates explanations than it does about women. Such an explanation ignores fundamental issues about the structure and purpose of higher education, the contribution it makes to society, and the way in which males exercise their control of their own continued advantage.

'Where women are the power is not' (Rendel 1980, p.144) and if more men than women enter universities it is an indication that universities exercise some power. If in universities women are concentrated in the social sciences, in language, literature and the arts then it is not unreasonable to suspect that these subjects are not a locus of power. If a greater number of women are to be found in taught courses as distinct from research courses then it can be assumed that it is the research courses that are prestigious and at least potentially powerful (among postgraduate students in Britain, women comprise 34.3 per cent of students on taught courses and 22.8 per cent of research students (current unpublished DES statistics)). If women are found to be predominantly teachers and not researchers within universities then it is possible to conclude that it is research which constitutes the power base and from which the policy-and decision-making candidates are likely to be drawn. This is the pattern of a male-controlled institution and a pattern which many women would like to see changed by terminating male control.

THOSE WHO RULE HAVE THE RULING IDEAS

For centuries it has been men who have ruled in the area of the construction and distribution of knowledge: men have attended to and treated as significant what men say, with the result that most of the public knowledge that is available to us today was encoded 'by men about men for men' (Smith 1978, p.281). This knowledge is based on the male experience of the world — including the male evaluation of 'the male' — and is biased and limited: this knowledge, however, is also based on the assumption that *male experience is the sum total of human experience* (Daly 1973; Janeway 1980; Baker Miller 1976; Rich 1979; Smith 1978; Spender 1981a).

'Those who rule' not only have the 'ruling ideas' states Sandra Acker (1980a) but also 'the ability to convince subordinates of the validity of these ideas' (p.86), so that all members of society, women and men, have been led to believe that the knowledge produced by men is complete and total, which has many significant repercussions for women and women's experience. Where women's experience of the world and themselves is different from the male definitions of the world, and women, then there is no conceptual space to accommodate women's experience (Spender 1980, 1981a; Stanley 1977). Women's experience — where it is articulated — may be dismissed or denied, treated as 'unreal' or 'aberrant' in the schemata designed by men. Within these schemata male experience is consistently being interpreted as authoritative and universal, possessing the potential for generalization, while female experience which is 'different' is devalued, treated as insignificant. One of the outcomes of this arrangement is that the problems perceived by men become the problems of society while the problems that originate in women's experience of the world — including the problem of male dominance — are more likely to be classified as individual in nature, attributed to the 'inadequacies' of the women who express them, and rendered 'invisible'. By such means is sexual inequality continually being realized.

That men could have come to be convinced of the totality of their own conceptualization of the world is in some respects not at all surprising. While the circles in which knowledge has been produced have been exclusively male it has been feasible for males to assume that their experience represented human experience, for who would perceive and protest at the limitations? The exclusion of women has meant that where women's experience is different from men's it has been structurally precluded and men, therefore, may not have encountered a challenge to their conceptualizations, and may have had no reason to suspect that the limits of their world are but the limits of the male world.

The presence of women could well have made a significant difference, not just in terms of the knowledge which has been produced but in terms of the authority of men to encode knowledge. If not sufficiently powerful to have unseated the rulers, women might at least have been able to cast doubt on the assumption of the universal nature of male experience, and have questioned the accuracy and credibility of male explanations for the objects and events of the world (Spender 1981a).

But women are not now and never have been part of the circle, and again, therefore, it is not surprising that males should have encoded themselves as the central reference point against which those who are not male are measured. Women have labelled this phenomenon 'the male-as-norm-bias' whereby men have described and explained the world in relation to themselves, where, consequently, women are conceptualized only as they relate to men. This male-as-norm-bias, which is fundamental in what we know and which is reflected across disciplines, helps to reinforce and reproduce the centrality of man and the 'otherness' of woman (de Beauvoir 1972) and helps to justify and legitimate men's authority to rule.

There are many reasons for suspecting that women's experience of the world is different from men's: in a society structured on sexual inequality men occupy a position which women do not: they are dominant. Most of what we know has been encoded by men from their perspective as the dominant sex and imposed on women without reference to its capacity to accurately represent and explain women's subordinate position. This, says Dorothy Smith, has significant ramifications for women because 'the means women have had available to them to think, image, and make actionable their experience of the world have been made for us and not by us. It means,' she says, 'that our experience has not been represented in the making of our culture. There is a gap between where we are and the means we have to express and act. It means that the concerns, interests, experiences forming "our" culture are those of men in positions of dominance whose perspectives are built on the silence of women . . .' (p.282).

What has been passed off as *our* knowledge, *our* descriptions, problems, explanations, *our* education, is in fact the knowledge, descriptions, problems, explanations and education of men: what has been represented to us as neutral, impartial and objective is in fact 'partial, limited, located in a particular position and permeated by special interest and concerns' of men (Smith 1978, p.283).

Among the most advantageous and efficacious of the 'ruling ideas' that men have produced is that of the objectivity of male experience.

Currently women are challenging the knowledge which men have produced and legitimated as the knowledge of society: women are challenging the classification scheme on which that knowledge is based (and in which males are central, the norm, and women are peripheral, and deviant) and the authority of men to be the sole arbiters and encoders. Women are identifying the massive bias that has operated against women in society and education while men control society and education. Like their predecessors, women today are demanding an end to male control.

'Until recently "mankind's" understandings have been the only understandings generally available to us' states Jean Baker Miller (1976) but 'as other perceptions arise — precisely those perceptions that men because of their dominant position could *not* perceive — the total vision of human possibilities enlarges and is transformed' (p.1). Women are beginning to describe and explain the 'underside' of human experience (Boulding 1976), to represent the world from the perspective of those who are dominated, and men, women, and the world are perceived very differently from this perspective: these new 'understandings' also severely challenge the old.

That men are the authorities, that their experience is universal, that they are the norm, that their truth constitutes the truth and their explanations *logic*, that their subjective experience is *objective* and their problems the *social* problems, are value judgements which have originated with men and are embedded in the public knowledge which largely forms the curriculum of educational institutions. This constitutes an enormous bias against women, who, while they may be permitted entry to such institutions, are required to 'learn' that males and male experience are more valuable. Women are required to adopt the 'ruling ideas' which devalue women, which define them as deviant and without authority, which classify women's truth as unreal, women's explanations as illogical and women's subjective experience as personal, idiosyncratic and unreliable. This is one of the ways sexual inequality is constructed, one of the ways dominance and subordination is realized, and it is a way which is routinely utilized in education, particularly higher education. While men retain the power which they currently possess in higher education they are able to use it to perpetuate their own, self-constructed 'superiority' and justification for dominance.

THE GATEKEEPERS
Within higher education it is the male system of values which prevails, it is men who decide what is important and what the issues will be, it is men who determine the agenda and the priorities. It is they who decide — on the basis of their own experience and their own logic — what the form and substance of education will be, the organization of the disciplines, the standards that will operate; and while ever universities have existed it can be substantiated that men have used this power to keep women and their concerns invisible. They have been the gatekeepers, admitting to their system only knowledge which is consistent with their experience as men. Women have been excluded from this process whether or not the universities, the professions, or the disciplines have been technically open to them (Spender 1981d).

Among the ranks of the professors, 2.3 per cent are indeed women, but this in no way suggests that they have any part in shaping the form and substance of education. Within the prevailing scheme of values it could even be argued that if women comprised 50 per cent of the policy and decision makers, men could still retain the power for, after all, women comprise 51 per cent of the population and are without power. It is erroneous to assume that there is a one-to-one relationship between women and men in a society predicated on sexual inequality.

Women who are but 2.3 per cent of the professorial population are in a powerless position and the problem of their minute representation is compounded by other facets of male power. First of all, for example, the presence of a woman in an influential position may indicate only that she has received the approval of men and does not necessarily suggest that she has any rights of her own. Within universities where men act as gatekeepers and determine what is to be recognized as proper scholarly work and suitable skills, where they distribute the rewards and punishments, then those few women who are admitted to influential positions 'are those who have passed through this very rigorous filter. They are those whose work and style of work and conduct have met the approval of judges who are largely men' (Smith 1978, p.289).

If such women do elect to expose the discrepancies between the legitimated male version of experience, and their own experience as women, there are many means available to dismiss and devalue them. The further women move from the schemata decreed by men the more evidence they can provide to validate them, for within them women are deviant, their processes irrational, their responses emotional and a woman, therefore, who persists in articulating her experience as a woman can provide men with confirmation of their own authority. Rather than being perceived as different and autonomous, as innovative and valid, a woman who continues to challenge or contradict the male view of the world and to assert her own, is more likely to be classified as incompetent (and to serve as evidence that women are unsuitable for posts of responsibility).

This typifies the perpetual dilemma that women face in a man-made world (and which remains outside the experience of most men), for the bias against women is so constructed that they are 'inferior' if they accept the male value system in which women are allocated an inferior place, yet also 'inferior' if they attempt to develop a value system of their own which departs from the male norm and is therefore perceived as 'deviant'.

Living within this framework generated and imposed by men is for women frequently a condition of existence and one which women in the academic community often have to deal with on a daily basis. Women must either accept the knowlege which has been constructed by men and where the more they learn the more they learn about their own inadequacy (Roberts 1976; Showalter 1976) or assert their 'deviancy', their 'irrationality' and 'illogicality' — hardly helpful characteristics in a university context as presently structured.

Understandably, some women have accepted the terms laid down by men. There is the woman, says Adrienne Rich (1979), who 'has for her own survival learned to vote against other women, absorb the masculine adversary style of discourse, and carefully avoid any style or method that could be condemned as "irrational" or "emotionally charged". She chooses for investigation subjects as remote as possible from her self-interest as a woman, or if women are the object of her investigation she manages to write about them as if they belonged to a distant tribe' (p.138).

Women who are concerned with describing and analysing the world from their perspective as women are continually required 'to defy the evidence' states Elaine Reuben (1978), for within higher education evidence has been produced that it is the male, and the male view of men and of women which is valid, and on the basis of this classification men are — by definition — the better candidates for positions of responsibility: women who defy this evidence can, paradoxically, help to vitiate the male definitions.

It is not unexpected that in the system which men have set up, where male values, male logic and male standards prevail, men should emerge as the 'better candidates' within their own institutions, and should be able to assert sincerely — in some circumstances — that there is no bias against women: it is simply that women do not meet their standards! It is not unexpected that men should declare that they detect no distortions in the knowledge they construct, no limitations in their logic or bias in their beliefs. It is perfectly possible that for men the knowledge they have consturcted fits well with their experience of the world (including the experience that education is beneficial, that it enhances one's life, that it promotes growth and development). But the male experience is the experience of less than half the population and it is partial. Until the experience of women — which includes the educational experience of being devalued, dismissed and denied — is fully taken into account in higher education, it can be asserted that men are in control, that they are acting as gatekeepers, that they are rendering women and women's experience 'invisible' and that this constitutes a bias against women and facilitates the continual reconstruction of sexual inequality.

THE FOUNDING FATHERS AND THE DISCIPLINES

'There is no discipline which does not obscure or devalue the history and experience of women as a group' states Adrienne Rich (1979, p.135) and this is an inevitable outcome of male control where the founding fathers have been able to formulate the structure of the disciplines free from female opposition to their decrees and challenges to their authority. From women's perspective it is as if the organization and composition of many of the modern disciplines were irrelevant, so absent are women from consideration.

In 1792 Mary Wollstonecraft raised most of the issues which relate to women, but despite the fact that this was a period when many of the burning issues and questions of the day became the parameters for new bodies of knowledge (political science, economics, sociology, psychology for example) the fundamental issues which Wollstonecraft raised about male dominance were not and never have been the substance of any discipline. It could be argued that male dominance did not constitute a problem for many men, hence no discipline emerged which addressed it while men were in control. The problems of men became the foundations of the modern disciplines, while the problems of women found no legitimated conceptual space. So women today raise many of the issues that Wollstonecraft raised, and in the two centuries in between the disciplines have produced very few insights that women could profitably use.

Across disciplines, women have mapped the invisibility and devaluation of women[1] which has been a consequence of women's exclusion from the production of knowledge. Says Dorothy Smith, it is because the disciplines have been created by men that 'women have had no written history until very recently, no share in making religious thoughts, no political philosophy, no representation of society from their view, no poetic tradition, no tradition in art' (Smith 1978, p.282). It is not because women have not made history, formulated religious schemata, engaged in philosophic activity, represented society as they saw it, been innovative in poetry and art, but because where women have engaged in these activities — and they have been different from men's — they have generally been perceived not merely as different but as deficient, as insignificant and unworthy of consideration or inclusion.

Analysing the paradigms of the various academic disciplines and their inherent exclusion of women is a task of considerable magnitude which has been undertaken elsewhere (Spender 1981a) but an overview of some of the disciplines and their underlying premises can help to suggest the nature and extent of the problem which has in so many respects and for so long gone unrecognized by many men.

For example, in history, Jane Lewis (1981) shows that what we have accepted as the history of society is the history of men, recorded by men, in which men have made sense of the world in relation to themselves. Reclaiming women's history, states Lewis, is no mere matter of adding them on to men's history, because the existing categories devised by men are not always appropriate: for example, two of the periods that men have nominated as periods of liberation — the American War of Independence and the French Revolution — curtailed, as distinct from extended, women's rights, and would therefore be classified as periods of restriction and not liberation by more than half the population.

Of course women have been recording women's history and providing it with a theoretical context but it has never been treated in the same way as men's history, partly because of the value system which is embedded in the discipline itself. Sometimes women's historical work has been temporarily acknowleged — as in the case of Mary Beard (1946) for example, but only to 'disappear' within the next generation.[2] Women's history has been evaluated against the yardstick of men's history and suffered from the conceptualization of male as norm and female as deficient, and has been treated as less intellectually interesting and rewarding, argues Berenice Carroll (1976); it is often 'justified' only insofar as it illuminates what "we" want to know about "other issues" ' (p.xi). Today, while there is an enormous amount of energy being devoted by women to reclaiming women's history, the nature of the discipline — and its control — is such that women are still being 'kept outside' as they encounter these 'ruling ideas' and the resistance of women that they embody. Carroll argues that women can be interested in their own history for its own sake, in precisely the same way that men are interested in their history for its own sake, and it is a mark of who formulated the present value system and who continues to enforce it that historians could seriously suggest that the purpose of women's history is to provide a more comprehensive context in which to locate the activities of men!

A comparable situation exists with regard to literature where men have been in control as the critics (and publishers), and have been able to formulate the aesthetic standards, decreeing what is laudable and what is not: a survey of most literary curricula readily reveals that it is men who are laudable and women who are not. (Elaine Showalter 1976 found in one prestigious American university that there were 313 male writers being studied and 17 women, which in no way corresponds to the availability of writing by men and women: likewise Anna Walters, 1978, found in her survey of prescribed texts for 'A' level examinations in London that there were 50 male writers and 2 female.) Annette Kolodny (1981) has commented on her own university education in literature and says 'where women writers were taught, as in the courses on the history of the English novel, a supposedly exceptional work might be remarked for its "large scope" or "masculine thrust", but more often than not women's novels were applauded for a certain elegance of style, an attention to detail or nuance, and they they were curtly dismissed for their inevitably "feminine" lack of humor, weighty truths or universal significance' (p.23).

Many women are currently reviving the issue that Virginia Woolf raised over fifty years ago when she said that men are the arbiters in literature and male standards prevail, so that when a women writes 'she will find that she is perpetually wishing to alter the established values — to make serious what appears insignificant to a man, and trivial what is to him important.' And, adds Woolf, 'for that, of course she will be criticized; for the critic of the opposite sex will be genuinely puzzled and surprised by the attempt to alter the current scale of values, and will see in it not merely a difference of view but a view that is weak or trivial, or sentimental because it differs from his own' (Woolf 1972, p.146).

This is an insight that women have about writing and its reception and it is an insight that dates back to Aphra Behn (Goreau 1980), but it has not been made the substance of literary study. Historically women have repeatedly asserted that when men enter women's literature they frequently enter a symbolic realm which is unfamiliar to them and which they dismiss rather than explore, thereby precluding if from becoming familiar. In these terms there is a fundamental sexual inequality encoded in the theory and practice of literary study which is more problematic to women than to men for it is a problem rarely raised by men of letters and incorporated into that study. Women can continue to explore and develop these understandings but it is unlikely that they will find conceptual space within the discipline while men remain in control and structure the discipline according to their own experience and priorities.

The position with language study is much the same. Lee Jenkins and Cheris Kramer.[3] (1978; 1981) have shown how male control has been used to exclude and devalue women: 'men make up the theory and the test situation,' they state, 'based on their experience and evaluate the behavior of women by their standards. The fact that women often behave differently . . . seems like an interesting curiosity rather than an indication of different modes of conduct based on different experiences and different ways of defining situations' (p.79). And so this enormous bias against women continues to be constructed as the disciplines continue to encode knowledge based on male experience. Women who enter these disciplines are initiated into ways of explaining the world in terms of the inadequacy of women so that 'mastering' a discipline frequently means accepting the deficiency of women.

Sheila Ruth (1981) has documented this bias as it has been encoded in philosophy, where 'a world view that constitutes humanity as male and relegates woman to the status of out-group, of "other" ' prevails (p.45). 'It is not difficult to understand how such confusion came about,' says Ruth, for the various disciplines have been historically owned and operated by and for men. 'Women were simply not an issue or a force. The construction of a universe where man (male) and human were coextensive was not problematic in a belief system that deemed women not quite human if it deemed them at all. Women simply did not function for the male conceptually because they did not function politically, economically or, for that matter intellectually. Women's perspectives are absent because they were permitted no entry into the club.' Ruth goes on to say that 'When "woman" does appear in the "sacred writings", she does not talk herself, but rather is talked about, usually in a subsidiary chapter that grudgingly gives some attention to the troublesome but persistent presence of the subsidiary of the human race. Aquinas, for example, inquires whether "in the first state, women would have been born" ' (p.45).

This is the discipline from which many of the modern disciplines have emerged and it is understandable perhaps that they should share common fundamental features: one discipline, however, which did not emerge was that which addressed the problem of male power, or which explored the nature and extent of the bias against women in the disciplines. Today, as that discipline does take shape in the form of 'Women's Studies', it is interesting to note the resistance that it meets in many circles, and the arguments that are used to deny its necessity and validity.

The social sciences have encoded no less a bias against women than the humanities, and Ann Oakley (1974, 1981) and Helen Roberts (1981a, b) have shown how the classification system and the categories of social science have been devised without reference to women, and cannot simply be extended to accommodate them. Along with Jessie Bernard (1973) they have exposed sociology as a male science and male experience which has contributed towards the creation of sexual inequality. Only males could have classified the work in which they were engaged as real work, and classified that which is allocated to women as non-work.

Only males could have explained the world in terms of production and ignored reproduction and made it invisible. Only males could have accepted that it was feasible and logical to construct the discipline of economics on the basis that it was fitting to pay men for their labour but not women, that it was proper to include men's work in the gross national product but not women's (unless, of course, as Gerda Lerner 1977 has pointed out, it was 'women's work' being performed by men, in which case they would be paid and included). Only males could continue to assert that western economies have moved from an indentured to a monetary base when a great percentage of the workforce is providing service in exchange for board and lodging.

From the perspective of women these issues are extremely problematic but they have no entry to economics — 'the oldest, the most established, the most quantitative of the social sciences — and the most dominated by men' (Ferber and Teiman 1981, p.125). That women the world over should be producing leisure for men (Leghorn and Parker 1981) is an issue which has not been entertained in a discipline which represents the interests of men; that the United Nations statistics indicate that women perform two-thirds of the world's work for less than 10 per cent of the world's salary and own less than 1 per cent of the world's wealth is problematic to many women but not a problem within economics.

Other disciplines in the social sciences are equally as culpable. Psychology which has assumed that the normal healthy adult is a male and that women's differences are deficiencies, so that an unhealthy male (who is represented as passive, dependent, weak) resembles a healthy female; where psychologists (and psychiatrists) have helped 'unhealthy' women (that is, autonomous, independent, self-determining women) to adjust to their 'femininity' and to conform to non-prestigious and unrewarding ways of behaving in our society (Walker 1981). Medicine, which has also assumed the male body to be the human body and has conceptualized the female as possessing 'additional parts' which are 'mysterious' and subject to disturbance, is equally biased against women and has played its part in producing knowledge which justifies sexual inequality (Elston, 1981).

And the natural sciences, where relevant, have also played a significant part in encoding a bias against women which can be readily used to explain and reinforce male dominance and male control. Ruth Hubbard (1981), for example, has asked why such selectivity has operated in terms of animal species that have been studied: 'Is it an accident,' she asks, 'that among billions of insect species, those whose social behaviour easily conforms to rigid roles are the ones who have caught the imaginations of naturalists from the nineteenth century onwards?' (p.214). Such studies can be used to justify existing social arrangements in society while animal species in which there is no easy interpretation of sexual asymmetry in favour of males are often neglected.

Hubbard analyses many of the scientific theories (including Darwin's theory of evolution) and indicates how much they owe to assumptions about the way the world works — including the assumption that men are more important than women. She shows how these values are embedded in some of the most established and 'objective' scientific explanations, and how they have been used politically, camouflaged as they may have been as 'laws of nature'. If there are some scientists who believe (or wish) 'that women's mental lives are controlled by the physical demands of their reproductive systems (or that blacks are intellectually inferior).' states Hubbard, and they 'proceed to "prove" these hypotheses by devising the necessary tests, asking the right questions, finding appropriate subjects, and then come to the obvious conclusions, sexism (or racism) becomes part of the scientific dogma' (p.215).

Kathy Overfield (1981) has also documented women's exclusion from science and the consequent results: 'Women, in fact, are excluded both in practice from scientific activity and — more importantly for us to realise — from and by the scientific ethic, ideology and image-making process' (p.238). Overfield goes so far as to assert that only men, who perceived themselves as dominant, could have evolved the scientific framework and ethic and elevated their form of rationality and logic to its present status at the expense of other forms of knowing or understanding.[4]

Justice has not been done to these critiques of the disciplines but this overview does serve to make the point that is widespread consensus — among women — that the disciplines are owned and operated by men and serve to enhance and justify the image of men at the expense of women. If this knowledge is *not* shared within the community of higher education, it is not because it does not exist or is not accessible, but because it is not being admitted or treated as significant, and it is this feature of the organization of higher education which is the focus of major criticism, because it illustrates the nature and extent of male control and the bias it constitutes against women.

RESEARCH: THE PROCESS OF MAKING ONE'S PREJUDICES COME TRUE

Ruth Hubbard (1981) has stated that researchers do not ask all possible questions but only those that are amenable to their methodology and which arouse their curiosity and interest (and the curiosity and interest of those prepared to fund research). Nor do they accept all possible answers but only those that fit with their implicit assumptions about the nature of the world (p.213). The objects which are selected for research — in the science and social science community — and the manner in which they are studied are used, states Hubbard, 'to reinforce the interests or preconceptions of the studiers. There is clearly not enough time for scientists to ask all possible questions, so one asks only those that promise to lead somewhere. The question is *who gets to decide where?*' (p.217). It is *who* and *where* which is the locus of a massive bias against women in research, for it is men primarily, if not exclusively, who decide, and they do so on the basis of what interests them and what is consistent with their interest.

Because men can choose the topics and the manner in which they are studied they are in a privileged position to legitimate the biases with which they began: they are in the position of being likely to make their prejudices 'come true'. In research, states Ruth Hubbard, there is the phenomenon of 'experimenter expectancy' and 'what is boils down to is more often than not, we find what we look for. Indeed one can prove almost any hypothesis if one gets to set the terms of the experiment,' she adds, 'to choose appropriate conditions, ask appropriate questions, select appropriate controls. And if one does a thorough job, the conclusion will have that quality of obviousness that scientists so enjoy at the end of meticulous research. And it really *is* obvious,' says Hubbard, 'for it fits what we believe about the world: but the reason that it fits so well is that it is founded on those very beliefs' (p.215).

When there are two sexes and knowledge is required about both sexes and their relationship to each other, then the stated tenets of 'good research' would suggest that it was mandatory that both sexes be equally represented in conceptualizing their own and each other's relationships. But one of the characteristics of research as currently conducted is that it is men who determine the parameters and points of reference and men begin with the understanding that they are primarily in control. This in itself requires explanation and justification yet the research process itself frequently permits this to 'materialize' without making it an object of inquiry.

Men have 'spoken for' themselves, and they have spoken for women; men have articulated their relationship to women and women's relationship to them. Women's voices have rarely been heard, they have been structurally excluded and will probably remain so while men retain control. While this situation persists it is possible for men to continue to 'prove' — without serious opposition or protest in their terms — that men are more central, authoritative and universal, for this 'value' is built into the research model with which they began and in which they are in a dominant position.

It is a very limited and distorted model and falls short of many of the stated requirements of good research which have been formulated under male control.

This is the 'politics of research', an area which many women are attempting to open up in order to explore the way men have used their power to justify and reinforce that power (Spender 1981a, c; Stanley and Wise in press). The response, however, from the male controlled research community has not always been positive. Often, not only is the political nature of conventional research disputed, but ironically, it seems that those who raise the issue are themselves frequently accused of being 'political' while those who deny it can insist on their own 'neutrality' and 'objectivity', a stance not inconsistent with the research model in which they are operating.

But if in the past the exclusion of women could be attributed to 'accident' or 'ignorance' the same explanations are unlikely to be convincing in the future, for while it must be acknowledged that women's protests and alternatives have not necessarily made their way into the 'mainstream' it must also be acknowledged that this is not because women have not produced a great deal of material on research nor because it has not been publicized (albeit in contexts which men have judged to be outside the central issues of concern).

The phenomenon of the exclusion of women from research (and the consequent bias which is established) is not confined to past practices but is today continually recreated and this gives rise to the puzzling question as to why this has not been a legitimate area of study within the discipline of education, for if any existing body of knowledge suggests itself as a potential base for such a topic, it is surely education. Rather than accommodating such study, however, education as a discipline can serve as a paradigmatic case for illustrating the way in which women continue to be excluded from research, and it can also help to indicate that unless radical and substantial changes are made, the bias against women in the future will be no less than it has been in the past.

Education as a discipline is also male controlled regardless of the number of women who are admitted to its ranks (see Byrne 1978 for further details). It continues to attach more significance to males and male experience and to produce more knowledge about males. In her study of the literature in the sociology of education, for example, Sandra Acker (1980b) has shown that the number of studies concerned exclusively with women is at least 5 per cent, while 37 per cent of the studies were concerned exclusively with males. To assume however that the remaining 58 per cent encompasses consideration of both sexes would not be advisable given the male bias that operates in research, for it may have been that among these studies were those in which it was so readily accepted that the male was the universal category, that it was not acknowledged that the sample was confined to males.

Certainly 'reputable' researchers are continuing to confine themselves to males without necessarily noting the limitations of the research. Halsey Heath and Ridge (1980) for example justified their exclusion of women on the grounds that women had not been included in previous studies, a practice which many women wish to take up as a central issue, but the significance of which appears to have escaped these researchers. (Sara Delamont 1981 has also pointed out that not only did these particular researchers assume the universality of male experience in their own research but they projected it on to the research of others by referring to their samples as 'male' when they did indeed include females: rather than interpreting this as carelessness or an aberration many women would be prepared to argue that this is all too frequently the consequence of women's exclusion.)

The issues which are 'interesting' and 'significant' and which are judged to be worthy of research are also more likely to be issues which relate to men and their interests, while those which concern women can remain at the periphery of research, unfunded, and unlikely to be taken seriously. This has been the case with the question of who is benefiting from mixed sex education. For many years women have been hypothesizing and asserting that boys are benefiting at the expense of girls and a number of research studies undertaken by women help to substantiate this thesis (Shaw 1980; Spender 1982; Stanworth 1981). But despite the documentation that women have provided and the frequency with which they have put their case, the issue has not been given priority in educational research: one wonders how long it would have remained invisible if the reverse were suggested and it was hypothesized that girls were benefiting at the expense of boys.

Topics which are given priority are those which are problematic to males, and as Sandra Acker (1980b) has indicated the absence of women in knowledge produced by men is astonishing. Using the literature of the sociology of education as a guide to social arrangements, states Acker, one would 'conclude that numerous boys but few girls go to secondary modern schools; that there are no girls' public schools; that there are almost no adult influentials of any sort; that most students in higher education study science and engineering; that women rarely make a ritual transition called "from school to work" and never go into further education colleges. Although some women go to university, most probably enter directly into motherhood where they are of some interest as transmitters of language codes to their children. And except for a small number of teachers, social workers and nurses, there are almost no adult women workers in the labour market' (p.5).

Yet this is the research that is often defended as 'neutral' and 'objective', while those who protest that it plays an active role in constructing sexual inequality are labelled as 'political' and accused of introducing 'values' into a 'value free' system.

Even where research is undertaken on women the double standard of male as norm and women as a deviant is often seen to be operating. Where women do not behave in the same way as men they can be excluded as subjects on the grounds that they are unreliable (Tobias 1978) or their behaviour can be consigned to the realm of the meaningless and treated as non-data. Acker (1980b) has also listed some of the 'explanations' of women's un-anticipated behaviour in educational research and they range from 'puzzlement' through 'contrary to expectation' and 'no supportable explanation' to the 'results for women students are bizarre' (Acker 1980b, p.9).

'One might expect that theories derived from males on the basis of male experience could well prove to be inappropriate and inaccurate for predicting and explaining female behaviour, but it appears that many researchers would rather modify humanity (and classify women as less than fully human) than modify their theories so that they take account of the full range of human experience. When women do not behave in the same way as men it is often assumed that there is something wrong with women, rather than the theory' (Spender 1982, in press).

At the same time as this model of research — with its inherent bias against women — persists, there is an enormous amount of research being undertaken in which women are central and in which the bias has been partly eliminated. This however could not be ascertained by reference to many of the 'offical records' of educational research: such research is often conducted outside institutions of higher education and almost always defined as 'outside the mainstream' so the pattern which has existed historically still continues today, where women are engaged in producing alternative and positive knowledge about women, but where such knowledge generally does not get admitted to the system of distribution.

For example, in her report *Research on Sex Differences in Schools in the U.K.,* Alison Kelly (1981) lists no less than seveny-nine individual researchers engaged in the area, and at the Women's Research and Resources Centre in London there are well over fifty women registered as undertaking research in education (Spender 1981, in press). It is doubtful whether any other area currently has so many researchers involved, but despite this impressive activity and a virtual explosion of publications in the area, many educational researchers located in the 'mainstream' can continue to undertake their work as if such knowledge did not exist.

It is not uncommon for women to raise the issue within the educational community, at conferences, meetings, staff discussions, to ask whether colleagues have read certain book and articles, become familiar with particular research studies or particular names. And it is not uncommon for such queries to be answered by blank stares of silence, or even admissions that such resources are unknown. As Sheila Ruth (1981) has stated, no researchers willingly admit to not knowing other important researchers and studies (p.50).

That William Taylor, Director of the University of London Institute of Education, can co-author a book *Education in the 80s: the Central Issues* in which little or no mention is made of women and where the bias against women in education is not raised as an issue (and where the index has no entries of women, or feminism, for example) is quite remarkable given the level of activity in his own institution, where not only is considerable research being undertaken but where the Women's Education Group (WEdG) has been meeting regularly and acting as a pressure group to try and bring about change in the biases that operate against women.

It is also remarkable to find that Pergamon Press is to publish a new *International Encyclopedia of Education. Research and Studies* in 1983 with fourteen special editors — all of them male. Some of the men who are involved would be unable to plead ignorance about the significance of this arrangement, for they have in the past been directly confronted with evidence of male control in education, and the undesirable consequences of that control. It seems, however, that *they* have not felt the need for change.

These are but two recent examples where the opportunity to include women did exist, but was not taken: there are however numerous other examples which could be cited to show the way women are still being excluded from educational research, and how males are using their authority and power to ensure that male issues are mainstream issues, and that official records are by and large the records of male endeavour.

There is the *British Research Index* for example, which purports to 'list and analyse the subject content of all articles of permanent educational interest' and which helps to make sure that the research undertaken by women on women does not become of permanent educational interest by *not* including women's publications in the sample of periodicals from which it selects its material. If future generations consult this *Index* in the attempt to find out what research was being undertaken in the 80s, they could be forgiven for assuming that the bias against women was not a significant issue, and that it attracted little interest. They would be far from correct, but they would be making a comparable mistake to the one we make today when we consult past official records and find that women are absent. Constructing the invisibility of women is an age-old activity which has served male control very well, for the absence of women from the record can help to imply that women have had no contribution to make and are therefore — justifiably — subordinate in education and society.

This is why women know so little about the history of women's protest against male control of education: it is why women are handicapped when they wish to assert their own positive heritage, for what women learn is 'approved' by men, and men have not approved of Aphra Behn, Mary Astell, 'Sophia, a person of quality', Catherine Macaulay, Mary Wollstonecraft, Emily Davies, Virginia Woolf — despite the fact that they all wrote impressive critiques of education. The official records point us to men, not women, and women who suspect that there have been positive women in the past and that there is a female heritage have the additional burden of *locating* these women even before they can begin studying them.

If women have been kept off the record, however, so too have some men, particularly those whose reasons for excluding women seem absurd today and are the source of some embarrassment. It will be interesting to note whether Joan Burstyn's book *Victorian Education and the Ideal of Womanhood* (1980), which documents the case against women's education, becomes adopted in the 'mainstream' for it does *not* portray men in a flattering light (Carol Dyhouse (1976) has provided similar information). What can be said with conviction is that women who read it will be much better equipped to resist contemporary arguments which attempt to justify the exclusion of women.

There is currently an enormous amount of research (including archivist research) which challenges traditional educational findings, but while the present power configurations persist in higher education it is possible that the existence of such research will do little to modify male control and to establish women as full members of the educational community. The charges which Mary Wollstonecraft levelled at educationalists in 1792 are no less relevant today, for men still control the education of men, *and of women*, and this works to the advantage of men and the disadvantage of women. Women are as far from influencing their own education, from producing and distributing within institutions authentic knowledge about women and men, as they were when Mary Astell (1694) called for a women's college free from the influence of men.

And many educationalists today make use of the same arguments as they did then to rebut the charges.

'In 1739, "Sophia, a person of quality" exposed the absurdities of male reasoning when she stated that men would not permit women to learn on the grounds that it was useless as they held no public office, and men would not permit women to hold public office because they had no learning. One might have expected that almost 250 years later this argument would have no credibility. Unfortunately, however, it still persists in many guises and is still used against women. "Blaming the victim" in this way helps mask the role which men have played in creating victims' (Spender 1982, in press).

That women lack experience and qualifications is still one of the major arguments used to explain women's absence from the citadels of power, that they are not the 'better candidates' is still put forward as a reason for all male editorial boards, all male speakers at a conference (see Research Intelligence *BERA Newsletter* April 1981, page 22 for an all-male list of contributors to the British Educational Research Conference of 1981), male professors, male research directors, etc. It should be argued that it was right and proper for education to provide those who lacked experience and qualifications with precisely that experience and qualification, but instead the exclusion of women is used to justify the continued exclusion of women. And while women are excluded from research — as theorists and subjects — this exclusion will continue to be practised and will continue to constitute a major bias against them.

BOYS OWN EDUCATION

Annie Cornbleet (1981) has stated that 'Boys *own* education', it belongs to them and is for them, and she echoes the statements of some of her predecessors such as Virginia Woolf and Mary Wollstonecraft. Higher education is a male domain where much positive knowledge about men and a little, negative knowledge about women is generated and transmitted, so that within the institutions both sexes learn about the justifiable 'superiority' of males and 'inferiority' of females. Both sexes receive a 'boys education' geared to the interests of boys (Hochschild 1975) and while this may have numerous advantages for boys it is a distinct liability for girls. Institutions of higher education are organized so that this arrangement will continue.

While institutions so carefully conserve and protect male control it seems that the struggle for an education of their own will be a long one for women: it has already been under way for three centuries. In these circumstances it seems that one possible alternative for women is to establish the college (or colleges) that Mary Astell proposed in 1694. In other countries where the problem seems comparable this has emerged as one solution for the elimination of bias against women in higher education. There is a women's university in Italy, and a women's university proposed in Norway, where women will control their own education, develop their own teaching and research, and gain the 'experience and qualifications' that men have denied them and then 'blamed' them for. (Ås 1981).

Where women do control their own education it is very different (Duelli-Klein unpublished). The values are different, the teaching styles different, the problems posed for research and the methods of study employed are different (Stanley and Wise in press): and the outcome is very different, for rather than learn about their own ostensible inadequacy, women can learn about their own strength[5]; rather than learn about the traditions of men, they can learn about the traditions of women and men and their inter-relationship. Sexual inequality is not so readily constructed under such conditions.

Many researchers have suggested that men are not willingly going to surrender their control in education (McWilliams-Tullberg 1980; Bryant 1979) but it must be noted that one of the 'ruling ideas' generated by the rulers is that where *they* are is the mainstream: rather than trying to dislodge the power configurations of the institutions perhaps it would be more profitable to dislodge the ruling ideas and to reconceptualize the 'mainstream' as a limited area, perhaps it would be more productive to *challenge* the belief that where women are the power is not. If numbers, energy and commitment are any guide, then women are in a strong position in education and educational research to re-label the present divisions in their own interest, and to eliminate some of the long-standing, deeply entrenched biases against women which have been generated and often condoned in higher education.

DISABILITY

Ronald Sturt

Is higher education ever able to assess an application only in terms of ability and to disregard evidence of disability?

The UCCA booklet *How to Apply for Admission to a University* has in the course of a few years changed the tone of its advice to candidates with physical or other disabilities in a way that appears to make superfluous the posing of the question above. For the 1976 entry UCCA informed such candidates that:

'some universities can make special provision for disabled or handicapped students. If you have a major physical disability (for example if you use a wheel chair)

(a) you are advised first to consult the universities to which you wish to apply to see whether they can offer you the special facilities you need; and

(b) you are invited, if you so wish, to mention your disability or handicap in section 16 of the application form.'

For the October 1981 entry the UCCA information reads:

'Universities are bound by the Health and Safety at Work Act 1974; they must ensure that no individual (student or otherwise) is put at undue risk. Candidates suffering from a disability or condition which could put themselves or others at risk must give details in section 5(d) of the application form. This is particularly important if courses involve laboratory or field work where incapacity of any sort (even temporary) could be hazardous. In addition, handicapped or disabled students may require special facilities, such as access to buildings by wheelchair. Universities are often able to make special provision in these cases, but if you are in this situation you are strongly advised to discuss the nature of your disability with universities before filling in your UCCA form, to see whether they can offer you the facilities you need.'

If the approach were to the University of Birmingham today the candidate would learn that the university 'is glad to consider physically handicapped students for admission to appropriate courses. The University believes that it is essential for such students to be given advice on an individual basis.' A photograph of wheelchair students active in the Sports Centre underlines the information. The University of Leeds would inform such a candidate that the subjects he or she can study depend 'on the nature and degree of handicap and on the current accessibility of teaching buildings. Accessibility for wheelchairs is rapidly being improved. . . .' The University of Southampton give 'sympathetic consideration' to applications from handicapped students, and 'the disabled student will be welcomed into the University community.'

DEFINITION. WHAT DOES HANDICAP MEAN?

'Handicap may come to lie in the eye of the beholder.'

Child and Markall (1976), quoted above, reported that observers of the research project in which he was engaged repeatedly emphasized that the question of definition was crucially important. The definition of disability he employed was 'explicitly confined to a condition, characterized by physical or sensory impairement, which could produce educational disadvantage in the tertiary sector.' This definition excluded the mentally handicapped. Child persisted:

'For physical or sensory impairment to become academically or vocationally significant somebody must perceive the condition as a departure from physical or sensory norms, must categorize that perception, must report it to others, negotiate the acceptance of this definition and obtain a response that conforms to it. Once these requirements are met the individuals designated handicapped become special kinds of person, are evaluated relative to others not deemed handicapped and have modes of activity and conduct prescribed for them.

'Thus, just as medical prognosis is founded upon certain assessments and routines so judgement is passed by the tertiary sector according to its own array of criteria.'

The survey over which Child and Markall spent two years was directed not at students medically designated disabled, but at 'the procedures and policies of institutions in reacting to those whom they perceived as disabled.'

Child's definition and his use of it marked a change from that used in earlier surveys such as the major study of the National Innovations Centre (1974) which used the following definition of full-time students in British universities and polytechnics with some form of physical disability:

'Any student with a physical or sensory impairment or chronic sickness, which could produce educational disadvantages, is considered to be disabled for the purpose of this survey. Thus students who are blind or partially sighted, have a hearing impairment, serious speech defect, paralysed limbs or defective control over limbs or bodily functions, epilepsy, haemophilia or other conditions requiring continuing attention, treatment or care are included. Students disadvantaged as a result only of psychiatric disorder are excluded' (on ground of difficulty of distinguishing between long-term conditions and short-term disorders due to stress).

Being interested also in the functional, not medical, aspect of the disability led the NIC researchers to a classification according to eight categories of functional impairment, and their analyses were based on that classification.

Barnett in Dixon (1979) pointed to a confusion between 'needs' and 'objectives' and advocated a redefinition of handicapped students in educational terms:

'Those sharing the common educational needs but, because of mental, physical or emotional conditions which impose learning parameters, requiring to have those needs met within situations which may include the setting of special objectives, the use of special resources and special expertise.'

A distinction between the terms 'disabled' and 'handicapped' was drawn by Jeffers (1980) who explained:

'For the purpose of this work the term handicapped is applied to people in the academic setting whose ability to study and benefit from the educational process is affected by a physical condition beyond their unaided control. It has been chosen because it implies not only restrictions imposed on the individual by his physical condition but also restrictions imposed from outside the individual by society and the environment.

'More and more frequently a handicap is considered to be the result of an interraction between a person's disability and his social and physical milieu.'

She chose not to use the term 'disabled' because 'in certain circumstances a disabled person is not necessarily handicapped.'

Definitions for purposes of investigation and report in higher education could themselves be said to cause bias or to enshrine it. It is however in legislation that the art of definition faces a rigorous future.

In America the Rehabilitation Act 1973, amended in 1974, amended in turn the definition of a handicapped individual according to Health (1977). Prior to that the definition was 'limited to the dimension of employability'. The new definition was:

'Any person who (a) has a physical or mental impairment which substantially limits one or more of such a person's major life activities, (b) has a record of such impairment, or (c) is regarded as having such an impairment.'

Major life activities were functions such as caring for one's self, performing manual tasks, walking, seeing, hearing, speaking, breathing, learning and working. This definition was amended for purposes of Section 504 of the Act for which Biehl (1978) compiled a guide to self-evaluation for colleges and universities.

Although the Chronically Sick and Disabled Persons Act 1970 provided in Section 28 for the interpretation of terms such as 'disabled', there was, in education, little guidance beyond the definitions of categories of handicapped pupils requiring special educational treatment embodied in Handicapped Pupils Regulations 1959 as amended from time to time. The Warnock Committee, whose report *Special Educational Needs* (1978) was a most extensive study of special education, adopted a concept of special educational need seen not in terms of a particular disability which a child may be judged to have, but in relation to everything about him, his abilities as well as his disabilities, and all factors which bear on his educational progress.

The concept was adopted and incorporated in the Education Bill 1981 in the House of Commons (1981) but there is no sign to date of any legislation which could extend the concept of special educational need to further and higher education. The House (1981) states:

'A child has "special educational needs" if he has a learning difficulty which calls for special educational provision to be made for him.

'. . . A child has a "learning difficulty" if

(a) he has a significantly greater difficulty in learning than the majority of children of his age; or

(b) he suffers from a disability which either prevents or hinders him from making use of educational facilities of a kind generally provided in schools, within the area of the local authority concerned, for children of his age, or

(c) he is under the age of five years and is, or would be if special educational provision were not made for him, likely to fall within (a) or (b) when over that age.

' "Special educational provision" means

(a) in relation to a child who has attained the age of two years, educational provision which is in addition to, or otherwise different from, the educational provision made generally for children of his age in schools maintained by the local education authority concerned.'

It is recognized that descriptive terms will be needed for particular groups who require special educational provision, but the effect of applying the new concept will serve to increase considerably the numbers of those with special educational needs at primary and secondary levels.

THE EXTENT OF NEED. WHO COUNTS?

The first measure of the failure of handicapped students to reach higher education in significant numbers was registered by Tuckey (1973) in the study of handicapped school-leavers, seven to eight thousand of whom left special schools each year. Of 788 school-leavers in the study 83 per cent were considered by head teachers to be suitable for further education: 34 per cent were successful, and five blind students and three physically handicapped went to university or college.

The National Innovations Centre (1974) reported that in the 1972-73 academic year universities and polytechnics had registered 554 disabled students, two in every thousand of the student population. The Amelia Harris survey in 1970 estimated that there were in the same age group nine disabled people in every thousand of the population as a whole.

One emphatic opinion was recorded in *The Disabled Student in Higher Education* (1974) when Dr. Richard Learner reported that over the previous few years admissions tutors in physics at Imperial College London had interviewed 5000 students for places of which one would have expected fifty or sixty to have been handicapped, by DES statistics. In the entire period one handicapped student — a blind candidate — had been interviewed. In Dr. Learner's opinion the supply of properly qualified handicapped students emerging from secondary education was 'wildly inadequate'.

Gunn (1976) noted that the National Innovations Centre figures in 1974 had proved to be underestimates. 'This . . . doubtless stems from the use of the definitions chosen, when the whole subject of physical handicap is assessed.' At 34 United Kingdom universities in 1974-75 there were recorded 258 disabled in a student population of 132,264. This was 1:513. He noted that twenty-three universities did not keep a register of any kind. Of the disabled students only fourteen had failed in the past five years, three withdrew for academic reasons, and four died.

There were two spheres where higher education attracted a greater percentage of the disabled. Butler (1978) surveyed nine years of work with blind students, and reported that 382 were enrolled on degree or professional courses. As there were two to three hundred seriously visually handicapped school leavers each year he considered 'the proportion entering further and higher education certainly appears to compare favourably with the national average.' According to the records of the Royal National Institute for the Blind all universities in England and Wales had accepted at least one seriously visually handicapped student, as had twenty-five of the thirty polytechnics, and forty-three of the two hundred colleges of education. Six per cent failed or withdrew, and Butler provided a valuable commentary on the problems faced by disabled students: eleven discontinued through failure to meet course standards; nineteen withdrew, ten having chosen the wrong course, and nine were unable or willing to change work methods. One of the nineteen was a girl student who gave up a social studies degree course because it was too theoretical; she enrolled on a catering course where, being the first and only blind student to do so, high expectations proved too great a strain. He reported that the student became a self-employed dressmaker.

The Vernon Committee report on the education of the visually handicapped, Education (1972), carried a statement that 'for many years the education of the partially sighted was restricted in the mistaken belief that sight would deteriorate through excessive use.'

The second variation was reported by Tomlinson in Dixon and Hutchinson (1979). The Open University had enrolled 1200 disabled students in a student population of 60,000. This represented two per cent of the OU population, and the failure rate of fourteen per cent was 'no greater among disabled students than among the general student population.'

The Open University had carried out analytical studies of all available records of disabled students, and Hales (1979a) reported that 3016 handicapped students had been registered and given a disability code in one of twenty-one categories. The tabulations showed, by disability code in each case, the year of entry, sex distribution, marital status, occupation, part-time education, highest educational attainment, regional distribution in the thirteen regions, credits gained, and degree studies completed.

UCCA (1981) has decided that, once the 1982 entry has been registered, disability will be entered on candidates' records in order to furnish details of the number of disabled applicants to universities and the number of acceptances.

Overseas the factors at work evoked similar conclusions. Bergh commented to the Stockholm international conference reported in *Opportunities for Handicapped in Higher Education* (1978) that an original theme on the lines of international exchange for the handicapped had been shelved when the planning committee realized it needed to know more of what was happening at home. The investigation produced disturbing results. In ten years progress has been made in the primary and secondary education of handicapped children but opportunities in higher education were 'almost non-existent.' Inquiries in other European countries revealed 'that this situation was not peculiar to Sweden.'

In New Zealand Bicheno (1981) recorded that the University of Auckland with a roll of 11,700 students had only fifteen students indentified as suffering from physical disabilities, although it was estimated that ten per cent of the population of the country was disabled.

In the United States Nugent (1978) suggested a lessening of adversity in his statement that for the past three decades 'program accessibility' has been a reality for thousands of severely handicapped students, over nine hundred of whom had gained degrees from the University of Illinois at Champaign-Urbana. Jeffers (1980) noted the effect of the 1974 Rehabilitation Act, effective date 3 June 1977. 'By September 1978 Indiana State University, Bloomington, had approximately double the number enrolled in 1977.' From an official source O'Neill (1977) expressed more modest expectations: it was unlikely that more than 30,000 students with handicaps requiring special building accessibility would be enrolled in higher education during any year. In 1974-5 total enrolment had been nine million students: one in three hundred had accessibility requirements. The estimates of handicapped children suggested that in any year about two hundred thousand handicapped people aged eighteen to twenty-three would be enrolled in colleges and universities. O'Neill reported that the 1970 American census data showed that only 3.3 per cent of persons aged eighteen to forty-four who reported they were severly disabled had obtained 'a college degree or more'. The same group had low 'labor force participation' and earnings, and against this bleak background he opined that, if the proportion of the group who were to finish college could increase to six per cent, the annual flow of benefits from this source would rise to a hundred million pounds.

INTENT: BY LAW OR DECLARATION
If special legislation or specific declarations were evidence of the existence of bias awaiting correction, the United States, Britain and other parts of Europe competed to apply the corrective.

In the United States, in Health, Education and Welfare (4 May 1977) the Rehabilitation Act 1973 (Public Law 93-112) Section 504 stated:

'No otherwise qualified handicapped individual in the United States . . . shall, solely by reason of his handicap, be excluded from the participation in, be denied the benefits of, or be subjected to discrimination under any program or activity receiving Federal financial assistance.'

With the amendment in 1974 (Public Law 93-516)

'it became clear that section 504 was intended to forbid discrimination against all handicapped individuals, regardless of their need for or ability to benefit from vocational rehabilitation services.

'It established a mandate to end discrimination and to bring handicapped persons into the mainstream of American life.'

Biehl (1978) explained that 'self evaluation under section 504' would be the principal process for assessing compliance and ensuring full participation, the process to be completed by 3 June 1978. Of some relevance was the advice that 'Federal financial assistance' was any grant, loan, contract, student aid or veterans assistance. 'Thus, virtually every college and university in the United States is covered by section 504.'

In Sweden the nations contributing to *Opportunities for Handicapped in Higher Education* (1978) referred to the declaration that 'higher education shall be equally accessible to all,' and asked why when the handicapped comprised 0.9 per cent of the population they represented only 0.2 per cent of the student body. There were nineteen European countries at the Stockholm Conference, together with the United States and the Philippines, and they concluded that 'ability to benefit' should replace 'ability to succeed' as the most important criterion for admitting a handicapped student. All post-secondary education should be orientated towards 'the full life' incorporating personal, academic and vocational interests.

In Britain the Open University's policy enunciated by Carver in Disabled (1974) was:

'to guarantee admission to those who in its opinion would not normally be able to attend a full-time degree course because of disability,'

provided that the necessary extra facilities could be supplied. This guaranteed admission was designed to enable the disabled student to jump the queue. Coe at the same conference reported that the academic board of the North East London Polytechnic had resolved that the admissions policy must be an open one and that physical disabilities should not be a bar to entry. Boyle also referred to a declaration of intent placed on record by the University of Leeds Senate and Council which guaranteed fair treatment for disabled students and staff:

'. . . all handicapped persons who are suitably qualified, shall for all purposes, including admission to university courses and appointment as members of staff, be treated fairly, and shall not be unnecessarily prejudiced on account of handicap; and, recognizing the special needs of handicapped persons, Senate and Council resolve *first* that all practicable steps shall be taken to ensure for them safe access and working conditions on the premises of the University; *secondly*, that no application for a student place or staff post from a handicapped person who seems otherwise suitable shall be rejected before he has been given an opportunity of discussing how he would overcome his difficulties with a relevant admissions officer or appointing committee; and, *thirdly*, that a joint Committee of Senate and Council shall be established to keep under review the needs of handicapped persons in the University and to advise on their implications.'

The Warnock Committee had been established, reported the National Innovations Centre (1974), by the Education Secretary, Mrs Thatcher, to review educational provision for children and young people handicapped by disabilities of body and mind, taking account of medical aspects together with arrangements to prepare them for entering into employment, and to consider and recommend the most effective use of resources for these purposes. The Committee's report, *Special Educational Needs* (1978), recommended that 'all universities and polytechnics as well as other establishments of higher education should formulate and publish a policy on the admission of students with disabilities or significant difficulties' in addition to making systematic arrangements to meet their needs once admitted.

Gunn (1976) in his analysis of university provision could find only three universities with a statement of positive intent, apart from the Open University with its precise nine point policy. Seventeen universities stated they had no policy at all.

Clarke, president of the National Union of Students, wrote in Child and Markall (1976) about

'the history of well-intentioned neglect, the lack of positive policy, the inadequate provision in most universities, colleges and polytechnics, — all this must be changed.'

He pledged the NUS — as well as students throughout the country — to fight to see that that was done.

Jeffers (1980) added a note of caution for Britain. The haste with which in the United States the Rehabilitation Act required institutions to complete modifications, adopt grievance procedures, and make programmes accessible within three years of the effective date could create problems for future generations.

'To be beneficial change has to be based on knowledge. Whether the United Kingdom adopts a more definitive approach as a result of permissive or mandatory legislation, education will be needed for the policy-makers, administrators and staff of academic institutions effecting change.

'It is fortunate that there exists, in both the USA and UK, an organization like the National Bureau for Handicapped Students to give advice, co-ordinate, initiate and investigate activities and services designed for the handicapped. Perhaps with their help and the assistance of the academic institutions the innovations of today will not be the follies of tomorrow.'

Marx and Hall (1978) had earlier expressed concern, at the first national conference at Dayton, Ohio: 'no-one is an expert on section 504. Attorneys . . . need a hundred years of case law and interpretation before they can provide an answer.' That Section 504 was the 'Civil Rights Act' for handicapped individuals seemed not to be in doubt, and 'the one general requirement that perhaps everyone is talking about in higher education is program accessibility. It seems to be on the minds and the tips of the tongues of everyone.'

INTEGRATION: RATIONALIZATION: SPECIAL PROVISION

The question whether or not the handicapped student should enjoy as much freedom in his or her choice of subject and site as do other students revealed in the nature of its answers wide differences between precept and practice.

Tuckey, Parfit and Tuckey (1973) pointed out that sending a child away from home and community to live in a specially designed school, 'often isolated in the country and protected from normal social conditions and life,' would not seem the best way to fit a child to live in that community or any adult community after he leaves school. Lord Boyle at the London conference, the *Disabled Student in Higher Education* (1974), in replying to speculation about scarce expertise such as careers advice being concentrated in a limited number — maybe a third or a quarter — of existing higher education institutions, expressed his unhappiness about such an idea: 'if you concentrate the facilities it lets the rest off.' Provision was a national responsibility. Child and Markall (1976) echoed those sentiments: 'As long as there are . . . isolated spheres of activity the problems of the disabled will be only partially solved. An additional danger is that there will be those who presume that a tendency towards isolated specialist centres . . . is to be encouraged.' The Warnock Committee, in *Special Educational Needs* (1978), stated that it had no wish

'to see prospective students deprived of any choice between institutions because of their disability. While this may be difficult to avoid for students who suffer from a relatively rare or particularly complex disability, we wish to see as many institutions as possible equipped to deal with students who are less severely handicapped.'

In the United States the requirement of the 1974 Act was reported in Health, Education and Welfare (1977) to be that each qualified handicapped person was to be educated with persons who are not handicapped to the 'maximum extent appropriate to the needs of the handicapped person.' Any institution in receipt of federal funds to which 'the post secondary education' sub-part applied should operate its programmes and activities 'in the most integrated setting appropriate.' Butler (1978) pointed out that in the UK only at five universities and one polytechnic had the number of handicapped students been sufficiently high — six to fifteen — to lead to any systematic college-based provision being made for them. The figures tended to disguise the fact that distribution was very irregular both in place and time, and 'even when there are several visually handicapped students at an establishment at the same time their common interest must not be taken for granted.' They may well have different degrees of vision, be on different courses, live at a distance from each other, and have no particular reasons to contact each other. Butler recognized the problem imposed by widespread and irregular dispersal of handicapped students in the planning and co-ordination of college-based and other services, including the dissemination of information. His survey of 248 undergraduates revealed:

43 read social studies
34 read combined arts
32 read law
29 read modern languages
13 read English
 8 read history
31 read other arts-based subjects
12 read economics
12 read psychology
34 read mathematics or science

Not only did these figures indicate a lack of common subject interests but also, as Butler pointed out, a bias towards courses in the arts and humanities although the numbers were increasing in mathematics, science and especially computing.

The European conference, reported in *Opportunities for Handicapped in Higher Education* (1978), agreed that integration should be a primary objective; but concern was expressed as to the inadequacy of the techniques available to make it work and the extent to which it was practicable or possible.

Gunn (1976) saw the dilemma more directly. The problem facing the physically disabled student

'is one of either finding a university that has accepted his or her kind of disability before, choosing a site that is suitable, as well as the course, or else summoning a powerful determination to convince the unconverted that they deserve an opportunity at least to try.'

Cooke's paper in Dixon and Hutchinson (1979) reported the Warnock Committee recommendations 'for the rest of this and into the twenty first century,' and emphasized that every college should designate a member of staff for the welfare of handicapped students, should formulate and publish a policy on admissions, and should make systematic arrangements after entry. Because of the small numbers his opinion was that special skills and facilities would probably be concentrated in a limited number of higher education institutions. The University Grants Committee's annual report for 1978-79, in the University Grants Committee Annual Survey (1980), contained comment on the Warnock proposals. The UGC

'reaffirmed their view that whilst provision should be made somewhere in the university system for all kinds of disability, it would be impracticable for special provision to be made everywhere. They thought that overall the facilities for the handicapped had been given fairly widespread attention by universities and these were steadily improving.'

Nugent (1978) furnished an account of the exuberant rehabilitation programme at the University of Illinois where, since 1947-48, disabled students had lived in twenty 'regular university residence halls' along with other students. Since 1951 Illinois had had an average of 225 to 250 severely physically disabled full-time residential students a year, with forty-five blind students in a given year. For the first seventeen years the programme was housed 'in temporary surplus tarpaper army barracks' and funds came from contracts with the Veterans Administration, the Illinois Divison of Vocational Rehabilitation and others. In its exuberance the Illinois programme lends weight to those who advocate the fullest possible integration of severely disabled students with others in regular campus conditions, and at the same time demonstrates the wealth of facilities which accrue to a dynamic specialist institution.

Jeffers (1980) traced the trend towards integration. The fore-runner, Sweden, moved steadily after 1902 towards an individualized, flexible concept of special education as part of its comprehensive education system, with seventy-five per cent of thalidomide children in 1969 being taught in ordinary classes. Norway had followed with legislation for integration in 1976, and Denmark a year later. In the UK the provision of special schools had not resulted in an academic institution being designed solely for students with handicaps, which meant that a form of integration became the normal practice when handicapped students gained admission to and attended higher education courses.

'No other approach to their inclusion in programmes has been considered at this level.

'Unfortunately in the past this has not been a positive policy decision affirming integration. Their inclusion was simply not given sufficient consideration by academic institutions, special schools or by the handicapped themselves.'

DISCRIMINATION — TO BEGIN OR TO END

Morris, author of the Chronically Sick and Disabled Persons Act 1970, expressed at the London conference in *The Disabled Student in Higher Education* (1974) his strongly held view that many students who have severe emotional problems, or are mentally ill, or have physical handicaps, received support at universities and polytechnics 'that is better than elsewhere in the community.' Yet there was still a long way to go.

'. . . we must not overlook other groups of people who also have difficulty in attaining their true academic potential.

'In today's universities and polytechnics acceptance no longer depends on conformity. Minority groups are treated neither with ignorance nor contempt. But mere acceptance is not enough. A measure of positive discrimination is needed.'

Carver at the same conference referred to 'guaranteed admission' at the Open University which was designed to enable the disabled student to jump the queue. Later at the same conference Savage, a disabled student, pointed out that handicapped students would not thank polytechnics or universities for allowing concessions such as lowering entrance qualifications: 'we wish to take our place in society as ordinary members.' Gunn (1976) pointed to the irony that the barrier of acceptance for university entry 'is often a higher one for the disabled. Given the intellectual endowment and pre-entry qualifications does not necessarily mean that they will obtain willing acceptance, or indeed any form of discrimination that is in their favour.'

In the United States positive legislation created uncertainty, as was reported in Health, Education and Welfare (1977). 'Commenters' from higher education suggested it would be appropriate for one post-secondary institution in an area to be made accessible and for colleges and universities in that area to participate, thereby developing a consortium. The Department of Health, Education and Welfare believed that such a consortium, when applied only to handicapped persons, would discriminate by restricting choice and therefore be inconsistent with the basic objectives of the statute.

'The Department has recognized that the problem of ending discrimination on the basis of handicap presents considerations that are extremely complex. . . . Eliminating gross exclusion and denials of equal treatment is not sufficient to assure genuine equal opportunity.

'In drafting a regulation to prohibit exclusion and discrimination, it became clear that different or special treatment of handicapped persons, because of their handicaps, may be necessary in a number of contexts in order to ensure equal opportunity.'

Redden (1979) saw the historical context.

'The 1970s will go down in history as the decade in which discrimination against the handicapped began to diminish.'

RELIGIOUS BIAS

John Gay

Any discussion about fairness or bias in higher education inevitably involves a series of value judgements as to what should count as evidence and how the evidence might be interpreted. Nowhere is this more true than in the case of the religious dimension. Indeed the whole issue of bias needs careful philosophical unravelling and it is hoped that such a conceptual analysis will be undertaken. This chapter restricts itself to looking at a range of material which might help the reader come to some interim conclusion about religious bias. Unfortunately, in this as in many areas it is the gaps in the evidence which are most prominent and so any conclusions are inevitably tentative.

The well-established distinction between the structures and the processes of higher education is used. It will be argued that while some of the institutional structures could be interpreted as being biased in favour of religion, the day-to-day processes of higher education are very much against religion.

In the first section on structures, an attempt will be made to describe the possible elements of the higher education system which might exhibit a religious bias. In historical terms the Church was the main provider of higher education, although this virtual monopoly was challenged from the Reformation onwards. The Catholic University is a crucial aspect of the international scene, and in the United States and parts of Europe Protestant universities and colleges are also important.

England has no Christian university, although in a number of ways Oxford and Cambridge approximate to this model. Apart from Oxbridge, Durham and King's College London, the main ecclesiastical bias at the university level resides in the Christian nature of the faculties of theology. The polytechnic sector is virtually free of religious bias, whereas the so-called third sector contains the Roman Catholic and the Church of England colleges of higher education: two coherent and explicitly value-laden groups of Church colleges. The Scottish, Welsh and Irish contexts are also examined.

The second section will examine the methodologically more difficult area of the place of the religious variable in the processes of higher education. Relatively little work has been done in Europe and so American evidence will be used. The areas discussed include the development of religious attitudes, religion in the curiculum, sex differences, student beliefs, staff beliefs, and the effects of the college environment on religion. The conclusion drawn is that in the majority of institutions the processes of higher education appear to work implicitly against religious beliefs and practices.

RELIGION AND THE STRUCTURES OF HIGHER EDUCATION
The Church's Historical Involvement
The main provider of higher education in the medieval period was the Church. She alone possessed the money, the manpower and the resources necessary to create universities, and so it was inevitable that the Church should have a predominant control over the contents and the methods of education. However, she did not have an exclusive monopoly and from the very earliest there was a strong tension between ecclesiastical control and academic automony. In 1395 Oxford was granted complete exemption from episcopal supervision and Cambridge followed suit in 1439. Not that this freedom placed the universities outside the Church: essentially they formed the educational arm of the Church and most of the university teachers were in holy orders.

After the Reformation the educational legacy of the medieval period came under question as the newly emergent nation states were not so keen on education being in the hands of a universalist church. However, it was not until the later stages of the Industrial Revolution that church control of education was challenged, and the resultant demand for university education in effect meant secular education. As a result of the variety of church-state influences in education, there have arisen a number of distinct types of educational patterns, and these are well documented in Bereday and Lauwerys (1966).

The International Context
Despite the Roman Catholic Church's long involvement in higher education, most of the Catholic universities are creations of the last one hundred years. The great universities founded in the Middle Ages by the Catholic Church were secularized following the Reformation and the French Revolution and it was not until the late nineteenth century that a concerted effort was made in Europe, Latin America and parts of the Third World to establish new Catholic universities. The history of the development of higher education in North America meant that both Catholic and Protestant universities were founded slightly earlier.

The United Kingdom has no explicitly Catholic or Protestant universities but in other European countries a number are to be found. In Belgium the two Catholic universities of Louvain, one French and one Walloon, have a total of about thirty thousand students. They are independent of direct state control and the titular head of both universities is the Archbishop of Malines. In terms of finance however, ninety per cent of their funding comes from the state. The University of Mons has a small Catholic faculty of 500 students and there is also a Catholic institute of commercial studies.

Spain, Italy and the Vatican City all have Catholic universities, and Holland has the Catholic university of Nijmegen as well as the Free University of Amsterdam which is based on the principles of Calvinism. The University of Fribourg, although it is a state-provided institution, is Catholic in character, and the faculties of theology in the other Swiss universities are either Protestant or Catholic in stance and allegiance.

France has no free-standing Catholic university and the state retains its monopoly over the awarding of degrees and qualifications. However, there are 'free' Catholic faculties attached to secular universities and these are grouped together in institutes. A proposal in the 1970s would have allowed the Catholic institutes to conduct exams and award degrees and other qualifications, but this proposal was eventually rejected.

In the United States, until 1950, institutes of higher education were mainly religious in foundation and by far the largest providers were the Protestant churches, having established over one thousand colleges in all. Pace (1972) examined the history and present status of these colleges for the Carnegie Commission and drew up a typology which enabled him to scale the colleges according to their degree of affiliation to their sponsoring Church. He found that some of these colleges had formally shed their legal ties with their founding Church and a large percentage of the rest remained only loosely associated. Interestingly it was this latter group of institutions, with environments which were 'tepid' both academically and spiritually, which he discovered to be having greatest recruitment difficulties and at most risk of closure. On the other hand those colleges which emphasized their Protestant links, and these were mainly the evangelical and fundamentalist colleges, appeared to have a secure future.

The Roman Catholic Church opened its first college in the United States in 1789, and throughout the nineteenth century there was a steady growth of small Catholic colleges designed largely to preserve the faith of the few Catholic laymen from the immigrant ghettoes who aspired to higher education (Greeley 1969). However, most of the growth in Catholic higher education took place this century and student enrolments rose from 32,000 in 1916 to almost half a million. Although there are about three hundred Roman Catholic colleges and universities, many of these are small and about forty per cent of the total Catholic student population attends one of the twenty-one big institutes such as Notre Dame, Fordham and St Louis.

In recent years, particularly following Vatican II, there has been considerable questioning within the Catholic university sector as to its place and purpose. This has been facilitated by such groups as the International Federation of Catholic Universities which have provided enabling services for debate and discussion (McCluskey 1970; International Federation of Catholic Universities 1974, 1979). Despite a significant element of secularization within many of these universities, they still remain recognizably religious institutions both in terms of their structures and their processes. Even if the truly Christian university is unlikely to be ever realized, nevertheless it remains an ideal type against which other religious institutions measure themselves.

The English Universities

Many have argued that there has been no need to establish a Christian university in England because in a number of very significant ways Oxford and Cambridge already approximate to this model. Certainly in terms of their history they could be described as Christian universities and although they have undergone a gradual process of secularization nevertheless the Christian ethos is still pervasive and evident.

A visitor looking down from the top of the university church in Oxford gains the distinct impression of an ecclesiastical landscape — quadrangles, towers, spires, stained glass windows, pointed arches and chapel buildings. He is quite likely to hear a bell: whether it is summoning the faithful to worship in the college chapel, or the hungry hordes to supper in the dining hall, it sounds religious.

To what extent is Oxford underpinned still by Christian assumptions, traditions and trappings? Somewhere in almost every college will be the chapel; not the centre of life for most students but nevertheless a close and accessible symbol of Christianity. Daily services and Sunday sermons preached by the distinguished are likely to impinge upon a high proportion of resident students in a way that would be impossible in a polytechnic. Although the norm of the resident chaplain who is also a teaching fellow has been abandoned in most colleges, and in some instances the chaplain's post is held in conjunction with a city curacy, still virtually every college has a designated chaplain who can get to know his people in a way that would be the envy of most other university chaplains. Three of the college chapels, Magdalen, New College and Christ Church, have choir schools attached, and as a result they draw congregations from outside the college.

The role of Visitor of a college has a symbolic importance which is easy to minimize. Most other universities choose a prominent secular member from 'the great and the good' but in Oxford sixteen of the colleges have a bishop. The Bishop of Winchester is Visitor to five colleges, the Archbishop of Canterbury to four and the Bishop of Lincoln to two. Many of the colleges are also patrons of a number of parishes, which involves finding new incumbents and maintaining satisfactory long-term links with those parishes.

The titles of twelve of the colleges are religious, comprising six saints; Jesus, Trinity, All Souls, Corpus Christi, Magdalen and Christ Church. The merging of the religious and the academic is highlighted by Christ Church. The position of Christ Church is unique in that the college chapel is also the cathedral for the Diocese of Oxford, and the head of the college is also dean of the cathedral. Apart from the Dean, and the Archdeacon of Oxford who is also sub dean of the college, four of the five residentiary canonries are annexed to chairs of theology. At the student level several places, academic clerkships, are awarded to those who sing in the cathedral choir.

Although the university consists of a federation of colleges, at the same time it has an over-arching structure of its own. This too has its quota of ecclesiastical symbols and customs. Right at the centre of the university, in Radcliffe Square, stands the university church. The University Statutes declare that 'in the week preceding each Full Term, the Holy Communion according to the Liturgy of the Church of England shall be celebrated by the Vice Chancellor or some person appointed by him in the Church at St. Mary the Virgin . . .' (*Statutes, Decrees and Regulations of the University of Oxford* 1980, p.659). Each Sunday in term a university sermon is preached at the morning service and the regulations limit the choice of preacher as follows: 'The Vice Chancellor and Committee may use such liberty in nominating Preachers as may be exercised by a Diocesan Bishop in accordance with the Resolutions of the Convocations of the Church of England' (Ibid, p.661).

Upon admission to the degree of MA, the ceremony in the Sheldonian has the distinct flavour of an ordination service. Candidates kneel in front of the vice-chancellor who inducts each of them into the MA status by tapping their heads with a book and pronouncing the admission formula which starts and ends with ecclesiastical language. When the vice-chancellor reaches the final words 'in the name of God, Father Son and Holy Spirit' he is to 'reverently bare his head'.

The faculty of theology is thoroughly Christian and implicitly Anglican in its style. The Lady Margaret Professor of Divinity is required to be a priest of the Church of England, and the other main chairs, in terms of their job descriptions, could not be held by non-Christians. For example the Nolloth Professor of the Philosophy of Religion is required to 'lecture and give instruction in the philosophy of the *Christian religion* including Apologetics, that is the setting forth of the *reasonableness* as well as the authority of the Christian religion . . .' (author's italics).

Whatever may be thought about these job designations at least they are consistent with the content of the courses to be taught. The Honours school of theology is specifically Christian in its content and assumptions. Each candidate is required to take four papers in biblical studies, four in Christian doctrine and one or two other papers from a list of subjects most of which are Christian in their orientation. There is but one option in world religions and even the sociology of religion paper is largely about the Christian religion or deviations thereof. The Diploma in Theology follows roughly the same balance although with fewer papers.

The original purpose of the faculty of theology was to provide an academic grounding in theology for prospective priests in the Church of England. In practical terms this is still a significant issue although the basis is more ecumenical now. If there is any truth in the dictum that 'the Church is being killed by degrees' then Oxford would carry a good share of the blame. The faculty of theology is closely linked with the various denominational theological colleges in Oxford for their increasingly rigorous academic training requirements have produced a constant flow of students into the faculty at both first degree and higher degree levels. The only degree in Oxford that can be studied on a completely non-residential basis is the Bachelor of Divinity: a higher degree specifically designed to enable clergy who are also Oxford graduates to continue their academic studies while working in a parish.

There are ten institutes for theological training in Oxford and each has a close association with the university varying from full college status to recognized institution rights. The three Anglican theological colleges are able to metriculate a total of twenty-five students each year into the university and these are in addition to Oxbridge students who would already have university membership. These three colleges were instrumental in negotiating a university-validated Certificate in Theology which covers most of the requirements of the Church of England's General Ordination Examination.

A number of other institutes of a Christian foundation exist. Perhaps the most prominent has been Pusey House, dedicated to the promotion of Anglo-Catholic ideals within the university. The house has provided residence, library and meeting facilities for students, and its chapel with its Anglo-Catholic ritual and range of impressive preachers has had a significant impact on many students. Several of the religious orders run hostels for students and there is the full range of central chaplaincy services provided by each of the denominations: noteworthy in terms of student drawing power is the Catholic Chaplaincy. The evangelical focus is to be found in the Christian Union, and the two Anglican Churches of St Aldates and St Ebbes.

Oxford has been examined in detail in order to illustrate some of the structural, institutional elements which suggest that in some very real senses it is a Christian university. The same study of Cambridge would reveal many similar features.

The two nineteenth-century foundations of Durham and King's College London, being modelled on Oxbridge, again reveal in their structures clear signs of ecclesiastical bias. In Durham there has been a tradition that both the bishop of the diocese and the dean of the cathedral should be persons of high academic standing in order that they can visibly link church and university. In recent years the University of London has accepted the Jesuit Heythrop College as a full college within the university. Indeed a collegiate structure allows a university to contain within itself a diversity of styles of institution.

A random sample of one thousand Church of England clergy taken from the 1979 edition of *Crockford's Clerical Directory* revealed that one in three are Oxbridge graduates (Cambridge 17 per cent and Oxford 16.7 per cent), a further 10.5 per cent are graduates of King's College London and 9.2 per cent are graduates of Durham. If one adds to this the number of clergy who were trained at the associated theological colleges but who are not graduates of any of these universities, then the importance within the ecclesiastical tradition of Oxbridge, King's College London and Durham becomes even clearer.

The other English universities reveal little in the way of structural bias: the only exception being in the teaching of theology. Where a university has a faculty of theology it is normal to find that the predominant concerns are with Christianity, but such a weighting could well be justified on educational grounds. Few would accuse the faculties of modern languages of racial bias for having a greater concentration on French than on Swahili. In the Universities of Manchester and Bristol the faculties of theology are closely related to the theological colleges: at Manchester to the three Free Church colleges and at Bristol to the combined Church of England college and the two Free Church colleges. The role of the universities in validating courses in teacher training has tended to heighten the Christian emphasis. Only at the University of Lancaster has there developed a department of religious studies in which Christianity is not the predominant concern. However, the long-term effects of the Lancaster style should not be under-estimated for their style was widely publicized and at a time when most university faculties of theology were experiencing recruitment difficulties, Lancaster was always over-subscribed. Furthermore the two major Schools Council projects on primary and secondary religious education were Lancaster based, and thus the diffusion of the Lancaster 'phenomenological' approach through the school system has been very significant. One university, Liverpool, is forbidden by statute to teach theology.

All universities have chaplaincy provision as part of their general service to students (General Synod 1980a). In one or two cases, such as the University of Exeter, this chaplaincy provision is formally integrated into the university structure, but in most instances chaplains are provided by the various Churches and work on a consumer-attraction basis. Where the chaplaincy is housed in a local church, its marginal position in relation to the central concerns of the university is particularly highlighted. On most campuses religion competes openly for student support with other interest areas and it is often the non-established forms of Christian involvement, such as the Christian Union and the charismatic groups, which are most evident.

The English Polytechnics and Institutes of Higher Education

It is difficult to find much structural bias in favour of religion in the polytechnic system. Their secular origins and predominant concerns mean that the religious dimension does not intrude much into the day-to-day work. Chaplaincy provision, in comparison to universities, is sparse, and the problems of relating to a scattered and mainly non-resident clientele are enormous. Since the mid-1970s a number of polytechnics have inherited a teacher-training role from a merged college of education and included in this has been a strong normative element of a Christian type. Most primary school teachers are expected to teach religious education along Christian lines and a proportion of them would take religious studies as a main academic subject. However, the progressive cut back in teacher training and the particular vulnerability of the polytechnic teacher training sector is likely to remove this temporary religious intrusion into an otherwise predominantly secular sector.

It is among the institutes of higher education, the so-called third sector, that the evidence of structural bias is most substantial. Until 1870 virtually all the schools in England were provided by the Church and so it was natural that the Church should also provide training institutions for teachers and it was not until after the Cross Commission of 1890 that the state began to provide its own training colleges.

During the period up to the Second World War both the Church of England and the Roman Catholic Church continued to expand the numbers in their colleges, although the proportion in Church colleges relative to those in state colleges gradually declined. The mushrooming demand during the 1960s for teacher-training places was a great challenge to both Churches and between 1963 and 1970 the Church of England's numbers doubled to 18,000 and the Roman Catholic Church's numbers went up from 4500 to 11,000. In addition were the two methodist colleges and the one of the Free Church, which in all gave the Church a total stake in teacher training of about twenty-eight per cent. This presented the high spot in the Church's numerical involvement in teacher training (Gedge 1974).

The events of the last ten years are too recent to need close documentation. Despite the so-called massacre of the colleges of education (Hencke 1978) the Church's structural involvement has remained, although at a reduced scale, through its surviving colleges of education, which have now become diversified colleges of higher education.

Both the Roman Catholic Church and the Church of England retain enough colleges to give them a formal stake in the future educational system of this country (see Table 20). In addition, the Methodists keep a toe-hold in the system through their small free-standing Westminster College, and also through Southlands College which is now a constituent element of the Roehampton Institute. The control structures for this newly-emerging third sector of higher education are still being developed and the futures of some of these institutions are now being seriously questioned. It is difficult therefore at this stage to know whether we are talking of a slimmed-down but viable Chuch sector for the future (Gay 1979) or of an historical remnant which will soon 'wither away on the vine'.

Scotland, Wales and Ireland

In Scotland, ministerial training for the Church of Scotland (Presbyterian) is totally integrated into the university system. The four universities of Edinburgh, St Andrews, Glasgow and Aberdeen have faculties of divinity and colleges of ministerial training and in each case the principal of the college is also a senior member of the faculty of divinity. The Church of Scotland has a committee for 'Church representation on the University

Boards of nomination'. Thus the faculties of theology are heavily Christian in their orientation and at a practical level concerned significantly with the academic element of ministerial training. Two of the present colleges of education are Roman Catholic and the rest are state controlled.

TABLE 20
The Church colleges of higher education

ROMAN CATHOLIC

1 Free-standing institutions

> De la Salle College, Manchester
> La Sainte Union, Southampton
> Newman, Birmingham
> St. Mary's, Strawberry Hill, London
> St. Mary's, Fenham, Newcastle upon Tyne
> Trinity and All Saints, Leeds

2 Colleges within a federal structure

> Christ's College `}` Liverpool Institute of Higher Education
> Notre Dame
> Digby Stuart: Roehampton Institute of Higher Education

CHURCH OF ENGLAND

1 Free-standing institutions

> Christ Church, Canterbury
> Trinity, Carmarthen
> St. Paul and St. Mary, Cheltenham
> The College, Chester
> St. Martin's, Lancaster
> Bishop Grosseteste, Lincoln
> St. Mark and St. John, Plymouth
> King Alfred's, Winchester
> Ripon and York St. John

2 Colleges within a federal structure

> St. Katharine's, Liverpool: Liverpool Institute of Higher Education
> Whitelands, London: Roehampton Institute of Higher Education

3 Colleges which have merged with another institution to form a new voluntary institute

> Bishop Otter, Chichester: part of the West Sussex Institute of
> Higher Education
> Derby Lonsdale, Derby: part of the Derby Lonsdale College of
> Higher Education

The Welsh system approximates more closely to the English one. The University of Wales is secular in orientation, although its theological faculties are Christian in emphasis, and through the schools of theology and associated theological colleges the faculties are significantly concerned with ministerial training. St David's College Lampeter, founded on the Oxbridge model by the Church of Wales in 1822, has a clear religious bias. For many years most of its graduates entered the ministry and until 1975 the principal had always been a cleric. There is a strong department of theology whose head carries the title of Professor of *Pastoral* Theology (author's italics). Trinity College Carmarthen is a Church of Wales college of higher education.

In Ireland it is extremely difficult to separate out the religious element from the general cultural and historical matrix within which it is set. Political ideologies are given religious form and thus issues which appear in religious clothing may in fact be expressions of something very different. However, it is beyond the scope of this paper to give a detailed analysis of education and society in Ireland.

In structural terms, schooling in Northern Ireland is segregated and teacher-training provision inevitably follows suit. Stranmillis College Belfast, founded in 1922, was intended to be inter-denominational, but from 1925 onwards Roman Catholic men ceased to attend and switched instead to the Roman Catholic women's college of St Mary's Belfast which had been opened in 1900. In 1961 the men's department transferred to separate premises at St Joseph's College Belfast, and so in practice Stranmillis College became a Protestant college. As long as the school system remains segregated, teacher training is likely to as well. The rest of higher education is integrated, although it could be argued that it is implicitly Protestant: eg the faculty of theology at Queen's University Belfast is staffed by recognized teachers from the Protestant theological colleges.

In the Republic, University College Dublin was founded in 1851 by John Henry Newman as the Catholic University in Ireland. Much has been written about Newman's educational ideals and it does seem that he visualized the Catholic university as being open and free, particularly when it was set in the context of a Catholic country (Newman 1910; Ker 1975; Coulson 1976). Newman was increasingly critical of attempts to exert ecclesiastical control over the university and he saw a clear distinction between a Catholic university and a clerical university. In 1908 the National University of Ireland was established, with its three constituent colleges of Dublin, Galway and Cork, and as the state was reluctant to encroach upon the Church's preserve there was to be no faculty of theology. Furthermore, religious education and moral education were not included in some of the university's professional teaching qualifications, and no provision was made for training specialist teachers in religious education (McClelland 1980). Such teaching in schools is normally done by teachers with first degrees in other subjects, by clerics and religious.

Trinity College Dublin was founded to educate the Protestant ruling class and at various periods the Roman Catholic bishops prohibited Catholics from attending. Fitzgibbon (1981) shows that with the lifting of this ban the proportion of Protestants to Catholics gradually balanced out during the 1960s. She concludes that in the near future the proportions in the college are likely to reflect the overall population structure in terms of religious composition.

St Patrick's College Maynooth is now recognized as a constituent college of the university and until recently was devoted entirely to seminary training. Since 1966 the college has diversified, although the clerical influence is still paramount. The four colleges of education are all Roman Catholic and are concerned primarily with providing catholic teachers for catholic schools.

RELIGION AND THE PROCESSES OF HIGHER EDUCATION

This section reviews some of the evidence relating to the way the religious variable operates within higher education. It is suggested that in a number of Church-related institutions a student's religious beliefs and practices may be maintained or even enhanced, but that in the majority of institutions strong secularizing forces are dominant. In a small minority of cases the processes are *explicitly* biased in favour of religion, whilst in the vast majority of instances they are *implicitly* biased against religion.

The Development of Religious Attitudes

Children's religious attitudes are largely a product of home and to a lesser extent of school influences. In terms of religious autonomy the critical time appears to be in the mid-teens. Argyle (1975, p.59) has described adolescence as 'the age of religious awakening, during which time people either become converted or decide to abandon their childhood faith, if they had one'. Studies of 'conversion' show a peak around the age of fifteen or sixteen and it is assumed that those who make a decision to become irreligious do so at about the same time.

Most investigations of college and university students' religious beliefs and practices bear out this hypothesis. Feldman (1969, p.47), reviewing a large number of surveys in the United States, concluded that according to students' self-reports, marked change in religious orientation is as likely to begin in high school as in college. Thalheimer (1973) discovered that most college staff had veered away from religion in their pre-college period of academic training, and similar conclusions were reached by Hoge and Keeter (1976) and Hastings and Hoge (1976).

British surveys have tended to replicate these American findings. Pilkington and Poppleton (1976, p.9) conclude that university does not have much effect on a student's religious beliefs, but rather 'it seems likely that the important factors bringing about a movement away from religious beliefs and practice occur before students enter the university at all.' Wright and Cox (1967, 1971) investigated the changes in religious and moral beliefs of sixth-formers between 1963 and 1970 and found that among these pupils a highly significant decline in religious belief and practice took place. Hornsby-Smith et al. (1976) attempted to follow up evidence that there was a major decline in attendance at Mass before the fifth year.

It has to be admitted that the techniques for investigating religious changes and for determining their causes are still at an early stage of development. Nevertheless there is sufficient evidence to suggest reasonably conclusively that major changes in religious orientation tend to occur around the age of fifteen or possibly earlier (Martin and Pluck 1976), and that while the change is multi-directional, it is predominantly away from religious belief and practice.

Religion and the Curriculum
There has been a long-standing fear that the *hidden* curriculum of higher education is strongly biased against religion. At an organizational level concern has been expressed through the University Teachers Group and the newly formed Higher Education Foundation. Sider (1976) argues that although the days of militant campus atheism are gone, most secular universities foster non-religious views in subtle ways. The increasingly common attitude is that one need only worry about small manageable questions and that no general world view is necessary. Moberley (1949) warned that practical atheism is normally much more effective than the more militant variety and by adopting a neutral stance the university implies that religion does not matter. Bereday and Lauwerys (1966, p.17) concluded that 'impartiality to all beliefs tends to have as its effect support for unbelief'. In a recent publication (Working Party on Christian Involvement in Higher Education 1978) the Church of England recognizes that education cannot be value-free and so attempts to draw guide-lines for the inclusion of Christian values in the curriculum. It also examines the type of curriculum a Christian college might offer. Indeed the whole area of values education has become a growth industry in American education.

That there is a direct relationship between religion and the *explicit* curriculum becomes clear upon reflection on the lack of Quaker military scientists or Christian Science doctors. But in most cases the relationship is more complex. There is generally assumed to be a logical conflict between science and religion, and this is borne out by surveys which show the disproportionate number of scientists to population as a whole who are atheists (Argyle 1975). Furthermore, Datta (1967, p.627) found that 'the results of a series of studies extending from 1926 to 1965 have indicated that eminent American scientists are not a random sample of the general population of Church members' and that Catholics, Baptists, Methodists and Lutherans were under-represented. Values attributed to Catholics are generally considered to be incongruent with scientific attitudes and those attributed to liberal Protestants and post-ghetto Judaism are generally considered congruent. Merton (1968, pp.628-660) found that Calvinistic doctrine was intrinsically hospitable to science.

However, although there is a higher proportion of atheists among scientists, and although it seems that certain forms of religious organization are in potential conflict with scientific developments, Lehman and Shriver (1968) found in a pilot study in one American university that the scientist/non-scientist dichotomy did not successfully predict religiosity scores. Consequently, further investigations were carried out in fifteen universities and he discovered that it was more useful to focus on subject matter than on method (Lehman 1974). His resultant scholarly distance theory took as the critical variable whether the discipline involved the study of religion. Those disciplines such as psychology which do study religion were termed 'low-distance' subjects, and those such as physics which do not study religion were 'high-distance' subjects. In high-distance fields, because religion is not an object of inquiry, it is not seen as problematic, whereas low-distance subjects tend to produce lower levels of religiosity. He found that among the secular universities and faculties scholarly distance was a predictive factor of levels of religiosity whereas the scientific/non-scientific dichotomy was not. On these campuses, faculty in low-distance disciplines share norms that tend to proscribe personal involvement in religious institutions. However, on Church-related campuses the concentration of clerics in non-science areas and in disciplines involving the study of religion meant that the scholarly distance theory was reversed and the norms in these faculties tended to prescribe traditional religious involvement.

Feldman and Newcomb (1969) quote two studies, both of which illustrate the apparent eroding force of the social sciences. At one college the curricula causing the most loss in traditional religious values were the humanities, the social sciences, and industrial administration, while those causing least loss were chemistry, physics and engineering. At the other college, social science caused the greater loss while physical education the least loss. Entwistle and Wilson's work in England (1977, p.108) accords with these findings in that 'sociologists showed distinctive social attitudes. They were tough minded radicals whose syllabus freedom was associated with unstable extraversion. They had high political and low religious values.' Argyle (1975, pp.92-3) feels that it is psychology in particular that produces low levels of religiosity and advances as reasons self-selection and the relativizing effect of the subject. In a study in this country McLeish (1970) found that students studying the physical sciences tended to be high on the religious values scores whereas students studying humanities were low. Pilkington and Poppleton (1976) show that both in 1961 and in 1972 students in education and medicine had high levels of religiosity.

Firm conclusions, in the light of the available evidence, are difficult to draw. Certainly the problems caused by self-selection and differential recruitment need careful examination: is it that potentially irreligious people are more likely to choose to study the social sciences? Some of the contradictions in the survey findings point to a need for a more broad-based and systematic analysis with more of the variables held constant. However the following basic patterns seem to emerge. After allowing for a small percentage of explicitly atheist scientists, the 'high-distance' effect of science tends to allow for higher levels of religiosity. The humane vocational subjects of medicine and education are also congruent with higher levels of religiosity. There appears to be a conflict in the evidence relating to the humanities, probably resulting from the varied usage of a term which covers such a wide variety of component elements. The social sciences, particularly sociology and psychology are strongly related to low levels of religiosity. Theology too is a 'low-distance' subject and the academic study of religion can have a very disturbing effect on a student's religious beliefs, but unfortunately there is little published empirical evidence in this area.

Sex Differences in Religious Behaviour and Beliefs
Available information on sex differences in religious practice and beliefs reveal that such differences are considerable. Argyle (1975, p.71), reviewing the evidence, concludes 'it is obvious that women are more religious on every criteria'. Similar conclusions are reached in America through work which synthesizes survey material. Feldman (1969a, pp.13-14) found that women scored high on the religious value scale and Parker (1971, p.731) decided that 'the overriding conclusion to be reached is that women are more religious and generally more conservative in their beliefs.' Moberg and McEnery (1976, p.54) sampled the students of Marquette University, one of the largest Catholic universities in the United States, in 1961 and again in 1971 and they comment 'typical patterns of higher conformity to Church norms among females than males . . . was observed.' In a study in England, Entwistle and Wilson (1977, p.104) found that women 'had overall higher scores on neuroticism, tender-mindedness and religious values . . . .'

While there seems to be a general agreement about women's higher religious base-line, there is some uncertainty about changes in religiosity while at college. Feldham (1969) found that women were more likely than men to report increased religiosity while at college and less likely to report decreased religiosity. A longitudinal study by Farley et al. (1977) found that both men and women increased in commitment to religion and also that in the two decades between 1950 and 1970 women's general religious values appeared to be changing faster than men's. However, in studies in this country Pilkington et al. and Poppleton (1965; 1976) found that women students moved away from religion more than men in their three years at college: a finding replicated for girl sixth-formers by Wright and Cox (1971). While this could be explained by an increased emphasis on equality and similarity between the sexes, and also in terms of a sex time-lag in a levelling-down process in religious commitment, Pilkington and Poppleton (1976, p.5) conclude 'it is significant, however, that it is the women who have tended to conform to the men's rather irreligious norms rather than the reverse . . . .' It may well be that this conformity to dominant norms is the crucial issue, for in America Feldman and Newcomb (1969) discovered that women had a strong tendency to move towards the college norms. In his study of an Anglican college of education Seaman (1978, p.119) comes to a similar conclusion. It would be interesting to know whether the sex ratio of a college exerts any impact on students' beliefs and practices. Astin (1977, p.69) found that attendance at an all-male college led to an increase in traditional religious affiliation.

Student Beliefs

There are great problems in attempting to assess student beliefs and the methodological complexities mean that most conclusions have to be treated with considerable caution.

A number of longitudinal studies indicate an element of decline in religious beliefs among the students investigated. Heath (1968) measured the religious attitudes of students in a small liberal arts college in the United States and found that between 1948 and 1968 there had been a clear decline in religious orthodoxy. Hoge (1974) carried out a replication of earlier studies in twelve United States colleges and universities, some dating back to 1906, and found a long-term liberalization of religious attitudes and a decrease in religious observance. He carried out a further more detailed survey in two colleges in the United States (Hoge 1976), using identical questionnaires. He found that feelings of need for some sort of religious faith or personal philosophy dropped consistently from 1952 to 1974: 'in sum, in the area of religion a sharp decline occurred in traditional religious beliefs from the early 1950s to the late 1960s, with little change since, but Church participation has declined since 1968-69' (p.158). However, when he looked at what he termed the 'basic' religious beliefs, he found that these had hardly altered from 1968 to 1974. Setting his findings against previous research, he concludes:

'All the research indicates that the trends towards less religious orthodoxy and Church participation during the 1960s are continuing in the 1970s . . . . Institutional religious life has dropped more than personal religious life. The new mood among students in the 1970s appears to be a retreat from the political activism of the 1960s, but no deviation from the trend towards individualism and experimentation in religion.' (Hastings and Hoge 1976, p.238)

However, a replication survey carried out at Michigan, Cornell and Dartmouth in the 1950s and again in 1972 found that in all three institutions the commitment to religion grew (Farley 1977).

In England, Pilkington and Poppleton (1976, p.2) quote a longitudinal survey of students at Sheffield University in 1961 and again in 1972 and conclude: 'it is quite clear . . . that by 1972 as compared with 1961, there had been a massive and statistically significant movement away from religion on the part of the students.' They were unable to assign any reasons to account for this decline. A similar movement away from religious belief and practice is reported by Wright and Cox (1967, 1971) in a study of sixth formers over the period 1963 to 1970. Although as yet the evidence is slender there does appear to be a distinction made in practice between being personally religious and participating at an institutional level in religion, and it is this latter element which has suffered the most erosion.

Staff Beliefs

In respect of staff beliefs much of the information once again relates to the American scene and so this will be examined first. Hoge and Keeter (1976) reviewing past research concluded that college teachers were less traditionally religious in their beliefs and practices than was the general population. The precise reasons for this were uncertain, although Thalheimer (1973) argued strongly that it was the result of a self-selection process: a higher percentage of agnostics tended to become academics rather than it being the direct result of academic activity. Hoge and Keeter (1976, p.230) found that teachers tended to be lower in religiosity who had a higher scholarly productivity, spent more time in basic research, saw themselves as intellectuals and felt uncomfortably different from non-academics. Conversely teachers had a higher religiosity who had been longer in their jobs, saw themselves as being relatively committed to their college, considered it important to be liked by different kinds of people and felt free to speak out on controversial issues.

De Jong and Faulkner (1972) interviewed a sample of the faculty at a large American state university and discovered that few of them totally rejected the traditional aspects of religion, so they could not fulfil the stereotype of the atheist professor. Over half of them belonged to a Church, attended services regularly and reckoned that church membership and prayer were important to their lives. However, when viewed against traditional Christian teachings, their beliefs showed a marked departure from the orthodox. De Jong and Faulkner conclude that what emerges is a picture of intellectuals who have rather thoroughly de-mythologized the core beliefs of the Christian faith but still continue to take part in church activities and worship.

The experience of Protestant colleges in the United States has been that when secular values become accepted into the normative structure of the college then most faculty quickly cease to take any explicit religious stance in their dealings with students, and any religious beliefs the staff may have become reserved for the private sphere. Kratcoski (1972, p.25), reviewing the present state of Catholic higher education, concludes that it is walking a tightrope between developing its academic standards and not abandoning the moral and spiritual sides. In this latter area he feels that the role of the faculty is crucial: 'If the value-specifics of Catholic higher education are to be retained and broadened, the faculty must play a major role, either directly through classroom instruction or indirectly through example and informal interaction with students.' He surveyed the faculty of five small Catholic colleges, and found that eighty-eight per cent considered it an important part of their teaching function to advance the aims of the college and eighty-four per cent were committed to influencing character development. A comparable survey by Hubery in a large state university found that only forty-six per cent of the faculty saw the moral development of students as part of their concern (quoted in Kratcoski 1972).

There is little empirical evidence relating to staff beliefs in England, but we may assume that some of the processes involved in American higher education are also found here. There is some information from studies of humanism in Britain that teachers and lecturers are disproportionately represented among the membership of groups such as the British Humanist Association (Campbell 1971, p.95). Whatever the factual basis of the recent debate over Marxist influence in British universities and colleges, it does reveal that in the popular imagination there is a deep-seated suspicion that many higher education teachers are atypical in their beliefs and attitudes. In this country, where church-going is not so much a part of the way of life as it is in America, a secularization of intellectual belief is likely to be accompanied by a cessation of religious practice.

The Effects of the College Environment on Religion

Does the college environment have an effect on the religious beliefs and practices of its students? An early study by Jacob (1957) queried the ability of higher education to change students' basic characteristics and he concluded that 'religious beliefs and the values thereto, have been remarkably persistent through college regardless of institution or the time when students were in college' (p.56). In 1961 Astin argued that the college 'product' was more dependent on the characteristics of the students entering than upon the influence of the college itself. Similarly Hastings and Hoge's (1976) research concluded that a lack of change in religiosity from college class to college class both in 1967 and in 1974 indicated that the impact of college on students' religion was quite weak. In this country, Pilkington and Poppleton (1976, p.9), examining the survey results over the three-year range of students at Sheffield University both in 1961 and 1972, suggested 'that the experience of university is not in itself an important factor in affecting religious attitudes.'

Feldman, following up his general work with Newcomb on the impact of American colleges upon their students, wrote two articles (1969a, 1969b) on the effect of colleges on religion. Taking as his research question, 'Do American students typically change in their orientation to religion in their undergraduate years?' he found that 'the average score on the religious scale decreases . . . with year in college' (1969a, p.42). A series of studies showed mean changes indicating that seniors, compared with freshmen, were somewhat less orthodox, fundamentalistic, or conventional in religious orientation, more sceptical about the existence of a Supreme Being, more likely to see God in impersonal terms and less favourable to the Church as an institution. This was reflected in change of religious practice, for Feldman found that church attendance and religious participation declined with time at college. These findings are echoed by Parker (1971), who found that of twenty-nine surveys examined, seventeen reported a predominant change from orthodox or conservative religious beliefs to liberal or secular ones during a student's time at college.

Unfortunately in this country the amount of similar material is rather slender. McLeish (1973, p.419), reporting on a survey of ten colleges of education in East Anglia, concluded that 'students over a period of three years, change in the direction of the lecturers' and tutors' views in so far as they tend to move from a religious conservatism to a secular humanism.' Generalizing from the evidence available, McLeish felt that the basic pattern of change as a result of the college experience was a tendency to lose faith in religion and to develop radical viewpoints (p.421).

It has been argued that such changes in religious stance could be a normal result of aging, but Argyle (1975, p.35), quoting from control studies of young people not at college, shows that parallel changes do occur in the non-student population but to a much smaller degree. Similarly Astin (1977, p.78), in an analysis of ten years of longitudinal data, found that dormitory students were no less religious than students living with parents at the beginning of the college course, but they were substantially less religious four years later.

Students vary greatly both between and within institutions, and statistics of general trends can mask some very significant counter-movements. Feldman (1969a), drawing on studies which use a methodology which does not mask these movements, found that religious change could be multi-directional. He discovered that in many cases the average trend away from religion was small and that 'at some colleges the number of students experiencing increased religiosity more than counterbalances the number manifesting a decline' (Feldman 1969b, p.123). As a result of this he decided that the influence of most college environments on students was neither direct nor uniform but rather indirect and diffuse (1969a, p.53).

That most college environments do not have a consistent unidirectional impact on student religion reflects the fact that most colleges and curricula are not designed to have any specified impact on religious views. Feldman (1969b, p.123) found that in the majority of American colleges there was 'a deliberate avoidance of institutional policies concerning the particular direction of change in religious outlook that the college should promote, although there might be statements about desired college outcomes in terms of the student character.' However, whatever the official intentions of the colleges, their environments do have considerable impact on students' religious beliefs as students themselves report direct challenges and direct reinforcements (Feldman 1969b, pp.123-4). The higher education scene in both the United States and in England consists of a diversity of types of institution varying along the spectrum from explicitly religious to implicitly anti-religious. Because of the opportunity for student choice, differential recruitment means that students may be already typically different in their religious outlooks and commitments as they enter different colleges.

Although the religious issues may not be the critical ones in reaching a decision, Feldman feels 'that the non-religious criteria students use in picking a college may be associated empirically with certain religious views' (1969b, p.106).

It would seem from the evidence that colleges, intentionally or otherwise, do have an impact on students' religion and although significant movements in the direction of increased religiosity are reported, on average the trend is towards a more liberal humanist position.

CONCLUSION

How is the evidence to be interpreted? There does seem to be a certain structural bias in favour of religion in so far as a few institutions have explicitly religious features embedded within themselves. However, whether this is unfair is a matter for debate. A pluralist system may need a sprinkling of value-laden institutions to challenge the predominantly neutral, secularist stance of the majority. Furthermore, a proportion of the English population is explicitly religious and so it might not be unfair to have institutions of higher education reflecting their world views. Although there has been a rumour around for the last ten years of a Moslem university or college being established in England, and although for a variety of reasons such a possibility is unlikely to be realized, nevertheless the founding of a Moslem institute of higher education could be justified in terms of fairness. Whether such an institute would be desirable or acceptable is another question. The author has argued elsewhere (Gay 1979) that there should be a place within the English higher education system for a few value-laden institutions.

Although bias and descrimination are often used as interchangeable terms, it is important to recognize the distinction between them. It is assumed that discrimination relates more to individuals or small groups, whereas bias refers to structural and process characteristics at a more general level and it is this latter area which has been investigated. However, a variety of organizations were contacted who might have had evidence of religious discrimination, but in most cases they were unable to report anything more than isolated incidents.

Evidence of religious discrimination against individuals or small groups is much easier to detect than more fundamental but less obvious structural and process biases. Discrimination is usually blatant whilst bias is deep-seated, subtle and complex. Perhaps one of the most important but least researched areas of religious bias in higher education is in the area of the curriculum. Interestingly this issue is being well researched at the school level where questions such as the selection of course content, teacher attitudes and expectations, styles of teaching, methods of examination and assessment, and a variety of other related areas have been under discussion. It is the author's hunch that much of the higher education curriculum is implicitly anti-religious, but as yet there is little available published evidence to relate to this assertion.

The interim conclusion reached is that in general terms higher education in Britian is biased against religion. With the partial exception of a handful of universities and the Church-related colleges of the third sector, most of the structures of higher education maintain a neutral stance towards religion. However, the processes of higher education, whether intentionally or otherwise, exert strong anti-religious pressures.

LANGUAGE BIAS

Gordon Brotherston

ACADEMIC PREJUDICES IN MATTERS OF LANGUAGE

What constitutes bias in, say, sex or religion is easily enough defined, in the first instance, within the liberal-bourgeois tradition. Indeed, not to recognize how disadvantaged women have been in higher education in Britain has by now become little short of criminal, while to suggest that Jews shouldn't be let in would brand one as a don of the type that officially vanished from Cambridge a century or so ago. With language and culture, speech and manners, things are less clear-cut. For possible biases stemming from this quarter can prove to be inseparable from the actual aims of higher education in this country, from the very ethos of certain university subjects. Of course this much could once have been said of all-male medicine and Anglican theology of the past. May we then regard linguistic bias, too, as anachronistic, something that in due course may be statistically exposed and rectified? Or is its resilience of another order?

At its simplest this bias occurs when the official language of study does not coincide with the student's first language. Yet even with this innocuous proposition, what do we mean by language? If taken to be just phonetic and social, is it to be identified as national, in the sense that German and French are, or as regional, in the sense that Lowland Scots (Lallans) and West Indian are? And then are we chiefly concerned with speech, or with script and its norms of grammar (which means 'written') and orthography? (a distinction which in the system of Saussure became that between 'langue' and 'parole'). Or again, do we wish to calibrate any or all of these more or less crude alternatives according to the language theories which have held sway in higher education from the days of the medieval trivium (of logic, grammar and rhetoric) through the 'new science' of Vico, Herder and Marx, to the Structuralism and Discourse theory of our day? A masterful exposition of this intellectual and educational history can be found in the chapter on language in Raymond William's *Marxism and Literature* (1977), which has the advantage of being complemented by an equally pertinent chapter on literature.

In the actual workings of higher education in Britain today, phonetic and social language, hereafter simply called 'language', inheres in quite different ways in different academic subjects. Hence any bias narrowly specific to language will be the easier to detect and measure the less language is essential to the subject, and the more it serves as a tool to other ends.

Examples here are pure mathematics, and music, which indeed have symbolic languages and scripts of their own. And the ability to handle such subject-languages can readily emerge in contradistinction to the ability to speak or write ordinary prose; hence a student will be practically disadvantaged only in so far as learning and assessment depend nonetheless on the prose medium. At the other extreme stand subjects to which language ability is essential, at all levels. In this category we find English literature and law, where not knowing the right words and expressions is not so much an inconvenience as a radical flaw that no amount of remedial instruction can compensate for. After all, literary critics and barristers excel academically because of their memory for and prowess in words, because of an accomplishment that is a fortiori verbal.

This much alone is enough to suggest that in the first instance the 'problem' of language bias is best approached, not as part of some global theory of human behaviour, as with respect for actual and institutional usage (could using the Greek alphabet in algebra, or Latin in anatomy, amount to a 'bias'?), and for the many ways it may be defined within and beyond the directly social. In particular it suggests that language bias can be measured between poles that correspond to the 'science versus arts' principle according to which higher education in Britain is founded. How these two terms acquired their present academic meaning goes back to the rationalism of enlightenment in Europe; institutionally it begins when theology, served by the 'handmaiden' philosophy, ceases to be the central discipline and is substituted on the one hand by the exact sciences, as in the pure Positivist model of Comte, and on the other by modern 'arts' like the English introduced into Oxford in the 19th century. Not fully spelt out in England and Wales as a whole until the 1944 Education Act and later in the two-fold choice at GCE 'A' level, this division of scholastic or medieval spoils had most practical effect on the middle- and working-class students at whom the Act was directed. And it is thanks to studies of what happened to them that we have our few, yet sensitive accounts in English of what language bias feels like in practice.

In the first place science subjects attracted the working class (boys and girls) just because they seemed classless, bodies of 'pure fact' that need have no more connection with people than Einstein's physics did with his complicity in nuclear murder. Taught mainly by rote, then as now these subjects required and encouraged little critical awareness, little questioning or uncomfortable definition of the self within language and culture. For that reason they also led to spectacular failures at university, which had nothing to do with sloth. Interviewing students from Huddersfield Jackson and Marsden (1966) reported such admissions as:

> 'Yes, at university you get the chance of mixing with people from all walks of life, but none of my friends were like that. They were all doing physics. It's hard to say when I really knew anyone who wasn't doing physics. Back at school in the sixth there were a couple of arts types I

argued with — but no, I didn't *know* them. Still perhaps they were the last two. . . . I just couldn't absorb any more facts. I think I was burnt out after so many years. I'd begun to lose interest, I'd been going on for all those years and I began to think about it. Yes, for the first time I began to think what was it for? — and I couldn't absorb any more.' (pp.168-9)

According to the same study, arts subjects from school onwards, especially English, were generally avoided by males but when tackled by either sex provoked a high degree of self-awareness in language. And since local speech was generally regarded as incompatible with that of 'cultured' people, a split in loyalties could occur tantamount to bi-lingualism, to use the authors' term:

'And there were those who struggled again with the old problem of accent. This ranged from strident over-imitation of upper-class timbre to straightforward discussions at home in which the natural shift to a more educated accent was plainly argued out. ("Mother, I shall have to start speaking correctly. I can't lecture to them unless I speak correctly.") There were those who reported living through waves of feeling in which they spoke broader Yorkshire at home than their parents and better English at university than their lecturers.' (p.165)

Observations in the same vein can be gleaned from such authors as Richard Hoggart and Raymond Williams, who, like Jackson and Marsden, draw directly on their own working-class experience; and taken together they point to a web of conflicts foreshadowed in literature by Thomas Hardy's most memorable *Jude the Obscure*. True, Jude tried to get into Balliol or Biblioll College, Christminster, rather before his time. As the Master put it to him: 'judging from your description of yourself as a workingman, I venture to think that you will have a much better chance of success in life by remaining in your own sphere and sticking to your trade than by adopting any other course.' Yet so much of this dilemma, even down to details like how to go about applying, fully anticipates what post-1944 sociologists have unearthed. As Hardy relates it, the core of Jude's endeavour was his learning up the qualifying language, in those days classical Greek and Latin rather than ruling-class or 'Kings' English. For studying his Griesbach with the spiritual Sue not too far away he would sit mumbling 'strange syllables' with fervour:

' — words that had for Jude an indescribable enchantment: inexplicable sounds something like these:-
"All hemm heis Theos ho Pater, ex hou ta panta, kai hemeis eis auton:" Till the sounds rolled with reverent loudness, as a book was heard to close:-
"Kai heis Kurios Iesous Christos, di hou ta panta kai hemeis di autou!" '

When it comes, the letter of rejection changes fervour into mockery and irreverence, and for a bet Jude declaims the Latin creed in a pub. Yet only to feel remorse, to feel that Greats had all along been too great for him and that his 'University hopes' were really an unworthy desire for social success. In reporting how the obscure Jude came to recognize his 'folly', Hardy presses home his darker irony.

In one key respect Hardy's work is more incisive than much modern sociology, despite and because of the early date at which it was written. For it clearly shows the university as a ruling-class privilege, drawing the line between that class, with its bishops, statesmen and generals, and all classes below it, rather than between the working class with its poverty and communal pride, and all classes above it. Of course this can be partly explained by the fact that most English universities were founded after *Jude* was published (1895) and that only later did Oxbridge allow the foundation of such 'popular' colleges as Ruskin, referred to by Hardy as Jude's in the preface to the second edition (1912). Yet dramatic as it was, particularly in the wake of the 1944 Act and in other areas of higher education, this growth left untouched the ruling class that spurned Jude and scarcely tampered with its privilege. The mechanisms by which the privilege is exercised will be well enough known and include contract between the college and a given private school, for which places are expressly or tacitly reserved. In any case, Oxford demands qualifications which the state system is so ill-equipped to provide that the majority of its entrants now in 1981 again come from private schools, just as before the 1944 Act.

Though tiny, this privileged group wields enormous power, and has as much hold as ever over the Civil Service, for example. Forged not just at Oxbridge but at the private schools which feed it, the ethos of the group is acerbically described by Alasdair MacIntyre (1967) in his three-class analysis of English society. He picks out such factors as 'loyalty to the group and the cultivation of a corresponding feeling that there are really no limits to what you may do to outsiders'; 'a very strong sense of continuity with a past which is largely the product of genealogical imagination'; and 'its antipathy to careerism, an antipathy which is accompanied by a feeling that members of this particular group have a *right* to a certain sort of job' (pp.38-9). And overall he emphasizes that 'it is the solidarizing function of the rituals that are important in binding the class together'. In this perspective 'higher education' and 'language bias' acquire quite different meanings. For Oxbridge proves to be not tutors who enlighten you but the place that teaches you the higher rituals of power, rituals to which are essential speech and manners that may be disguised or played down but may never be appropriated by outsiders. Testified to by every true statistic of English capital, the distinctive and superior role of Oxbridge is confirmed by the tendency for ruling-class sons who fail to get in to be sent somewhere quite else rather than to another university or institute of higher education.

Leaving this traditional hegemony largely to one side, educational sociologists of recent decades have tended to concentrate on inequalities within the state system alone. Exposing the linguistic and other more or less covert biases against the working class has historically gone hand in hand with the introduction of comprehensive schools. This is certainly the case with Jackson and Marsden, who tease out such elusive factors as the 'shrewd' cultural complicity between the erstwhile grammar-school teacher and the middle-class parent. Similar points, for example on the difference between the old and the new middle-class parent, appear in the work of Basil Bernstein (1971-75), though in guise of rigorous analysis. So rigorous in fact that language bias as such is approached only through a theory of codes which distinguishes the 'elaborated' from the 'restricted' and between levels of complexity. Whatever view is taken of the usefulness of (or need for) this particular classification there can be no doubt that Bernstein, as he so often claims on his own behalf, quite surpasses his theoretical predecessors in US linguistics, especially the behaviourists.[1] By the same token he has received and awoken ready echoes in west Europe, for example in Ulrich Ammon's *Dialekt, Soziale Ungleichheit und Schule* (1973), and in the fundamental *Rapport Pédagogique* by P. Bourdieu and J.C. Passeron (1965).

In response to Bourdieu and Passeron's work has come a critique of both it and Bernstein's which conveniently returns us to the question raised right at the start of this essay, about the possible anachronism of language bias. This is *Education, Class Language and Ideology* by Noelle Bisseret (1979), who while acknowledging her predecessors' critical advances charges them both with what she calls 'essentialist ideology'. By this is meant any attempt educationally to distinguish between language- and say sex- or class-bias or any account of dominant language which fails to insist on its superiority as non-essential, as no more than economically and socially induced. With model clarity she starts off by showing what the term 'aptitude' has meant successively in the theory and practice of French higher education, form the 18th to the 20th centuries, dwelling on how the 19th-century bourgeois, like the post-1944 English middle class, were able to turn such definitions to their advantage in a nominally open system. She then shows how rules of grammar and conversation relate to social control, concluding her analysis with the claim that it does show

'. . . how one could stop treating language practices as if they existed in themselves, independent of the way in which they relate to one another and to the social organization of the referent. Concrete and symbolic domination is one and the same thing; power relations also exist in and through the most ordinary and everyday utterances. They do not exist before language and do not exist without language. This kind of approach breaks with the notion that a language is a neutral tool, independent of dominance relations. That linguistic unification exists does not mean that linguistic homogeneity exists, and one should give up the idea that there is a reality, 'language', considered as a factor of internal cohesion despite social conflicts. Of course one can speak of cohesion, of communication between the dominant and dominated: they can communicate with each other because their speech relates to the same referent.

'It is because they fail to recognize this that specialists in the scientific enquiry on class languges have not managed to avoid the trap of prevailing ideology according to which the dominant class sets up its own language habits as an absolute standard.' (p.143)

In principle there is nothing wrong with this scholarly hypothesis; and according to it language bias may truly be taken to be as arbitrary as that in sex, creed or class. In practice, however, the very language that conveys the statement itself assumes a kind of 'essence': that of centrality. All the examples of dominated language discussed by Bisseret and by her predecessors are defined negatively and seriatim against a central norm. However unattractive the political origins of that norm may appear, it nonetheless exists and, without it, its dependent dialects could cease to be mutually intelligible, say Lallans and West Indian in the case of written English. The practical limits here are those of translation. For example, in fostering Lallans against the class dominance of standard English, Tom Scott and Hugh McDiarmid set about translating other languages into it (eg the French of Villon), but with the one glaring exception of English itself (eg Shakespeare). That 'English' in this respect amounts to an essentially literary cannon, which indeed itself relies heavily on translated authority (above all via the King James Bible), does not and cannot modify the fact of its centrality and dominance. Certainly, any attempt to define 'national' languages like French and English without ultimate reference to their consecrated and official literature, into which Bisseret's own work of necessity incorporates itself, leads to the most arbitrary and absurd socio-linguistics of all (ie of 'native speech', 'mother tongue' etc.).

Furthermore, reluctance to admit any of this amounts to dominance in itself, for in the non-essentialist argument we are actively prevented from distinguishing between *types* of dominated language. For whatever their political similarities, Welsh and Yorkshire shepherds have linguistic resources and use linguistic codes that clearly differ in kind, vis-à-vis standard English; in no circumstances could the former be called 'dialect'. The difference Welsh represents is of the kind which since the Middle Ages has issued into nationalism and which even in recent decades has promoted cultural separatism throughout the world from the most various of socio-economic bases — among Ibo, Quechua, Hebrew, Basque, Flemish and so on. To dismiss these modern movements as sentimental or archaic or to deny the importance of language to them in practice serves just the cultural imperialism which in Britain has rigorously upheld the dominance of English, discriminating at every turn against even the most legitimate alternatives to it. Indeed the enterprise has succeeded so overwhelmingly that few English would naturally identify the Welsh with the British who formerly owned their territory or would imagine that Lear actually ruled over a British Kingdom older than Rome. And it is telling that Dr Samuel Johnson, the grammarian who largely invented what is now known as Eng. Lit., should also have devoted vast energy in the wake of the 1748 massacres to deriding the cultural integrity of the Scots. His long and uncomfortable journey to the Western Islands of Scotland in 1773 was undertaken mainly in order to deny Ossian, the hero whom English academics would never, but whom continental Europe unaminously did see as the token of a culture devoured by English greed. (The embarrassment that he could not but feel, in his own terms, before the truth and law engraved so early at Iona was avoided by the device of claiming inscriptions there to be illegible, 'incumbered with mud and rubbish'.) Only with this kind of literary awareness can language teaching in higher education ever hope to be more than the mouthpiece of political dominance (or more than simply mindless as it so often is). And only through this kind of literary inquiry can the roots of language bias be at all exposed, in the fetish of national written language, inclusive of 'dominant' and 'dominated' dialects alike.

The starkest example of language dominance in modern history in part defines that history: that begun with the invasion of the New World by Spanish and Portuguese, English and French. It is a dominance which those languages announced was complete almost from the first; already in 1492 Columbus forecast that his new hosts would not long withstand the onslaught he had begun. Yet despite massive slaughter and seizure of land, the job still hasn't been done, even now. The governments of most American states are still busy either exterminating Indians or persuading them to give up their culture. It is true that native languages have offical status in certain countries, like Guarani in Paraguay and Quechua in Peru, and in the latter case there have been attempts to revive the chair in Quechua which flourished in colonial Lima and helped actually to spread that language, through missioneering, beyond its Inca limits. Also, as a footnote to the protracted War of the Castes in Yucatan, which the Maya never formally lost, their language was declared a prerequisite for certain courses at the University of Merida. Yet overall it would be fair to say that throughout higher education in Latin America independence from Europe in fact increased the dominance of Spanish and Portuguese.

In this the example of Mexico deserves attention for several reasons. Partly because of the general dominance of Spanish and partly because of an acute historical fear of federal secession, native languages have always been heavily discriminated against, except for isolated cases like that of Maya mentioned above (which in fact has amounted to very little academically). And although with Guatemala it has the strongest pre-Columbian literary tradition of any American country, only recently has the fact been formally acknowledged, in university departments of anthropology, archeology and 'letras'. Moreover, while Nahua and Maya speakers long ago worked out their own versions of the alphabet imported from Spain (even before Tihoo became Merida in the case of the Yucatecan Maya), a proper sense of continuity, from classic precedents, is practically obscured by the scientific use of the International Phonetic and other modern alphabets to transcribe

Maya; what is gained in phonetic precision is lost culturally, as it is when King Lear is transcribed into the Initial Teaching Alphabet.

As the centre of New-World book production before the European invasion, Mexico is also the home of two scripts, unrivalled anywhere in what they can teach us about the phenomenon of written language. The one is the hieroglyphic script peculiar to the lowland Maya and tied phonetically to their language[2]; the other, iconographic, was international and used by speakers of quite different languages (Nahua, Maya, Otomonguan). Inextricable from shamanist practices still very much alive in rural Mexico, books written in the latter script still serve to educate, and pre-Columbian codes that unite number, concept and sign persist still in ritual (eg of healing) and the moral history of those rituals. In their first efforts to combat Mexico's pagan culture, Christian missionaries simply burnt these books, sensing in them, correctly, the heart of the opposition to the culture they sought to impose. And to the extent that they were right these priests were wiser than educationalists engaged in 'literacy' campaigns today who assume that technological and economic dominance means intellectual superiority and who interpret passive resistance to their efforts as stupidity. At once the subject and the teaching aid in the pre-Columbian academies (for students between 15 and 22), the pages and chapters of these books reveal the huge pedagogic power of script which is not phonetic. Its dream symbols and syntax are what the pedagogue Ezra Pound (1936) hoped to find (with Fenellosa's help) in the ideograms of China and Japan. In no circumstances can they be deemed 'non-essential', according to our earlier definition of language; and by the same token they carry none of the intellectual limitations and bias imposed of necessity by phonetic language differentiated into national norms like those of English and French.

None of the approaches to language bias taken so far has pointed to what must here be a final example and test case. This involves the distinctions between (phonetic) language that is 'good' or 'bad', in terms not just of syntax or grammar and still less of 'linguistic capital' but of diction. Traditionally uncodified in English or classified according to notions of 'style', such distinctions nonetheless play a large part in assessment at all levels of higher education, notably in 'general essay' papers. Moreover newspapers and the press clearly presuppose public awareness of what badness in such cases is, by paying readers to hunt out examples of it for the amusement of others. Hence this recent specimen in *Private Eye* (19 June 1981)

'A fourth model, called on *interactionist model* has been formulated. A basic element in this model is the focus on the ongoing multidirectional interaction between an individual and his or her environment, especially the situations in which behaviour occurs. Persons and situations are regarded as indispensably linked to one another during the process of interaction. Neither the person factors nor the situation factors per se determine behaviour in isolation; it is determined by inseparable person

by situation interactions.
Personality at the crossroads. D. Magnuson & N.S. Endler (eds).'

At one level this kind of prose can be objected to simply because it uses 'long words', that it prefers the Latinate to the homegrown, the pretentious to the everyday. And with this we enter the arena of the Fowlers,[3] the Potters (1950) and the Mitfords, who each in their way testify to a deep-seated English distrust of imported language first felt by the Saxons in 1066. So powerful that it obliged the Norman ruling class to switch speech, this brand of Englishness is still palpably perceived as the 'heart' of the language, as the jingles of TV commercials attest, with their Anglo-Saxon alliteration (works wonders; they're golden, they're goodness; washes whiter; etc.)

Significant in itself, and unparalleled in European philology, this atavism in English has been historically bound up with a yet deeper prejudice of a moral order, cogently stated by George Orwell (1957) in his famous essay *Politics and the English Language*:

> 'Now, it is clear that the decline of a language must ultimately have political and economic causes: it is not due simply to the bad influence of this or that individual writer. But an effect can become a cause, reinforcing the original cause and producing the same effect in an intensified form, and so on indefinitely. A man may take to drink because he feels himself to be a failure, and then fail all the more completely because he drinks. It is rather the same thing that is happening to the English language. It becomes ugly and inaccurate because our thoughts are foolish, but the slovenliness of our language makes it easier for us to have foolish thoughts.' (p.143)

Going on to make a didactic or educational point, Orwell says that how we use language affects everything, not least the ease with which we may lie to ourselves and may be lied to officially (eg about nuclear war — his example already in 1946). Such a philosophy of language turns bias, against 'bad' language, into nothing less than a moral necessity; and Orwell's critics would dismiss it as self-deluding, a Puritan nostalgia for the word of God. Yet the remarkable fact about Orwell is that while insisting on language as a moral and political medium for every speaker and writer he still respects it, for itself, no less than would a poet. At the very least he may be said to raise, in acute fashion, a problem inseparable from the whole concept of liberal education in English (and the hopes expressed by Robbins that British higher education would form 'not merely good producers but good men and women').

We began by pinpointing two major difficulties that beset any discussion of language bias in higher education. First, how do we know when and whether bias of this sort is necessarily a bad thing, academically? Second, how can we best define 'language' as the medium biased this way or that, when the term refers to so many different sorts of phenomena? Looking back, we may now add a third, which concerns the amount and type of evidence available, above all that there is little. And what little there is tends to relate to aspects of but one type of language bias, that against 'dominated' groups within national languages. Moreover, this evidence has been interpreted quite contradictorily, according to the particular theory it is supposed to support, a point made several times by Bisseret (1979). In these circumstances, no attempt could be made to present a straightforward statistical survey of language bias: the mere definition of the problem proves to be a major philosophical task while hard data collected so far are scanty. Instead, we have tried to anticipate and draw out the main factors which need to be considered in a comprehensive account of language bias, focusing in particular on four. These are its function as a demarcation not so much against the working class as for the ruling classes; the centrality acquired historically by 'national' language, which is rarely questioned in those terms; the different relations of speech to script, alphabetic, hieroglyphic and iconographic; and the discrimination between language that is either 'good' or 'bad'.

NOTES

INTRODUCTION

1   It is interesting to note that the *Education World Yearbook* for 1981 has also taken as its main theme the education of minority groups. It is a far larger collection of papers than this volume, with a wider spread, looking not just at higher education, but at all levels and in a number of countries. The editor is Jacquetta Megarry, the publisher Kogan Page.

RACE BIAS

1   The adjectives 'black', 'black and brown', ethnic minority, and New Commonwealth and Pakistani are used interchangeably here to refer to the population of Great Britain which is of New Commonwealth and Pakistani origin, estimated at 1,642,000 for 1976 (OPCS 1979). This group (NCWP) provides the best estimate of the black population of Great Britain — something over 3% of the total, of which it is estimated that about 40% (CSO 1979) were born in this country, and are still *mainly children*.

2   See particularly: CRC Reference Series and Annual Reports; Crispin Cross (1978) *Ethnic Minorities in the Inner City: the Ethnic Dimension in Urban Deprivation in England*; White Paper (1975) *Racial Discrimination* HMSO Cmnd. 6234, which recognized that, while other groups were disadvantaged, '. . . few other groups in society display all the accumulated disadvantages' found among ethnic minorities.

3   Bell, A., Jnr. (1972) 'The Dred Scott Case: Mr. Chief Justice Torney delivered the opinion of the Court. . . .'

4   See Freeman's bibliographical note for further research along these lines.

5   'No State shall deny to any person within its jurisdiction the equal protection of the laws.' Section 1, Fourteenth Amendment to the Constitution.

6   'Strict scrutiny' is an especially stringent standard of judicial review operated by the US Supreme Court in some kinds of 'Equal Protection' cases.

SEX BIAS

1   For further discussion of the disciplines as 'men's studies' see Dale Spender 1981b, where practitioners of a range of academic disciplines have documented the nature and extent of male control (and female exclusion) and have developed remarkably similar evaluations.

2   For further discussion of this process of the 'disappearance' of women and their intellectual work see Dale Spender (forthcoming) *Women of Ideas and What Men have Done to Them: from Mary Wollstonecraft to Mary Daly* London and Boston: (Routledge & Kegan Paul.

3   Cheris Kramer is now Cheris Kramarae.

4   Space does not permit a detailed analysis of the complex and significant critiques of Overfield and Hubbard and their work is highly recommended as further reading.

5   Women's *strength* is an hypothesis that is almost unknown in the research community and has not formed the basis of any systematic study, unlike that of men's strength.

LANGUAGE BIAS

1   An example being K.L. Pike (1967); for an irreverent account of how I.A. Richards, as a language teacher, was seduced by behaviourism and Skinner, see Young's review of I.A. Richards in the *New York Times Book Review* 26 May 1974; on other 'advances', see Fishman 1972.

2   For a brief — and demeaning — note on Maya literacy, see Goody 1968; on this aspect of the New World generally see my study of 1979.

3   The Fowlers open their account of the English language with five rules, the last of which is said to be a compendium of the others:
> Prefer the familiar word to the far-fetched
> Prefer the concrete word to the abstract
> Prefer the single word to the circumlocution
> Prefer the short word to the long
> Prefer the Saxon word to the Romance.
> (1931:11)

REFERENCES

ACACE (1979) *Links to Learning* Leicester: Advisory Council for Adult and Continuing Education

ACACE (1981) Untitled policy document on a system of continuing education. Leicester: Advisory Council for Adult and Continuing Education (Available Autumn 1981)

Acker, Sandra (1978) *Sex Differences in Graduate Student Ambition* University of Bristol, unpublished PhD

Acker, Sandra (1980a) Women, the other academics *British Journal of Sociology of Education* 1 (1) 81-91

Acker, Sandra (1980b) *Feminist Perspectives and the British Sociology of Education* Paper presented at BSA Annual Conference, Lancaster

Aitken, R (1966) *Administration of a University* University of London Press

Allen, S. (1979) Pre-school children: ethnic minorities in England *New Community* Summer London: Commission for Racial Equality

Althusser, L. (1971) Ideology and ideological state apparatuses. In Cosin, B.R. (1972)

Alves, C. (1979) *The Church Colleges into the 1990s* The College of Ripon and York St John, Occasional Paper 2

Ammon, U. (1973) *Dialekt, Soziale Ungleichheit und Schule* Weinheim und Basel: Beltz

Argyle, M. (1975) *The Social Psychology of Religion* RKP

Armytage, W.H.G. and Peel, J. (1978) *Perimeters of Social Repair* London: Academic Press

Ås, Berit (1981) Private communication

Astell, Mary (1694) *A Serious Proposal to the Ladies* London: publisher unknown

Astin, A.W. (1975) *Preventing Students from Dropping Out* San Francisco: Jossey Bass

Astin, A.W. (1977) *Four Critical Years: the Effects of College on Beliefs, Attitudes and Knowledge* San Francisco: Jossey Bass

Ballerstedt, E. and Glatzer, W. (1979) *Sociologischer Almanach Handbuch gesellschaftlicher Daten und Indikatoren* Frankfurt: Campus Verlag

Banks, O. and Finlayson, D. (1973) *Success and Failure in the Secondary School* London: Methuen

Barnett, V.D., Holder, R.L. and Lewis, T. (1968) Some new results on the association between students' ages and their degree results *Journal of the Royal Statistical Society* A (131)

Barnett, V.D. and Lewis, T. (1963) A study of the relation between GCE and degree results *Journal of the Royal Statistical Society* A (126) 187-226

Beard R.M. and Bligh, D.A. (1971) *Research into Teaching Methods in Higher Education* (Third edition) Guildford: Society for Research into Higher Education

de Beauvoir, Simone (1972) *The Second Sex* Harmondsworth: Penguin

Beard, Mary (1946) *Women as Force in History: a study in traditions and realities* New York: Macmillan

Beezer, R.H. and Hjelm, H.F. (1961) *Factors Related to College Attendance* Washington: US Government Printing Office

Bell, D.A. (Jnr) (1972) *Race, Racism and the American Law* Boston: Little Brown & Co.

Bereday, G.Z.F. (1973) *Universities for All: international perspectives on mass higher education* San Francisco: Jossey Bass

Bereday, G. and Lauwerys, J. (1966) *Church and State in Education* World Yearbook in Education

Berkove, G.F. (1979) Perceptions of husband support by returning women students *The Family Co-ordinator* October

Bernard, Jessie (1973) My four revolutions: an autobiographical history of the ASA. In Joan Huber (Editor) *Changing Women in a Changing Society* Chicago and London: University of Chicago Press

Bernstein, B. (1971-75) *Class Codes and Control* London: Routledge and Kegan Paul

Bicheno, M. and Davis, A. (1981) *New Start for Disabled People* Auckland: University of Auckland

Biehl, G. (1978) *Guide to Section 504 Self-Evaluation for Colleges and Universities* Washington DC: National Association of College and University Business Officers

Bindman, G. and Grosz, S. (1979) Indirect discrimination and the Race Relations Act. In Runnymede Trust *A Review of the Race Relations Act 1976* London: Runnymede Trust

Bisseret, N. (1979) *Education, Class Language and Ideology* London and Boston: Routledge and Kegan Paul

Bolton, C. and Kammeyer, K. (1967) *The University Student* New Haven, US

Boning, E. and Roeloffs, K. (1970) *Innovation in Higher Education: three German universities, Aachen, Bochum, Konstanz* Paris: OECD

Boudon, R. (1974) *Education Opportunity and Social Inequality* London: John Wiley

Boulding, Elise (1976) *The Underside of History: a view of women through time* Boulder, Colorado: Westview Press

Bourdieu, P. (1974) The school as a conservative force. In Eggleston, J. (Editor) (1974)

174   References

Bourdieu, P. and Passeron, J.C. (1965) *Rapport Pedagogique et Communication* Paris

Bourdieu, P. and Passeron, J.C. (1977) *Reproduction in Education, Society and Culture* London: Sage Publications

Bowles, F. (1962) Access to education — A global view *College Board Review No 48* Autumn. The full report appears as Bowles (1963)

Bowles, F. (1963) *Access to Higher Education* UNESCO and the International Association of Universities

Bowles, S. and Gintis, H. (1976) *Schooling in Capitalist America* London: Routledge and Kegan Paul

Brandis, W. and Henderson, D. (1970) *Social Class, Language and Communication* London: Routledge and Kegan Paul

Briggs, A. (1969) Development in higher education in the United Kingdom: nineteenth and twentieth centuries. In Niblet, W.R. (1969)

British Dyslexia Association (1980) *Dyslexic Applicants for Admission to Universities and Institutes of Higher Education* BDA

British Standards Institution (1979) *Code of Practice for Access for the Disabled to Buildings* London: BSI

Brock-Utne, Birgit (1981) *What are the Effects of Curricula Options?* Paper presented at the Council for Cultural Cooperation educational research workshop on sex stereotyping in school education, Hønefoss, Oslo

Brotherston, G. (1979) *Image of the New World: the American continent portrayed in native texts* London and New York; Thames and Hudson

Bryant, Margaret (1979) *The Unexpected Revolution: a study in the history of the education of women and girls in the nineteenth century* London: University of London Institute of Education Studies in Education 10

Burgess, T. and Pratt, J. (1970) *Policy and Practice: The Colleges of Advanced Technology* London: Allen Lane

Burgess, T. (1977) *Education After School* London: Gollancz; Harmondsworth: Penguin

Burgess, T. and Pratt, J. (1971) *Innovation in Higher Education: Technical Education in the United Kingdom* OECD

Burstyn, Joan N. (1980) *Victorian Education and the Ideal of Womanhood* London: Croom Helm

Butler, M. (1978) *Visually Handicapped Students: a survey* London: Royal National Institute for the Blind

Byrne, D.S., Williamson, B. and Fletcher, B.G. (1975) *The Poverty of Education, A Study in the Politics of Opportunity* London: Martin Robertson

Byrne, Eileen (1978) *Women and Education* London: Tavistock

California State Postsecondary Education Commission (1978) *Access in a Broader Context: college-going rates in California* Sacramento: California Postsecondary Education Commission

Callaghan, D. (1964) The Catholic university: the American experience. In Coulson, J. *Theology and the University* DLT

Campbell, C. (1971) *Towards a Sociology of Irreligion* Macmillan

Caplovitz, D. and Sherrow, F. (1977) *The Religious Drop Outs: apostasy among college graduates* California: Sage

Carroll, Berenice A. (Editor) (1976) *Liberating Women's History: theoretical and critical essays* Urbana, Chicago, London: University of Illinois Press

Carter, C. (1980) *Higher Education for the Future* Basil Blackwell

Carter, B.L. and Newman, D.K. (1978) Perceptions about black Americans *The Annals of the American Academy* January

Carnegie (1973) *Priorities for Action: Final Report of the Carnegie Commission in Higher Education* McGraw-Hill

Central Statistical Office (1979) *Social Trends 9* London: HMSO

Challis, R. (1976) The experience of mature students *Studies in Higher Education* 1 (2)

Charnley, A., Osborn, M. and Withnall, A. (1980) *Review of Research on Mature Students* National Institute of Adult Education

Cheetham, J. (1981) *Social Work Services for Ethnic Minorities in Britain and the USA* Oxford: OUP

Child, D. and Markall, G. (1976) *The Disabled Student* London: National Union of Students and Action Research for the Crippled Child

Christensen, H.T. and Cannon, K.L. (1978) The fundamentalist emphasis at Brigham Young University 1935-1973 *Journal for the Scientific Study of Religion* March, 53-57

Cleugh, M.F. (1972) Stresses of mature students *British Journal of Educational Studies* 20, 76-79

Cobban, A.B. (1975) *The Mediaeval Universities* Methuen

Coleman, C.J. and Toomey, W.C. (1974) Commitment and credibility in a religious institution *Religion in Life* 1974, 494-500

Collins, R. (1971) Functional and conflict theories of educational stratification *American Sociological Review* 36

Collins, R. (1977) Some comparative principles of educational stratification *Harvard Education Review* 47

Community Relations Commission (1973) *Multiple Deprivation and Minority Groups* Mimeo, CRC/73/113

Community Relations Commission (1977) *Urban Deprivation, Racial Inequality and Social Policy: a report* London: HMSO

Conference of Ministers of Education and European Member States of UNESCO (1968) *Access to Higher Education in Europe* Paris: UNESCO

Cornbleet, Annie (1981) *School Girls — Realities and Possibilities* WEdG (Women's Education Group) seminar; London

Cosin, B.R. (1972) *Education: Structure and Society* London: Penguin

Crossland, F.E. (1971) *Minority Access to College: a Ford Foundation report* New York: Shocken Books

Coulson, J. (1964) *Theology and the University* DLT

Coulson, J. (1976) Newman's idea of an open university and its consequences today *Downside Review* April

Cross, C. (1978) *Ethnic Minorities in the Inner City: the ethnic dimension in urban deprivation in England* London: Commission for Racial Equality

Daly, Mary (1973) *Beyond God the Father: toward a philosophy of women's liberation* Boston: Beacon Press

Datta, L. (1967) Family religious background and early scientific creativity *American Sociological Review* 1967, 626-635

David, R.L. (1979) Full-time faculty resistance to adult and higher education *Lifelong Learning* 2 (6)

Davidson, J. (1980) Article in *Journal of the Association of Colleges Implementing Dip. H.E. Programmes* (ACID) July

Deem, R. (Editor), (1980) *Schooling for Women's Work* London: Routledge

Delamont, Sara (1981) Letter to the editor *Network* 19 Jan, p.2

De Jong, G.F. and Faulkner, J.E. (1972) Religion and intellectuals: findings from a sample of university faculty *Review of Religious Research* 1972, 15-24

Department of Education and Science (DES) (1979) *Access for the Physically Disabled to Educational Buildings* London: DES. Design Note 18

Department of Education and Science (DES) (1978) *Special Courses in Preparation for Entry to Higher Education* Press Notice, 2 August

Derbyshire Education Committee (1966) *Awards to Students* (mimeo)

The Disabled Student in Higher Education (1974) London: North East London Polytechnic and Central Council for the Disabled

Dixon, K. and Hutchison, D. (1979) *Further Education for Handicapped Students* Bolton: Bolton College of Technology

Douglas, J.B. (1964) *The Home and the School* London: McGibbon and Kee

Dore, R. (1976) *The Diploma Disease* London: George Allen and Unwin

Downing, P.M. (1978) *Arguments for and against Affirmative Action to Promote Equal Employment Opportunity* Washington: Congressional Research Service

Downton, A. and Newell, A. (1979) An assessment of Palantype transcription as an aid for the deaf *International Journal of Man-Machine Studies* 11, 667-680

Duelli-Klein, Renate (1981) Unpublished research on growth and development of women's studies in Britain and the USA. University of London Institute of Education

Dworkin, R. (1977) *Taking Rights Seriously* London: Duckworth

Dworkin, R. (1978) The Bakke decision: did it decide anything? *New York Review of Books* 17 August

Dyhouse, Carol (1976) Social Darwinistic ideas and the development of women's education in England, 1800-1920 *History of Education* V (1) 41-58

Eaton, E.G. (1980) The academic performance of mature age students: a review of the general literature. In Hore, T. and West, L.H.T. (Editor) *Mature Age Students in Australian Higher Education* Higher Education Advisory and Research Unit, Monash University, Australia

Eaton, E.G. and West, L.H.T. (1980) Academic performance of mature age students: recent research in Australia. In T. Hore and L.H.T. West (Editors) *Mature Age Students in Australian Higher Education* Higher Education Advisory and Research Unit, Monash University, Australia

The Economist (1981) *Right to be white — and male?* 28 March

Eddy, E.D. (1959) *The College Influence on Student Character* Washington: American Council of Education

The Education of the Visually Handicapped (1972) London: HMSO, The Vernon Report

Edwards, G. and Roberts, I.J. (1980) British higher education: long term trends in student enrolment *Higher Education Review* 12 (2)

Edwards, J. and Batley, R. (1977) *Inner Area Studies: Summaries of Consultants' Final Reports* 2 London: HMSO

Edwards, J. and Batley, R. (1978) *The Politics of Positive Discrimination: An Evaluation of the Urban Programme 1967-77* London: Methuen

Eggleston, J. (Editor) (1974) *Contemporary Research in the Sociology of Education* London: Methuen

Elston, Mary Ann (1981) Medicine as 'Old Husbands' Tales': The impact of feminism. In Dale Spender (Editor) *Men's Studies Modified: the impact of feminism on the academic disciplines* Oxford: Pergamon Press

Elton, L.R.B. (1975) Mature students: OU and non-OU. In Leedham J. (Editor) *Aspects of Educational Technology* London: Kogan Page

Embling, J. (1974) *A Fresh Look at Higher Education: European Implications of the Carnegie Commission Reports* Amsterdam: Elsevier

Entwistle, N.J. and Wilson, J.D. (1977) *Degrees of Excellence* Hodder and Stoughton

Espy, R.H.E. (1951) *The Religion of College Teachers* New York

Essen, J. and Ghodsian, M. (1979) The children of immigrants: social performance *New Community* Winter

Essen, J. and Ghodsian, M. (1980) The children of immigrants: social and home circumstances *New Community* Winter

European Centre for Higher Education (1978) *Statistical Study on Higher Education in Europe* Bucharest: UNESCO

Fagin, M.C. (1971) *Life Experience has Academic Value* ERIC Document Reproduction Service, EDO47219

Farley, J. et al. (1977) Women's values changing faster than men's? *Sociology of Education* April, 151

Feinstein, O. (1979) *A Humanities-Based Curriculum for Working Adults* Detroit: Wayne State University

Feldman, K.A. (1969a) Change and stability of religious orientations during college: freshmen-senior comparisions *Review of Religious Research* Fall, 40-60

Feldman, K.A. (1969b) Change and stability of religious orientations during college: social structural correlates *Review of Religious Research* Winter, 1969-70, 103-128

Feldon, K.A. (1972) *College and Student* Pergamon

Feldman, K.A. and Newcomb, T.M. (1969) *The Impact of College on Students* San Francisco

Ferber, Marianne A. and Teiman, Michelle L. (1981) The oldest, the most established, the most quantitative of the social sciences and the most dominated by men: the impact of feminism on economics. In Dale Spender (1981b) op. cit. 125-139

Fishman, J.A. (1972) *Advances in the Sociology of Language* The Hague: Mouton. 2 volumes

Fitzgibbon, A. (1981) *Religious Affiliation in an Irish University: Changes in the Period 1960-1980* Paper submitted to the SRHE annual conference 1981

Flecker, R. (1959) Characteristics of passing and failing students in first year university mathematics *The Educand* 3 (3)

Fleming, W.G. (1959) *Personal and Academic Factors as Predictors of First Year Success in Ontario Universities* Atkinson Study Report Number 5, University of Toronto, Department Of Educational Research

Fletcher, R. (1973) *The Teaching of Science and Mathematics to the Blind* Worcester: Worcester College for the Blind

Folter, J.F. and Nam, C.B. (1967) *Education of the American Population* Washington: US Government Printing Office

Forster, M. (1959) *An Audit of Academic Performance* Belfast: Queens University

Fowler, H.W. and Fowler, F.G. (1931) *The King's English* (Third edition) Oxford: OUP

Fox, W.S. and Jackson, E.F. (1973) Protestant and Catholic differences in educational achievement and persistence in school *Journal for the Scientific Study of Religion* 12, 65-85

Freeman, R.B. (1976) *The Over-Educated American* New York: Academic Press

Freeman, R. (1978) Black economic progress since 1964 *Public Interest* Summer

Galler, S. (1977) *Women Graduate Returnees and Their Husbands* Northwestern University, unpublished PhD thesis

Gay, J.L. (1971) *The Geography of Religion in England* Duckworth

Gay, J.D. (1979) *The Christian Campus? The Role of the English Churches in Higher Education* Abingdon: Culham College Institute

Gedge, P.S. (1964) *The Role of a Church of England College of Education* University of Birmingham, MEd thesis

General Synod Board of Education (1980a) *Partners in Understanding: an account of Church of England Chaplaincy in Higher Education* Church House, Westminster

General Synod Board of Education (1980b) *The Church Colleges of Higher Education* G.S.417. Church House, Westminster

Gerth, H., Mills, C. and Wright, N. (Editors) (1970) *Essays From Max Weber* London: Routledge and Kegan Paul

Ginsburg, H. (1972) *The Myth of the Deprived Child* New Jersey: Prentice-Hall Inc.

Girard, A. (1964) *Le Choix du Conoint* Paris: PUF

Glazer, N. (1975) *Affirmative Discrimination: ethnic inequality and public policy* New York: Basic Books

Glazer, N. (1976) Equal opportunity gone wrong *New Society* 22 January

Goody, J. (1968) *Literacy in Traditional Societies* Cambridge: OUP

Goreau, Angeline (1980) *Reconstructing Alphra: a social biography of Aphra Behn* New York: The Dial Press

Gross, B.R. (Editor) (1977) *Reverse Discrimination* Buffalo: Prometheus Books

Greeley, A.M. (1967) *The Changing Catholic College* Chicago: NORC Monographs in Social Research

Greeley, A.M. (1969) *From Backwater to Mainstream: A Profile of Catholic Higher Education* New York: Carnegie Commission on Higher Education, McGraw Hill

Greeley, A.M. and Rossi, P.H. (1966) *The Education of American Catholics* Chicago: Aldine

Greeley, A.M. et al. [1976] Catholic Schools in a Declining Church Kansas City: Andrews and McNeel

The Guardian (1979) *Selection by Race Approved* 11 October

Gunn, A. (1976) *The Opportunities of the Physically Disabled Patient for a University Education* Reading: University Health Service

Habermas, J. (1975) *Legitimation Crisis* Boston: Beacon Press

Hales, G. (1976) Communicating with the deaf by conventional orthography: the case for a non-verbatim approach *British Journal of Audiology* 10, 83-86

Hales, G. (1977) *The Progress of Hearing Impaired Students in the Open University* Milton Keynes: The Open University

Hales, G. (1978) *Survey of Students at Additional Examination Centres for Disabled Students in the London Region* Milton Keynes: The Open University

Hales, G. (1979A) *The Disabled Student Population: A Demographic Profile* Milton Keynes: The Open University

Hales, G. (1979B) *Two Communication Developments for Hearing Impaired Students* Milton Keynes: The Open University

Hales, G. and Gauntlett, D. (1981) *Experience of Adults with Dyslexia in Tertiary Education* Milton Keynes: The Open University

Halsey, A.H. (1977) Towards meritocracy: the case of Britain. In Karabel, J. and Halsey, A.H. (Editors) (1977)

Halsey, A.H., Heath, A.F. and Ridge, J.M. (1980) *Origins and Destinations: family, class and education in modern Britain* Oxford: Oxford University Press

Halsey, A.H. and Trow, M. (1971) *The British Academic* London: Faber and Faber

Hansard (1979) 12 March

Harris, D. (1940) Factors affecting college grades: a review of the literature *Psychology Bulletin* 37

Hastings, P.K. and Hoge, D.R. (1976) Changes in religion among college students 1948-1974 *Journal for the Scientific Study of Religion* September, 237-249

Health, Education and Welfare, Department of (1977) Non discrimination on basis of handicap and programs and activities receiving or benefitting from Federal financial assistance *Federal Register* 42 (86)

Health, Education and Welfare, Department of (1978) Implementation of executive order 11914: non discrimination on the basis of handicap and Federally assisted programs *Federal Register* 43 (9)

Heath, D. (1968) *Growing up in College* San Francisco: Jossey Bass

Henike, D. (1978) *Colleges in Crisis: the Reorganization of Teacher Training 1971-1977* London: Penguin

Higginbotham, A.L. (Jnr) (1978) *In the Matter of Color* Oxford and New York: OUP

Hochschild, Arlie Russell (1975) Inside the clockwork of male careers. In Florence Howe (Editor) *Women and the Power to Change* New York: McGraw Hill

Hoge, D.R. (1974) *Commitment on Campus: Changes in Religion and Values over Five Decades* California: Westminster

Hoge, D.R. (1976) Changes in college students' value patterns in the late 1950s, 1960s and 1970s *Sociology of Education* April, 155-163

Hoge, D.R. and Keeter, L.A. (1976) Determinants of college teachers' religious beliefs and participation *Journal for the Scientific Study of Religion* Sept, 221-235

Hoggart, R. (1958) *The Uses of Literacy* (Second edition) Harmondsworth: Penguin

Hood, R.W. (1973) Forms of religious commitment and internal religious experience *Review of Religious Research* Fall, 29-36

Hooper, J.D. (1979) My wife, the student *The Family Co-ordinator* October

Hopper, E. (1971) *Readings in the Theory of Educational Systems* London: Hutchinson University Library

Hopper, E. and Osborn, M. (1975) *Adult Students: Education, Selection and Control* London: Frances Pinter

Hornsby-Smith, M.P. (1978) *Catholic Education: the Unobtrusive Partner* London: Sheed & Ward

Hornsby-Smith M.P. et. al. (1976) Catholic students in higher education *The Month* June, 191-198

House of Commons (1981) *Bill 48 Education: a Bill to Make Provision with Respect to Children with Special Educational Needs* London

Howell, D.A. (1962) *A Study of the 1955 Entry to British Universities* Evidence to the Robbins Committee on Higher Education, University of London (mimeo)

Hubbard, Ruth (1981) The emperor doesn't wear any clothes: the impact of feminism on biology. In Dale Spender (1981b) op, cit. 213-236

Hunsberger, B. (1978) The religiosity of college students: stability and change over years at university *Journal for the Scientific Study of Religion* June, 159-164

Husen, T. (1979) *The School in Question. A Comparative Study of the School and the future in Western Societies* London: Oxford University Press

Initial teacher training: DES statement (1981) *Educare* 11, 17-18

International Federation of Catholic Universities (1974) *The Spiritual Function of the Catholic University and its Function as a Critic* Paris: IFCU Report

International Federation of Catholic Universities (1979) *The Catholic University: Instrument of Cultural Pluralism to the Service of Church and Society* Paris: IFCU

Jackson, B. and Marsden, D. (1966) *Education and the Working Class* (Revised edition) Harmondsworth: Penguin

Jacob, P. (1957) *Changing Values in College* New York: Harper and Row

Janeway, Elizabeth (1980) *Powers of the Weak* New York: Alfred Knopf

Jeffers, M. (1980) *Academic Library Services for the Handicapped in Northern Ireland* Loughborough University

Jencks, C. et al. (1972) *Inequality: A Re-assessment of the Effects of Family and Schooling in America* New York: Basic Books

Jenkins, Lee and Kramer, Cheris (1978) Small group processes: learning from women *Women's Studies International Quarterly* 1 (1) 67-84

Jenkins, Mercille and Kramarae, Cheris (1981) A thief in the house: women and language. In Dale Spender (1981b) *op. cit.* 10-22

Jensen, M.D. (1980) Access to higher education through distant-learning *Contemporary Education* 51 (2) 71-73

Johnson, S. (1963) Preface to a dictionary of the English language (1755); A journey to the Western Islands of Scotland (1775). In Wilson, M. (Editor) *Johnson. Prose and Poetry* London: Renard Press

Jones, C. (1976) *Immigration & Social Policy in Britain 1976* London: Tavistock

Jones, C., Kirp, D. (1979) *Doing Good by Doing Little* University of California Press

Jones, H.A. and Williams, K.E. (1979) *Adult Students and Higher Education* Leicester: Advisory Council for Adult and Continuing Education

Kapur, K.L. (1972) Student wastage at Edinburgh University, I. Factors related to failure and drop-out *Universities Quarterly* Summer

Karabel, J. and Halsey, A.H. (Editors) (1977) *Power and Ideology in Education* London: Oxford University Press

Kassman, J. (1978) *Lone Mothers in Higher Education* London: National Council for One Parent Families

Katz, J. (1976) Home life of women in continuing education. In Astin, H. (Editor) *Some action of her own* Toronto: D.C. Heath & Co.

Keeble, D.E. (1968) Regional representation at a 'National' university *Universities Quarterly* 23 (2) 66-73

Kelly, Alison (1981) *Research on Sex Differences in Schools in the UK* UK National Report to the Council for Cultural Co-operation educational research workshop on sex stereotyping in schools, Hønefoss, Oslo

Kelly, S. (1980) *Changing Parent-Child Relationships: An Outcome of Mother Returning to College* Paper presented at the Fifteenth Annual Australian Psychological Society Conference, Toowoomba, Queensland

Kelsall, R.K., Poole, A. and Kuhn, A. (1972) *Graduates: The Sociology of an Elite* London: Methuen

Ker, I.T. (1975) Did Newman believe in the idea of a Catholic university? *Downside Review* 1975, 39-42

King, M. (1980) *The Mature Student of Chemistry in Higher Education* University of Sussex, unpublished PhD thesis

Kirkwood, A. (1979) *The Institute Bibliography* IET Monograph Number 2 (third edition). Milton Keynes: Institute of Educational Technology, The Open University

Knight, S. and McDonald, R. (1978) Adult learners in university courses. In *The Proceedings of the Thirteenth Annual Conference of the Society for Research into Higher Education* Guildford: SRHE

Knoell, D.M. (1970) *People Who Need College: A Report on Students We Have Yet to Serve* Washington: American Association of Junior Colleges

Knox, J. (1971) The Church in higher education *Religion in Life* Winter, 489-499

Kogan, M. (1979) *Educational Policies in Perspective: An Appraisal of OECD Country Educational Policy Reviews* Paris: OECD

Kolodny, Annette (1981) Dancing through the minefield: some observations on the theory, practice and politics of a feminist literary criticism. In Dale Spender (1981b) *op. cit.* 23-42

Kozubal, S.X. and Flatter, C. (1977) Traditional and non-traditional religious interests among female college age Christians *Review of Religious Research* Winter 163-167

Kramnick, Mariam (Editor) (1978) *Vindication of the Rights of Women* Penguin

Kratcoski, P.C. (1972) The sources and strength of professorial value commitments *Review of Religious Research* Fall, 25-29

Kuper, L. (Editor) (1974) *Race, Science and Society* London: Allen and Unwin

Labov, W. (1970) The logic of non standard English. In The Open University — Language and Learning Course Team *Language and Education* London: Routledge and Kegan Paul

Laurence, D.H. (1972) *Bernard Shaw. Collected Letters 1898-1910* London: Max Reinhardt

Layard, R., King, J. and Moser, C. (1969) *The impact of Robbins* London: Penguin

Legge, C.D. (1972-77) *Register of Research in Progress in Adult Education* University of Manchester

Leghorn, Lisa and Parker Kathy (1981 in press) *Women's Worth* London and Boston: Routledge & Kegan Paul

Lehman, E.C. (1972) The scholarly perspective and religious commitment *Sociological Analysis* 1972, 199-216

Lehman, E.C. (1974) Academic discipline and faculty religiosity in secular and church related colleges *Journal for the Scientific Study of Religion* June, 205-220

Lehman, E.C. and Shriver, D.W. (1968) Academic discipline as predictive of faculty religiosity *Social Forces* Dec, 171-182

Lerner, Gerda (1977) *The Female Experience: an American Documentary* Indianapolis: Boobs Merrill

Lester, A. and Bindman, G. (1972) *Race and the Law* Harvard University Press

Levin, H.M. (1976a) Equal Educational Opportunity in Western Europe: a contradictory relation. Paper presented to the Annual Meeting of the American Political Science Association, Chicago

Levin, H. (1976b) Educational opportunity and social inequality in Western Europe *Social Problems* 24 (2)

Levitan, S.A., Johnston, W.B. and Taggart, R. (1975) *Still a Dream: the Changing Status of Blacks since 1960* Harvard University Press

Lewis, Jane (1981) Women lost and found: the impact of feminism on history. In Dale Spender (1981b) *op. cit.* 55-72

Lipset, S.M. and Schneider, W. (1978) Racial equality in America *New Society* 20 April

Little, Alan (1978) *Educational Policies for Multi-racial Areas* Goldsmiths' College Inaugural Lecture, University of London

Little, A. and Willey, R. (1981) *Multi-ethnic Education: the Way Forward* Schools Council Pamphlet 18

Livingston, J.C. (1979) *Fair Game? Inequality and Affirmative Action* San Francisco: W.H. Freeman

Locke, M. (1978) The Hinterland of North East London Polytechnic *Higher Education Review* 10 (2) 17-31

Macaulay, Catherine (1790) *Letters on Education* London

MacIntyre, A. (1967) *Secularization and Moral Change* Oxford: OUP

Malleson, N.B. (1959) University Student, 1953. I - Profile *Universities Quarterly* 13, 287-298

Marceau, J. (1977) *Class and Status in France* London: Oxford University Press

Marino, C. (1971) Cross national comparisons of Catholic and Protestant creativity differences *British Journal of Social and Clinical Psychology* 1971, 132-137

Marshall, R., Knapp, C.B., Liggett, M.H. and Glover, R.W. (1979) *Employment Discrimination: The Impact of Legal and Administrative Remedies* New York: Praeger

Martin, B. and Pluck, R. (1976) *Young People's Beliefs* General Synod, Church House, Westminster

Marx, P. and Hall, P. (1978) *Proceedings of the Disabled Student in American Campuses: Services and the State of the Art* Dayton: Wright State University

Masclet, J.C. (1976) *The Intra-European Mobility of Undergraduate Students* Amsterdam; European Cultural Foundation

Mayor, B. (1979) *Register of Institutional Research and Development* Milton: The Open University

McClelland, V.A. (1980) The Church and R.E. In Cumming, J. and Burns, P. *The Church Now: an Inquiry into the Present State of the Catholic Church in Britain and Ireland* London: Gill & Macmillan

McCluskey, N.G. (1970) *The Catholic University: a Modern Appraisal* University of Notre Dame Press

McCracken, D. (1969) *University Student Performance* Report of the Student Health Department, University of Leeds

McGregor, G.P. (1981) *Bishop Otter College and Policy for Teacher Education* London: Pembridge Press

McIntosh, N.E. (1981) *Demand and Supply in the Education of Adults* Paper presented to the Annual Meeting of the Association of College Vice Principals, March 20th, 1981

McIntosh, N.E.S. (1978) Access to higher education in England and Wales. In *Innovation in Access to Higher Education* New York: International Council for Educational Development

McIntosh, N.E. and Woodley, A. (1974) The Open University and second chance education *Paedogogica Europaea* II

McIntosh, N.E. and Woodley, A. (1978) *Combining Education with Working Life or: The Working Student* Paper presented at the fourth International Conference on Higher Education, University of Lancaster

McKay, D.D. (1977) *Housing and Race in Industrial Society* London: Croom Helm

McLeish, J. (1970) *Students' Attitudes and College Environments* Cambridge Institute of Education

McLeish, J. (1962) The age factor in adult learning *International Review of Adult and Youth Education* 14, 26-45

McLeish, J. (1973) College environment and student characteristics. In Lomax, D.E. *The Education of Teachers in Britain* John Wiley, 411-423

McWilliams-Tullberg, Rita (1975) *Women at Cambridge: a men's university — though of a mixed type* London: Victor Gollancz

McWilliams-Tullberg, Rita (1980) Women and degrees at Cambridge University. In Martha Vicinus (Editor) *A Widening Sphere changing roles of Victorian Women* London New York: Methuen

Melia, T. and Kitching, J. (1981) Initiatives for the educationally disadvantaged in the USA: an example of student affirmative action *Imperial College Education Forum* 11 March

Merton, R.K. (1968) *Social Theory and Social Structure* New York: Free Press

Miller, Jean Baker (1976) *Toward a New Psychology of Women* Harmondsworth: Penguin

Miller, S.M. (1978a) The recapitalization of capitalism *International Journal of Urban and Regional Studies* 2 (2)

Miller, S.M. (1978b) Look back in apathy *New Society* 23 February

Moberg, D.O. and McEnery, J.N. (1976) Changes in church related behaviour and attitudes of Catholic students 1961-1971 *Sociological Analysis* 1976, 53-62

Moberley, W. (1949) *The Crisis in the University* SCM

Morgan, A., Gibbs, G. and Taylor, E. (1980) *Students' Approaches to Studying the Social Science and Technology Foundation Courses: Preliminary Studies* Study Methods Group Report Number 4. Milton Keynes: Institute of Educational Technology, The Open University

Mountford, Sir J. (1957) *How They Fared — A Survey of a Three-Year Student Entry* Liverpool University Press

Moynihan, D. (1975) *The Negro Family: the Case for National Action* New York: Office of Policy Planning and Research, US Department of Labor

Muradbegovic, M. (1978) Problems of access to higher education in Yugoslavia. In *Consultation for the Preparation of a Study on Access to Higher Education in Europe* Bucharest: UNESCO

Murphy, J. (1971) *Church, State and Schools in Britain, 1800-1970* RKP

National Innovations Centre (1974) *Disabled Students in Higher Education* London: NIC

Neave, G. (1976) *Patterns of Inequality* Windsor: NFER Publishing Co. Ltd.

Neave, G. (1979) Academic drift: Some views from Europe *Studies in Higher Education* 4 (2)

Newcomb, T.M. and Wilson, E.K. (1966) *College Peer Groups* Chicago

Newcomb, T.M. et al. (1967) *Persistence and Change: Bennington College and its Students after Twenty Five Years* New York: Wiley

Newman, D.K. et al. (1978) *Protest, Politics and Prosperity: Black Americans and White Institutions, 1940-1975* Pantheon

Newman, J.H. (1910) *The Idea of a University* Longmans

Newson, J. (1963) *Half our Future* A report of the Central Advisory Council for Education, England, under the chairmanship of Sir John Newson, London: HMSO

The New York Times (1979) *High Court Backs a Preference Plan for Blacks in Jobs* 28 June

NFER (1979) *Register of Educational Research in the United Kingdom Volume 3 1977-78* Windsor: NFER Publishing Co. Ltd.

Nias, J. (1972) Value persistence and utility in colleges of education *Education for Learning* Autumn, 29-34

Niblett, W.R. (1969) *Higher Education: Demand and Response* London: Tavistock Publications

Niblett, W.R. (1974) *Universities between Two Worlds* University of London Press

Niblett, W.R. (1976) *The Church's Colleges of Higher Education* Independent Publication: Church Information Office, Westminster

Nisbet, J. and Welsh, J. (1972) The mature student *Educational Research* 14

Nugent, T. (1978) More than ramps and braille *American Education* 14 (7) 11-18

Oakley, Ann (1974) *The Sociology of Housework* Oxford: Martin Robertson

Oakley, Ann (1981) *Subject Women* Oxford: Martin Robertson

OECD (1972) *Interdisciplinarity* A report of a seminar organized by the centre for Educational Research and Innovations and the French Ministry of Education. OECD

OECD (1974) *Towards Mass Higher Education. Issues and Dilemmas* Paris

OECD (1977a) *Selection and Certification in Education and Employment* Paris

OECD (1977b) *Learning Opportunities for Adults, Vol. IV Participation in Adult Education* Paris

Office & Population Censuses and Surveys (OPCS) (1979) *Population Trends 16* London: HMSO

O'Neill, D. (1977) *Discrimination against Handicapped Persons. The Costs, Benefits and Economic Impact of Implementing Section 504.* Washington: Government Printing Office

Open University (1972) *Language and Education: A Source Book* London: Routledge and Kegan Paul

Open University (1981) *Open University Digest of Statistics 1971-1980, Volume 1 — Students and courses* Milton Keynes: The Open University

Opportunities for Handicapped in Higher Education (1978) Stockholm: Swedish Central Committee for Rehabilitation

Orfield, G. (1978) *Must we Bus?* Brookings

Orr, L. (1974) *A Year between School and University* Slough: NFER Publishing Co. Ltd.

Orwell, G. (1957) Politics and the English language (1946) *Selected Essays* Harmondsworth: Penguin

Overfield, Kathy (1981) Dirty fingers, grime and slag heaps: purity and the scientific eithic. In Dale Spender (1981b) *op. cit.* 234-247

Pace, C.R. (1972) *Education and Evangelism: A Profile of Protestant Colleges* Carnegie Commission on Higher Education, McGraw Hill

Pankhurst, J. (1980a) *Focus on Physical Handicap: Provision for Young Please with Special Needs in Further Education* Slough: NFER Publishing Co. Ltd.

Pankhurst, J. and McAllister, A. (1980B) *An Approach to the Further Education of the Physically Handicapped* Slough: NFER Publishing Co. Ltd.

Patterson, M. (1976-77) Government policy and equality in higher education: The junior collegization of the French university *Social Problems* 24

Pattillo, M.M. and Mackenzie, D.M. (1966) *Church Sponsored Higher Education in the United States* Washington DC: American Council of Education

Parker, C.A. (1971) Changes in religious beliefs of college students. In Strommen, M.P. *Research on Religious Development* New York, 724-76

Pedersen, O.K. (1978) Access to higher education in other countries. In *The Right to Education and Access to Higher Education* Paris: International Association of Universities

PEP (Political and Economic Planning) (June 1974) *Racial Disadvantage in Employment*

PEP (Political and Economic Planning) (September 1974) *The Extent of Racial Discrimination*

PEP (Political and Economic Planning) (September 1975) *Racial Minorities and Public Housing*

PEP (Political and Economic Planning) (February 1976) *The Facts of Racial Disadvantage: a national survey*

Pettigrew, T.F. and Green, R.L. (1976) The legitimizing of racial segregation *New Society* 29 January

Philips, H. and Cullen, A. (1955) Age and academic success *Forum of Education* 14

Pike, K.L. (1967) *Language in Relation to a Unified Theory of the Structure of Human Behaviour* (Second edition) The Hague: Menton

Pike, R.M. (1970) *Who Doesn't Get to University — And Why: A Study on Accessibility to Higher Education in Canada* Ottawa: Association of Universities and Colleges of Canada

Pilkington, G.W. and Poppleton, P.K. (1976) Changes in religious beliefs, practices and attitudes among university students over an eleven-year period in relation to sex differences, denominational differences and differences between faculties and years of study *British Journal of Social and Clinical Psychology* 1976, 1-9

Pilkington, G.W. et al. (1965) Changes in religious attitude and practices among students during university degree courses *British Journal of Educational Psychology* 35, 150-7

Pipher, J.A. (1962) *Barriers to University: A Study of Students Prevented from or Delayed in Attending University* Toronto: Department of Education Research, Ontario College of Education

Popper, K.R. (1959) *The Logic of Scientific Discover* Hutchinson

Popper, K.R. (1976) *Unended Quest: an intellectual autobiography* Fontana

Poppleton, P.K. and Pilkington, G.W. (1963) The measurement of religious attitudes in a university population *British Journal of Social and Clinical Psychology* 1963, 20-36

Potter, S. (1950) *Our Language* Harmonsworth: Penguin

Pound, E. (1936) *The Chinese Written Character as a Medium for Poetry* San Francisco: City Lights

Pratt, J. and Burgess, T. (1974) *Polytechnics: a report* Pitman

Pringle, M. and Fiddes, D. (1970) *The Challenge of Thalidomide* London: Longman

Provision Within F.E. for Students with Special Education Needs (1981) London: London and Home Counties Regional Advisory Council for Technological Education

Pye, M. (1977) *The Language of the Church in Higher and Further Education: An Account of the Bradwell Consultation* Church House, Westminster

Rampton Committee (June 1981) *West Indian Children in our Schools* London: HMSO Cmnd. 8273

Ramsey, P. and Wilson, J.F. (1970) *The Study of Religion in Colleges and Universities* Princeton University Press

Redden, M. (1979) *Assuring Access for the Handicapped* San Francisco: Jossey Bass

Rendel, Margherita (1980) How many women academics 1912-76? In Rosemary Deem (Editor) *Schooling for Women's Work* London and Boston: Routledge and Kegan Paul

Reuben, Elaine (1978) In defiance of the evidence: notes on feminist scholarship *Women's Studies International Quarterly* 1 (3) 215-218

Rex, J. (date unknown) *Racialism and the Urban Crisis* UNESCO

Rich, Adrienne (1979) Toward a woman-centred university. In *On Lies Secrets and Silence* London: Virago

Richards, I.A. (1974) *Essays in His Honor* Edited by Brower, R. et al. Oxford: OUP

Ringer, F. (1969) *The Decline of the German Mandarins* Cambridge, Mass: Harvard University Press

Robbins Report (1963) *Committee on Higher Education Report* London: HMSO Cmnd. 2154

Roberts, Helen (Editor) (1981a) *Doing Feminist Research* London and Boston: Routledge and Kegan Paul

Roberts, Helen (1981b) Some of the boys won't play any more: the impact of feminism on sociology. In Dale Spender *op. cit.* 73-81

Roberts, Joan (Editor) (1976) *Beyond Intellectual Sexism: a new woman a new reality* New York: David McKay

Robertson, J.S. (1971) Voluntary colleges. In Hewett, S. *The Training of Teachers: A Factual Survey* University of London Press

Roderick, G., Bell, J., Turner, R. and Wellings, A. (1981) *Mature Students in Sheffield: A DES funded report* University of Sheffield

Rogers, J. (1977) *Adults Learning* Second Edition. Milton Keynes: Open University Press

Rossi, Alice S. and Calderwood A. (Editors) (1973) *Academic Women on the Move* New York: Russell Sage

Royal National Institute for the Blind (1978-9) *Notes for the Guidance of Staff Concerned with Visually Handicapped Students* London: RNIB

Ruth, Sheila (1981) Methodocracy, misogyny and bad faith: the response of philosophy. In Dale Spender (1981b) *op. cit.* 43-53

Rutter, M. and Madge, N. (1976) *Cycles of Disadvantage* London: Heinermann

Sanders, C. (1961) *Psychological and Educational Bases of Academic Performance* Brisbane: Australian Council for Educational Research

Sanders, C. (1963) Australian universities and their educational problems *The Australian University* 1, 2

Scarman, Rt. Hon. Lord, (1977) *Minority Rights in a Plural Society* The Sixth Minority Rights Group Lecture 16 November

Scheffknecht, J.J. (1978) Permanent education: A European framework for higher education. In Stephens, M. and Roderick, G.W. (Editors) *Higher Education Alternatives* London: Longmans

Seaman, R.D.H. (1978) *St. Peter's College Saltley, 1944-1978* Saltley: St. Peter's College

Select Committee on Race Relations and Immigration (1977) *The West Indian Community* London: HMSO 1976/7 HC 180

Sewell, W.H. (1964) Community of residence and college plans *American Sociological Review* 29 (1) 24-38

Sewell, W.H. and Armer, J.M. (1966) Neighborhood context and college plans *American Sociological Review* 31 (2) 159-168

Shaw, Jennifer (1980) Education and the individual: schooling for girls, or mixed schooling — a mixed blessing? In Rosemary Deem *op. cit.* 66-75

Sharon, A.T. (1971) Adult academic achievement in relation to formal education and age *Adult Education Journal* 21

Sheffield, E. (1969) Response to Dean McHenry. In Niblett, W.R. (Editor) *Higher Education: Demand and Response* London: Tavistock

Sheffield, E. (1978) The national scene. In Sheffield, E. et al. *Systems of Higher Education: Canada* New York: International Council for Educational Development

Showalter, Elaine (1976) Women and the literary curriculum. In Judith Stacey et al. (Editors) *And Jill Came Tumbling After: sexism in American education* New York: Dell

Sider, R.J. (1976) The values-oriented cluster college: A new model for Christian higher education *Religion in Life* Winter, 436-448

Siemens, L.B. (1965) *The Influence of Selected Family Factors on the Educational and Occupational Aspiration Levels of High School Boys and Girls* Winnipeg: Faculty of Agriculture and Home Economics, University of Manitoba

Sindler, A.P. (1978) *Bakke, De Funis and Minority Admissions: the Quest for Equal Opportunity* New York: Longmans

Sizemore, D.R. and Spilka, B. (1973) Christian higher education: consensus and dissensus in student behaviour codes *Review of Religious Research* 1973, 10-15

Small, J.J. (1966) *Achievement and Adjustment in the First Year at University* Wellington: New Zealand Council for Educational Research

Smith, D.J. (1977) *Racial Disadvantage in Britain* Harmondsworth: Penguin

Smith, Dorothy (1978) A peculiar eclipsing: women's exclusion from man's culture *Women's Studies International Quarterly* 1 (4) 281-296

Smith, S.A. (1969) *Study of 1,543 Women Twenty-one Years of Age and Over at the Manitoba University* OISE Monographs in Adult Education, No.4

'Sophia, a person of quality' (1739) *Women not Inferior to Man* London: John Hawkins

Sorenson, H. (1930) Adult ages as a factor in learning *Journal of Educational Psychology* 21, 451-459

Special Educational Needs (1978) London: HMSO. The Warnock Report

Spender, Dale (1980) *Man Made Language* London and Boston: Routledge and Kegan Paul

Spender, Dale (1981a) Introduction. In Dale Spender (1981b) *op. cit.* 1-9

Spender, Date (editor) (1981b) *Men's Studies Modified: the impact of feminism on the academic disciplines*

Spender, Dale (1981c) Education: the patriarchal paradigm and the response to feminism. In Dale Spender (1981b) *op. cit.* 155-173

Spender, Dale (1981d) The gatekeepers: a feminist critique of academic publishing. In Helen Roberts (Editor) *op. cit.* 186-202

Spender, Dale (1981 in press) *Sexism: School for Scandal* (provisional title) London: Writers' and Readers' Cooperative

Spender, Dale (1982 in press) Who made the exclusive judge? The exclusion of women from educational research *journal of the Nordic Society for Educational Research*

Spender, Dale (1982 forthcoming) *Women of Ideas and What Men have Done to Them: from Mary Wollstonecraft to Mary Daly* London and Boston: Routledge and Kegan Paul

Sprandel, H. and Schmidt, M. (1980) *Serving Handicapped Students* San Francisco: Jossey Bass

Squires, G. (1979) Innovations in British higher education and their implications for adult education *Learning opportunities for Adults Volume 2: New structures, Programmes and Methods* Strasbourg: OECD

Stanley, Julia (1977) Gender marking in American English: usage and reference. In Alleen Pace Nilsen et al. *Sexism and Language* Urbana, Illinois: National Council of Teachers of English

Stanley, Liz and Wise, Sue (1981 in press) *Breaking Out: feminist research and feminist consciousness* Oxford: Pergamon Press

Stanworth, E. and Giddens, A. (1974) *Elites and Power in British Society* London: Cambridge University Press

Stanworth, Michelle (1981) *Gender and Schooling: a study of sexual divisions in the classroom* London: Women's Research and Resources Centre Publication 190

Stark, R. (1963) On the incompatibility of religion and science: a survey of American graduate students *Journal for the Scientific Study of Religion* 1963, 3-20

Steinberg, S. (1973) The changing religious composition of American higher education. In Glock, C.Y. *Religion in Sociological Perspective* Belmont, California

Steinberg, S. (1974) *The Academic Melting Pot* New York

Stock, Phyllis (1978) *Better than Rubies: a history of women's education* New York: G.P. Putnam's Sons

Stowell, R. (1981) *Is the Complexity of Financial Provision Handicapping Disabled Students?* London:National Bureau for Handicapped Students

Straubenzee, W. van (1973) Report and Recommendations of the Working Party on Discrimination in the Private Sector of Employment, HMSO. Quoted from Nathan,

Swift, B. (1980) *Trends in Awareness and Beliefs about the Open University among the General Public* Milton Keynes: Survey Research Department, The Open University (mimeo)

Swift, B. (1981) *Outcomes of Open University Studies — some statistics from a 1980 survey of graduates* Milton Keynes: Survey Research Department, The Open University

Swift, D.J. and Acland, H.D. (1967) *Some Data on Mature University Students* Unpublished report

Syson, L. (1975) *Poverty in Camden* London: Institute of Community Studies

Tapper, T. and Chamberlain, A. (1970) *Mature Students at the University of Sussex* University of Sussex, unpublished

Tawney, P.H. (1931) *Equality* London: George Allen and Unwin

Taylor, W. (1970) *Half a Million Teachers* University of Bristol, Lyndale House Papers

Thalheimer, F. (1973) Religiosity and secularisation in the academic professions *Sociology of Education* 1973, 183-202

THES (1977) Most mature students would prefer shorter courses *Times Higher Education Supplement* No. 312

THES (1981) Adults champion slams universities *Times Higher Education Supplement* 27 March 1981

Thomas, W., Beeby, C.E. and Oram, M.H. (1939) *Entrance to the University* Wellington: New Zealand Council for Educational Research

Thompson, E.P. (1968) *The Making of the English Working Class* London: Penguin Books

Thorndike, E.L. (1928) *Adult Learning* New York: Macmillan

Tobias, Sheila (1978) Women's studies: its origins, its organization and its prospects *Women's Studies International Quarterly* 1 (1) 85-98

Tomlinson, R. (1979) The development of services for disabled students at the Open University *Teaching at a Distance* 16

Tomlinson, R. (1980) *The Development of Support Programmes for Disabled Students at the Open University* Milton Keynes: The Open University

Tornes, Kristin (1981) *Sex stereotyping and schooling: a general overview* Paper presented at the Council for Cultural Cooperation educational research workshop on sex stereotyping in schools, Hønefoss, Oslo

Townsend, P. (1979) *Poverty in the UK: a survey of household resources and standards of living* Harmondsworth: Penguin

Trent, J.W. and Golds, J. (1967) *Catholics in College: Religious Commitment and Intellectual Life* University of Chicago Press

Tuckey, L., Parfit, J. and Tuckey, B. (1973) *Handicapped School Leavers: Their Further Education, Training and Employment* Slough: NFER Publishing Co. Ltd

Turner, R. (1971) Sponsored and contest mobility and the school system. In Hopper, E. (1971)

Tyler, W. (1977) *The Sociology of Educational Inequality* London: Methuen

UCCA (1980) *Statistical Supplement to the 17th Report*

University Grants Committee (1972) *Provision for the Disabled at Universities. Notes in implementation of the Chronically Sick and Disabled Persons Act 1970* London: UGC

University Grants Committee Annual Survey: Academic Year 1978-79 (1980) London: HMSO

US Commission on Civil Rights (1979) *Desegregation of the Nation's Schools: a status report*

Velleman, R. (1979) *Serving Physically Disabled People: An Information Handbook for all Libraries* New York: R.R. Bowker Company

Vincent, A. (1981) *Computer Assisted Support for Blind Students: A Micro-Computer Linked Voice Synthesizer* Milton Keynes: The Open University

Walker, Beverly (1981) Psychology and feminism: if you can't beat them, join them. In Dale Spender (1981b) *op. cit.* 111-124

Walker, P. (1975) The university performance of mature students *Research in education* 14, 1-13

Walters, Anna (1978) *The Value of the Work of Elizabeth Gaskell for Study at Advanced Level* University of London, unpublished MA thesis

Weber, M. (1970) The Chinese Literati. In Gerth, Mills and Wright (Editors) (1970)

Westerhoff, J.H. (1980) *The Church's Ministry in Higher Education* New York

Whitburn, J., Mealing, M. and Cox, C. (1976) *People in Polytechnics* London: Society for Research into Higher Education

Williams, R. (1961) *Culture and Society 1780-1950* (Second edition) Harmondsworth: Penguin

Williams, R. (1965) *The Long Revolution* London: Penguin Books

Williams, R. (1977) *Marxism and Literature* Oxford: OUP

Williamson, W. (1978) Centre-periphery models of educational attainment; a critique. In Armytage and Peel (1978)

Williamson, W. (1979) *Education, Social Structure and Development* London: Macmillan

Willingham, W.W. (1970) *Free-Access Higher Education* New York: College Entrance Examination Board

Willingham, W.W. (1971) Educational opportunity and the organization of higher education. In *Barriers to Higher Education* New York: College Entrance Examination Board

Wilson, W.J. (1978) *The Declining Significance of Race* Chicago

Wollstonecraft, Mary (1792) *A Vindication of the Rights of Women* London: J. Johnson; (reprinted 1978) Kramnick, Miriam (Editor) Harmondsworth: Penguin

Woodley, A. (1978) *Applicants who Decline the Offer of a Place* Milton Keynes: The Open University (mimeo)

Woodley, A. (1979) *The Prediction of Degree Performance among Undergraduates in the Commerce and Social Science Faculty* University of Birmingham, unpublished

Woodley, A. and McIntosh, N.E. (1976) *People who Decide not to Apply to the Open University* Milton Keynes: The Open University (mimeo)

Woodley, A. and McIntosh, N.E. (1980) *The Door Stood Open: An Evaluation of the Open University Younger Student Pilot Scheme* The Falmer Press

Woolf, Virginia (1972) Women and fiction. In Leonard Woolf (Editor) *Collected Essays: Virginia Woolf Vol II* London: Chatto and Windus. First published *The Forum* 29 March 1929

Woolf, Virginia (1974) *A Room of One's Own* Harmondsworth: Penguin

Woolf, Virginia (1977) *Three Guineas* Harmondsworth: Penguin

Working Party on Christian Involvement in Higher and Further Education (1978) *Christian Involvement in Higher Education* National Society, Church House Westminster

Working Party on Discrimination in the Private Sector of Employment (1973) *Report and Recommendations: Appendix 2* Belfast: HMSO

Wright, D. and Cox, E. (1967) Religious belief and co-education in a sample of sixth-form boys and girls *British Journal of Social and Clinical Psychology* 1967, 23-31

Wright, D. and Cox, E. (1971) Changes in moral belief among sixth-form boys and girls over a seven-year period in relation to religious belief, age and sex differences *British Jounral of Social and Clinical Psychology* 1971, *332-341*

Wuthnow, R. (1977) Is there an academic melting pot? *Sociology of Education* January, 7-15

Wynne, R. (1979) *The Adult Student and British Higher Education* Paris: European Cultural Foundation, Institute of Education

Wyatt, J.F. (1977) 'Collegiality' during a period of rapid change in higher education: an examination of a distinctive feature claimed by a group of colleges of education in the 1960s and 1970s *Oxford Review of Education* 1977, 147-155